DO THIS FOR
LOVE

FREE BURMA RANGERS
IN THE BATTLE OF MOSUL

DAVID EUBANK

WITH HOSANNAH VALENTINE

FIDELIS
BOOKS

FIDELIS BOOKS BOOK
An Imprint of Post Hill Press
ISBN: 978-1-64293-503-5
ISBN (eBook): 978-1-64293-504-2

Cover Design by Cody Corcoran

Interior photos courtesy of David Eubank, unless otherwise noted.

Maps and battlefield sketches provided by Justin DeMaranville and David Eubank.

Unless otherwise indicated, all Scripture taken from THE HOLY BIBLE, NEW INTERNATIONAL VERSION®, NIV® Copyright © 1973, 1978, 1984, 2011 by Biblica, Inc.® Used with permission. All rights reserved worldwide.

The views, opinions, and theological expressions contained herein do not necessarily reflect those of Fidelis Books or its other authors.

Post Hill Press
New York • Nashville
posthillpress.com

Published in the United States of America

*This book is dedicated to all the Rangers
who have given their lives for others.*

Most recently, we lost Zau Seng, our Kachin medic and cameraman, who was killed in an attack by the combined Turk and Free Syrian Army (FSA, Turkish proxy) forces in Syria on November 3, 2019, while on a relief mission. Zau Seng was a Kachin Ranger who served fourteen years with us in Burma, Iraq, and Syria. Along with being one of our top FBR leaders, he helped raise Sahale, Suu, and Peter and was a brother to all of us.

Before his last mission to Syria, he said, "I want to go back and help, just as others have helped me. I want to help tell the story with my camera and put a light on the people." We miss Zau greatly, and he leaves behind a young wife and a daughter who turned one year old on the day he was killed. The world is poorer for his loss, but we will continue his legacy of love, joy, courage, and service. We believe the things of the world are fatal but not final. We will see him again with Jesus in what the tribal people of Burma call the "undiscovered land." One day, we will all discover this land and enter the same new life Zau has now. Until then, we are here to love, to serve, to stand against evil, and to add to the beauty of the world.

Thank you, Zau Seng and all Rangers who have gone before us, for showing us how.

Table of Contents

Author's Note

The battle of Mosul, which lasted from October 2016 to July 2017, brought to a point all the lessons we have learned in over twenty years of Free Burma Ranger service in Burma, Sudan, Kurdistan, Iraq, and Syria. Old lessons about love, courage, commitment, practical service, and faith were reinforced under fire while new lessons, relationships, and battlefields taught us new ways to live, serve, forgive, and love.

The Free Burma Rangers (FBR) was founded by me and my wife Karen, along with ethnic leaders in Burma, in 1997 in response to a Burma Army offensive that displaced over five hundred thousand people. Since then, it has grown to include many different ethnic groups across Burma and the world. FBR is made up of Christians, Buddhists, Muslims, animists, Yezidis, agnostics, and atheists. We are not a religious organization, yet we are all united in the mission of bringing help, hope, and love to people of all faiths and ethnicities in conflict areas, shining a light on the actions of oppressors, standing with the oppressed, and supporting leaders and organizations committed to liberty, justice, and reconciliation. We believe love is the most powerful force in the world and try to serve others in love.

FBR is not a militia and most of our team members are unarmed. Our role is to give humanitarian help and get the news out in those conflict areas where we are called to go. We are not an attacking force, but we abide by this rule: an FBR member cannot leave someone who is in danger or run away if the people they are with cannot run away. Each individual decides whether or not to use weapons for protection, but cannot abandon anyone, no matter how dangerous the situation is.

We have over ninety relief teams in Burma, with each team composed of four to six people, as well as teams in Iraq and Syria. I am a follower of Jesus, and I have felt Him change my heart and help me do what, for me at least, would otherwise be impossible. I am thankful to all who have helped us by their love, actions, support, and prayers.

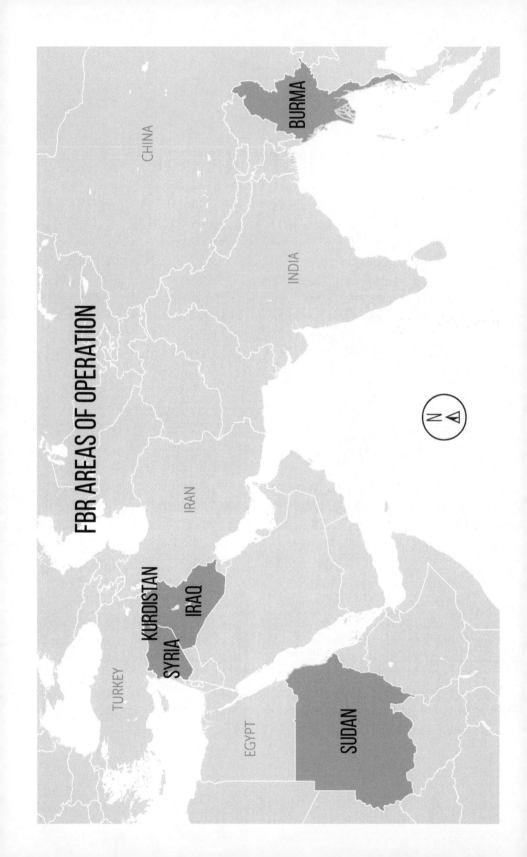

Introduction

Wreathed in smoke and dust, the tank raced forward, tracks screaming, jet turbine engine whining, main gun blasting, coaxial machine gun firing, and ISIS shooting back. We ran behind, past the bodies of men, women, and children as the tank zigzagged around them. Bullets smashed into the tank and ricocheted by us; others crackled in from the side, narrowly missing. An ISIS rocket-propelled grenade crashed to our left. Running with our team, I was also trying to make myself heard on my phone as I called for a smokescreen from the American battle commander.

War is loud. That's one way it's different than the movies. Another way is you can die. I was feeling both differences, running behind the revving Abrams tank as it blasted away at a gutted three-story hospital just two hundred meters from us, where hundreds of heavily armed ISIS fighters overwatched the road, firing at anything that moved. At the moment, my team and I were the only things moving, and machine gun and sniper rounds screamed by all around us as we sheltered behind the roaring tank. Layers of noise, from the high-pitched scream of bullets one meter away to the deep concussive explosions of air strikes five hundred meters away to the roar of the tank's engine and guns, along with heat, smoke, and dust, enveloped us under the merciless June sun.

The Iraqis had been trying to cross this road for a week; it was littered with Iraqi military vehicles destroyed by ISIS fire from the hospital. A few days before, the unit we were with was reinforced by another Iraqi battalion, which was immediately decimated: twenty-two soldiers were shot in one attempted movement across this thoroughfare. Our team helped recover the wounded that day, sprinting into the open under fire and dragging them back to safety. ISIS had repulsed every attempt by the Iraqi Army to cross this road. But now, five of us had crossed it, running behind a lone Iraqi tank toward ISIS lines, and were stopped on the other side, looking straight at the hospital just two football field lengths away.

All around us were the dead, more than fifty bodies strewn across the road in the graceless poses of desperation. An old man slouched, killed in his wheelchair; the young man who had been pushing him crumpled on the ground behind. Two young girls, maybe eight and ten years old, looked as if they'd been flung like dice to the ground by a giant hand; one of them was missing the top of her head. An old woman who'd carried a bundle was curled up beside it, dead in the middle of the street. A young man was sprawled full length, one arm stretched forward as if reaching for something just out of his grasp. His other hand reached back toward a young boy fallen at his side. And on and on.

I could die here today. Easy.

Just fifteen meters from my team and me was a concrete wall, bullet-riddled but still standing. Behind it was a soft drink factory that air strikes had reduced to a mangled mess of rebar and massive, broken concrete slabs. At the base of the wall were more bodies. But there was also life: two wounded men lay beside each other, sheltered by the wall from the relentless ISIS fire coming from the hospital. They waved feebly at us. A young girl who wore a pink shirt and pigtails sat next to a fallen, lifeless woman, probably her mother, hiding under her black hijab and peeking out; the ribbons in her pigtails fluttered in the hot breeze. Any move those survivors made away from the wall would expose them to the ISIS sharpshooters. Behind them was ISIS territory; in front of them, the safety of Iraqi Army lines. Between, one hundred and fifty meters of corpse-strewn street—and us.

And we were there to save them, these two men and one girl. It was June 2, 2017, the ninth month of the battle to retake Mosul from ISIS. We had been present on nearly every front of this fight. My team, family, and I had treated the wounded and helped care for thousands of fleeing civilians with the Kurds as ISIS was pushed out of Kurdistan. Then our team had embedded with the Iraqi Army. We met and partnered with the 36th Mechanized Brigade, 9th Armored Division, and followed them as the front line circled the east side of the city, moving south to north, from Sharazad to Tel Kayf and Al Rashidiya, through the fall of 2016 and into 2017.

It was a new dawn when we crossed the Tigris River south of Mosul and the front moved to the west side of the river and city. With the

Iraqis, we pushed through to Badush and thought we might keep moving west to Tal Afar, but the fighting in the old part of Mosul proved to be more difficult than anticipated, so—still embedded with the 36th—we moved in to support the attack on the northwest side of the city. We gave food to thousands of hungry and desperate civilians escaping the fighting. We treated hundreds of wounded soldiers and civilians.

We lost friends. Men I had eaten with, laughed with, fought alongside, and prayed with were shot down next to me. I couldn't save them. Children died in our arms, and the wailing of their grieving parents echoed in my heart as I thought of my own kids: Sahale, sixteen; Suuzanne, fourteen; and Peter, eleven. They were here too, just behind the front lines with my wife Karen and others on our team, helping with food and clothing distributions, or at the casualty collection points the Iraqi Army set up to give immediate help to wounded soldiers and civilians, and with kids' programs when we were able.

I thought of them now as I scanned the fifteen meters of unprotected ground between where I stood behind the tank and where those we were here to rescue sheltered at the base of the wall. There was so much destruction. So many people we couldn't save. So much death. Yet here, in front of us, was a chance to beat death. This was why we—me, my family, and my team—were here: because every life counts. The life of that little girl is just as valuable as my life, or those of my family's. *They will understand*, I thought. *If I die trying to save this little girl, my wife and kids will understand.*

We had turned onto this exposed street just as U.S. Army artillery had dropped several 155mm smoke canisters in front of the hospital. The ensuing cloud mostly blocked the view of our progress from the ISIS fighters inside. I had been on the phone with the Americans all day to help coordinate this. Now the cloud was dissipating, and we were taking more fire. We were protected from small-arms fire by the tank, but ISIS was also firing RPGs, antitank rounds, and mortars. We needed more smoke.

I got back on the phone with the Americans, shouting to be heard above the noise of the tank and incoming ISIS fire. "Sorry I'm yelling. It's loud here! The smoke was awesome, but it's dissipating, and we need more! If we don't have it now there are kids who are gonna die. The tank's gonna get blown up. We're all gonna die! How much longer before you get more smoke?" The battle captain told me ten minutes, and eight minutes later, a new barrage of smoke came. It was beautiful. The moment was now.

I turned to my team: Sky Barkley, a former U.S. Marine, had been volunteering with us for eight months, first in Burma and now here; Ephraim Mattos, a former U.S. Navy SEAL we had first met in Thailand three months earlier and who later joined us in Mosul; Mahmood, a Syrian refugee we first met at a church in Erbil, then again when he was selling ice cream at the mall there, was helping us as a translator; and Monkey, one of the original Rangers and now one of our leaders, an ethnic Karen (pronounced ka-REN) from Burma, who was also a cameraman and chaplain. I put my hands on Sky's and Ephraim's shoulders, pulling them in, and shouted, "OK, this is what I'm gonna do. You guys give me cover, I'm gonna run." It was a simple plan.

What I thought was, *There's no way I'm gonna live through this.*

Sometimes you do something and you think, "I might get hurt, but I have a chance." This wasn't one of those times. This was, "You're not going to get hurt. You're going to get killed." But I looked at the little girl by the wall and thought, *What would I want for my kids?* And I prayed and said to myself, "It's now or never." I prayed again, "Jesus, help me," and took off at a run.

Bullets cracked by my head. The tank's main gun and coaxial machine gun were firing to my left. Sky and Ephraim had stepped out from behind the tank and were giving covering fire behind me. ISIS bullets ricocheted off the wall to my right and hit at my feet. I ran by a young boy in a blue soccer jersey where he lay twisted around on his back, lifeless eyes pointed at the sky. I reached the girl, where she sat clinging to her dead mother, surrounded by crumpled bodies. My eyes locked on hers, which were fixed on me in blank terror. I shouted, "I'm here to help you!" and grabbed her arm, but she hung on tightly to her mother. I yanked at her, hard, pulling her away, and tucked her under my right arm; then I turned at a run and headed back to the tank.

And then I went down, down in the dirt and broken pavement. It happened so fast that I didn't fully realize what had happened, but also in slow motion so that, as I tumbled with this little girl in my arm who I wasn't going to let go of, I thought, ruefully, *Sorry. Sorry, little girl. If I was younger, a better athlete, I could twist and move so you wouldn't be hurt. I could save you pain. I'm sorry.* Eight meters from the tank, we slammed, face-first, hard, to the ground.

+

"We must take sides. Neutrality helps the oppressor, never the victim. Silence encourages the tormentor, never the tormented. Sometimes we must interfere. When human lives are endangered, when human dignity is in jeopardy, national borders and sensitivities become irrelevant. Wherever men and women are persecuted…that place must—at that moment—become the center of the universe."
—ELIE WIESEL, NOBEL PEACE PRIZE ACCEPTANCE SPEECH[1]

War is not a natural disaster; it is man-made, and there are always sides. To provide relief in war means you have to work with or through one of the sides. Entering a conflict zone to help puts you in the domain of one of the factions. The ability to provide humanitarian relief is dependent on one of those factions and there is no neutral space in combat.

Insisting on neutrality will only aid the oppressor or whoever is in control.

ISIS did not offer an option of neutrality—you were either for or against them. The humanitarian community was challenged. How do we help people when no one's playing by the rules? One report analyzing the difficulties of the humanitarian response in the Battle of Mosul, by researchers at Johns Hopkins University, said (italics mine), "…this response took place not only within the highly charged geopolitical landscape of Iraq, but also within the context of a rapidly shifting global environment for humanitarian actors. In the past three years, nearly 1,000 health workers have been killed in conflict settings, at times deliberately, an alarming figure that has raised serious questions about *whether traditional notions of humanitarian action remain tenable.*"[2] Humanitarian aid cannot always be effectively founded on the principle of neutrality.

This is not new and has always been the case. While I was working in Burma, a U.S. government official once said to me, "You should not be with the armed ethnic groups, or at the front lines in Burma. That is not the humanitarian way. When we were in Bosnia, we had a clear separation. A U.S. battalion provided security on the hill above while we distributed food in the valley below."

I replied, "That is good. Please send that U.S. battalion to stop the Burma Army from attacking the Karen, and we all will gladly provide humanitarian assistance in safety." There are many approaches to take when we are faced with humanitarian needs in war zones. But any role taken is dependent on one military or the other to make access and relief work possible.

Under international humanitarian law, combatants have a responsibility and duty to allow humanitarian access to vulnerable civilian populations—but, as noted in the Johns Hopkins report above, many combatants do not do this. This is for a variety of reasons: in combat, military forces usually are completely engaged and have a limited mission, capacity, or, sometimes, desire to provide humanitarian relief. In some cases, combatants actively target humanitarian workers.

This is true of all the areas we have worked: humanitarian organizations are targeted, and individuals providing relief are at risk of death, injury, or capture. War is deadly and unpredictable, especially on the front lines, so most relief organizations try to stay away from these fronts. They have certain lines they will not cross, including being armed or going to the front lines. This is partly to fulfill their duty to care for staff who are not trained for front-line environments or because there are liability concerns. They do life-giving and lifesaving work and serve a crucial role, but not at the front.

This means that, in war, there is a gap between the front lines and the humanitarian relief available to those in need. Fully recognizing the moral and physical dangers and desiring to always act in love, FBR serves in these humanitarian gaps.

The gap between the front lines and the nearest humanitarian relief can extend from a few blocks to one hundred miles or more. In the Battle of Mosul, as in most battles, humanitarian organizations were generally not at the front lines. This was due to the mortal danger present at the front, security protocols, the complex, ever-shifting environment, and the personalities, specialized training, equipment, and relationships needed to provide assistance at any front line. This meant civilians who required medical treatment, food, shelter, or transport had to escape one of the sides—here, ISIS—and pass on foot or be carried through to the other side, to the Iraqi military lines.

In Syria, we saw that sometimes the gap between the front lines and the nearest relief was over one hundred miles of desert. While we were on a relief mission in Africa, in the Nuba Mountains of Sudan, where the Sudanese government attacked daily, there were hundreds of miles of desert people had to cross to get help. In Burma, the longest civil war in the world rages on at seventy years at this writing as a relentless government, through the military, attacks and attempts to block assistance to displaced people at the front lines. Relief often takes arduous days of walking, and the medical wings of armed groups, if they exist, have limited capacity.

It is important to recognize that whether there is assistance or not, people will do their best to help themselves. Often, as is the case in Burma, families and villagers have only each other to rely on when they are attacked. Their tenacity, foresight, teamwork, love, courage, generosity, and resilience are the main reasons they survive.

Each individual and organization must decide what their role is in helping these people and what lines they will not cross. Any choice made incurs a cost. For those who will not work at the front lines or defend others, this means people they could have helped will suffer and die. For those who decide to go into this gap, this means they risk their lives and risk becoming part of the conflict in bad ways. There are no simple solutions, and both choices are fraught with moral, and mortal, danger. The response to every conflict, relief mission, and action must be weighed. For us, that means seeking advice and having discussion about the best ways to meet needs as well as honesty about our motives—and it means prayer, asking God what to do. Finally, our actions must always be motivated by love.

In our work at FBR, we have found we cannot be neutral, but the principle of impartiality is less negotiable: we help all we can as impartially as possible. FBR attempts to be impartial as we provide humanitarian assistance. We want to help all who are suffering if we can. At times we have treated, fed, prayed for, and shown love to wounded Burmese soldiers as well as to ISIS members who were captured or who surrendered. We provide aid equally to all who need it, regardless of religion, ethnicity, gender, age, or affiliation.

FBR feels called to help those at the front lines and in the humanitarian gaps. This puts us in danger and sometimes face-to-face with those who want to kill us. We are realistic about this and don't enter danger naively, nor do we add to the burdens of the front-line soldiers.

Rather, we are particularly equipped for this kind of operation due to our years of experience on the front lines.

When face-to-face with those who would kill us or those we are trying to help, FBR or anyone who serves in this dangerous gap must decide if they will try to defend themselves or others when they or the people they are helping are attacked. This does not mean we are a paramilitary force; rather, some of our members have the ability and competency to defend themselves and others. Whether or not one is armed is up to the individual, and if arms are chosen, they are strictly for defense. In carrying out the mission of helping the people and getting the news out at the front lines, FBR has a rule: you cannot run if the people cannot run. Knowing we must stay and help those in need no matter the danger, we do not lightly go on any mission. We pray, listen, and go in love.

CHAPTER ONE

The Making of a Ranger

"We are a warrior people…but what we really need is God."

—U Saw Lu, Wa foreign minister

"Mir·a·cle: a surprising and welcome event that is not explicable by natural or scientific laws and is therefore considered to be the work of a divine agency."[3]

This is a story of undeserved miracles. Some of them were immediate: moments when I knew I should be dead, like when a fight had just happened, and I realized afterward, almost with surprise, that I was still alive, somehow, despite statistics and physics that would predict a different outcome. Some of them I'm still in the middle of—these are the kind where you look back and see the many small things that led you to this exact point and prepared you for it, even though in the moment, none of it seemed to make sense. Sometimes, I feel like the player called off the bench in a close football game—as I am going in to score, I fumble the ball as I fall across the goal line. But, when all seems lost, the ball bounces back into my arms—touchdown! Wow, not what I deserve and nothing I can take credit for. Just this: God did not give up on me.

I was born on September 29, 1960, in Fort Worth, Texas, to Allan and Joan Eubank, just months before they followed God's call to Thailand and an adventure to which they would dedicate the rest of their lives and which would inevitably shape mine. They were both children of the American West, Texans, with foundational values of freedom and independence, and were part of that "greatest generation" who knew nothing in life comes easy but expected that hard work would yield success. They believed in duty, responsibility, and integrity. More than this, they were followers of Jesus. They pursued their faith like everything else: seriously, thoughtfully, humbly, with love, exuberance, and the determination to follow it through all its implications.

Dad graduated from Texas A&M in Geological Engineering in 1951 and served in the Army as Captain CO (commanding officer) of a combat engineer company in the Korean War. Mom was an up-and-coming Broadway and Hollywood star. They met in Korea while he was deployed and she was on tour with the USO (an organization founded in 1941 to provide live entertainment to members of the U.S. Military). As soon as he saw her, Dad knew she was the one he would marry. He offered her a tour of the base, and she talked him into letting her drive the Jeep, promptly sliding it into a ditch. Dad was in love, and they stayed in touch off and on as Dad left the military after the war for the oil business and Mom's career progressed.

But neither their relationship nor their careers was their driving force as they tried to figure out what it meant to put their faith in God first. Dad felt he was to be a missionary and pragmatically decided he'd be most valuable if he could first earn a million dollars in the oil business. In the Texas of the '50s with a geological engineering degree under his belt, and a lot of determination, it seemed to be more a question of when than if he'd make his fortune. But after a few years of working for various oil companies, he felt God give him Matthew 6:33: "But seek first his kingdom and his righteousness." It felt like God was telling him, "I trust other people with a million dollars, but not you." He needed to put God first, and God would take care of him. Dad left the oil business and started seminary at Texas Christian University in Fort Worth, with an invitation to do missions work in Thailand.

Mom had gradually lost touch with him as her growing career took her all over the world and his career in the oil business took him in a different direction. She was the lead in *Oklahoma, Plain and Fancy,* and *Carousel* and was named by *Theater World* as one of the top ten "promising personalities" on Broadway. But she too was wondering if she was headed in the direction God had planned for her. Always learning, seeking, she traveled from show to show with books like Kierkegaard's *Fear and Trembling*—not normal starlet reading material. She was on contract with Richard Rodgers of Rodgers and Hammerstein when they performed in Fort Worth, where Dad was in seminary. He came to every show, and she was surprised to find that the oil man had switched courses and was on the path to full-time mission work. Dad's new path now aligned with the direction her questions were sending her.

They married in December of 1959. I was born nine months later, and just a few months after that, they were off to Thailand. They settled down in a little village called Sam Yaek to help the local Thai Christians and share the love Jesus gave them. I was their firstborn, and three girls, Ruthanne, Laurie, and Suwannee, followed. In Sam Yaek, we ran around with the village kids, learning Thai as our first language. My sisters and I were very close, and to this day, they encourage and inspire me.

Sometimes I went with Dad on his jungle treks to remote villages. By the time I was five, he had taught me how to shoot a rifle, swim, and ride horses, and I was always riding, hunting, or playing army. I became a child of the outdoors and loved the freedom, wildness, and challenge I found there with a love that would never leave me.

There were no schools where we were, so, when I was seven years old, I left my parents and sisters and went to boarding school in Chiang Mai, which was five hundred kilometers north. Homesickness was my first sharp sorrow; it was also when I had my first personal experience with Jesus. On that day, I was sick with dengue fever. When you're sick, it can weaken you in other ways, too, so I was also really lonely. My parents were far away, and I was alone in a boarding house dorm room, feeling terrible. I decided to pray. I knew about Jesus; my parents were missionaries and prayed all the time. I knew He was supposed to help you when you needed it. So I prayed to Him. It was one of my first acts of faith, and it was an act of desperation.

I said, "Jesus, Mom and Dad believe in you, but they aren't here. If you're real, help me." Instantly, I felt the room become lighter, and I felt love. I knew it was Him. He heard my prayer and came. God is love. He came to help me, and I felt that love. That was my first experience of Jesus, and it came to me when I was alone and desperate. I went home for Christmas that year, and when Dad gave an altar call in church on Sunday, I walked forward and he baptized me soon after.

Though my first experience of faith was love, I prided myself on never surrendering in anything, and the easiest way to measure that was physical competition. I became fiercely competitive and, to further that, fiercely disciplined. Dad started running with me when I was seven, and I soon began my own self-designed workouts, mostly consisting of push-ups, pull-ups, and running. I loved to fight and would not give

Allan, my dad, travels through Burma at age 82, with our kids, 2010.

My mom, Joan, sings with the team and our girls for IDPs in Shan State, 2011.

up. I wasn't big, but I would not stop. In fact, this is how I met my best friend, now also my brother-in-law, Pete Dawson.

He started at Chiang Mai International School when I was in eighth grade; he was the new kid and bigger than me. But I was the undisputed tough guy at school—though maybe I just loved fighting more than anyone else. Either way, I was going to fight this guy and keep my title. Other kids egged us on all day, but I didn't need any extra motivation. When the time came, I decided to take an advantage—surprise. I walked up to him in an open area of the schoolyard. We both knew what was going to happen. He smirked and started trash-talking: "I hear you think you're tough…." I didn't talk. I punched him as hard as I could, first in the throat, then an uppercut to the stomach. Before he could do anything, I slid behind him, got my arms around his neck and started choking him for all I was worth.

Most of my fights ended right there. As I expected, Pete went down to his knees, and I was confident—but then he came back up. Whoa. I knew he was for real then, and I had a battle on my hands. He started slamming me as hard as he could against the hardest, sharpest things he could find, which were the concrete pillars of the school. It was a matter of if he could seriously hurt me before I made him pass out. I kept choking him, and he kept slamming me into the pillars. Before either of us won, teachers came rushing over and broke us up.

We were best friends from that day on. He would join me in early morning workouts and wrestling matches. Pete was a better athlete than me and could push me, compete with me, and still be my friend. Our competition never went beyond the specific event and we helped each other prepare for the challenges of the future. By then, my parents and sisters had moved to Chiang Mai, where Dad and Mom taught at a seminary.

Thailand was like the Wild West in those days. I could ride my horse to school and would go hunting in the hills surrounding Chiang Mai for days at a time. Pete and I hunted with Dad and the local tribesmen that lived in those hills, most of whom were Lahu or Karen. We learned how to track, hunt, and live in the jungle. My sisters and I raised horses, baby monkeys, leopards, and a bear. Being each other's best playmates, we were a tight-knit team.

We all traveled with my dad on evangelism trips to tribal villages in the jungle, far from modern development. I joined the Boy Scouts and Dad volunteered as scoutmaster. With Dad in charge, my life was harder as I had to pass every test and badge at a higher level to ensure there was no favoritism. But I also got special attention, meaning not just more punishment but more personal time, learning knots and other skills from my dad, who was a master.

At the same time, the Vietnam War was raging next door to Thailand. This gave extra scope and motivation to our training—I was determined to get in the fight as soon as possible. It also gave rise to unique opportunities; our Scout troop had volunteers from U.S. Special Forces and the CIA who helped train us and provided aircraft for resupply on jungle treks. One of the CIA men was Bob Brewer, who jumped into combat in World War II with the 101st Airborne and was depicted in an episode of *Band of Brothers*. He was shot in the throat in Eindhoven, Holland, during Operation Market Garden (depicted in the movie *A Bridge Too Far*). He survived when he was rescued by Dutch Boy Scouts and hidden from the Nazis. He promised then to always help the Boy Scouts.

We also had help from Harold, Gordon, and Bill Young, a pioneering missionary family from Burma who had survived the Japanese there in World War II and grew up to be famous hunters and conservationists. They helped start the modern conservation movement in Thailand and the Chiang Mai Zoo, where I did my Eagle Scout project. Along with Bob Brewer, Gordon and Bill worked with the U.S. and Thai governments against communist forces in the region. They were heroes to me, as they were masters of the jungle and spoke multiple tribal languages while loving God and people. Gordon wrote wonderful books, among them *Tracks of an Intruder* and *Journey from Banna*. Both are classics of adventure and life. The Morse family, also from Burma, taught us how to live in the jungle and serve God.

Chiang Mai had no high school yet, so eventually I was off to boarding school again, this time at the International School of Bangkok (ISB). Bangkok was a big city. There were more rules and less wildness. On weekends, after we finished our homework, Pete and I would roam Bangkok's streets, looking for the wild side: disturbances, thugs, anyone we could find an excuse to fight. We'd sometimes run ten miles through the hot, sticky nights, up and down luridly lit streets, touring the places everyone else tried to avoid, hoping to catch criminals in the act—but mostly looking for a fight. I was becoming an educated punk.

I also played sports, and it wasn't just a game to me; it was war. ISB didn't have football, so basketball was my favorite. I ran a full-court press the entire game.

As I went through high school, I was self-sufficient, lettered in sports, got top grades, and kept pushing myself physically. I didn't get into drugs and alcohol. Pete and I got drunk only once, after we won the Thai national high school basketball championship. We celebrated our win with a full bottle of whiskey each, punched each other in the face a few times, laughed a lot, and woke up feeling terrible. After that, I could not stand even the smell of whiskey for years, but my love of sports and competition only grew.

All this was to prepare me for what I really wanted to do: go to war as an American soldier, to fight for freedom and for the ideals of my country and to be in what I thought would be the greatest adventure. Combat presented the ultimate challenge. As I graduated from ISB, this was where I next turned my steps.

I always felt a need for God, but He was a sort of background entity who needed to be addressed occasionally. My prayers were usually something like, "Dear God, please bless me and this thing I want to do." I never thought of asking God what He might want me to do, as if it could be different.

I received a full ROTC scholarship to Texas A&M, following in the footsteps of my father and grandfather (Louis Charles Eubank, class of 1922). The Corps of Cadets at A&M was a hard and excellent training ground for future officers, and it was brutal. In addition to a full class load, we freshmen cadets, or "fish," were at the mercy of the upperclassmen, who could make us do basically whatever they wanted—clean their shoes, run around campus for three hours, or even stand naked in the hallway late into the night while upperclassmen beat us with ax handles. Although it was officially against all A&M rules, hazing got physical and violent. By my senior year, I found myself in the rare role of trying to introduce some perspective into the situation. I was the brigade commander and we got rid of the ax-handle beatings. We enforced push-ups as punishment rather than beatings—those also hurt but made you stronger. A&M prepared me well for future challenges.

I went in with a clear goal: to be an officer and ultimately join the Army Special Forces. I saw no point in doing anything unless I could be part of the best. There were a few options: Army Special Forces, Army

I was inducted into the Texas A&M Hall of Honor in 2019; my family and Dad and Mom were all there to see it.

Rangers, Navy SEALs, and Marine Force Recon, but the Army Special Forces had the behind-the-lines work with indigenous people I wanted to do the most. Only one time do I remember a doubt about my trajectory and that was during a summer break while in Chiang Mai for a visit home. At a prayer meeting at our house, my mind turned to God for the first time in a while, and the question suddenly came: "What if this isn't God's will for me?"

I hadn't thought of that. I only talked to God when I was desperate, and I hadn't been desperate since I was about seven years old. But the thought that He might have a different idea for my life suddenly felt like a punch in the gut. When was the last time I asked God what He wanted me to do, rather than informing Him of my plans? I remembered the stories of how He called Mom and Dad away right at the beginning of promising careers. My military career was right on that same brink.

At this meeting I prayed and said, "God, thank you for letting me join the Army and get my paratrooper wings as a cadet. I give all this up and will be a missionary if you want me to." I immediately felt God's presence come with reassurance. Another missionary who was there standing next to me, put his hand on my shoulder and told me God gave him these words for me: "Keep doing what I have called you to do. I'm preparing you for future service. Something will happen that will crush you, but you will not be broken. And, my son, you will know it is me when I'm speaking to you."

Wow! What a confirmation, and not just from my own head. I was cleared for full speed ahead in the army.

By the time I was twenty-two, I had my first command of a platoon of forty men in Panama. I competed in and won several endurance events while in Panama, which helped me get noticed by commanding officers; I was chosen to be the scout platoon leader. I tried out and was selected to the 75th Ranger Regiment and led Ranger units for three years in the 2nd Ranger Battalion, based out of Fort Lewis in Washington State. I then tried out for the Special Forces, and after selection and the qualification course, I was assigned as an A-team detachment commander.

I had always loved climbing—I took "getting to the top" literally as well as figuratively and climbed everything I could in Thailand; on family trips to Europe, I veered off of our hikes and got lost in cliffs but figured out how to scale them. In Central America, I climbed when the Army allowed me time. Then, being stationed in western Washington at the base of the Cascades gave ample opportunity to become a mountaineer. Between missions, while most of my men rested, partied, or hung out with their girlfriends or families, I climbed mountains. In cargo holds of C-130s, as we flew back from deployments, I'd plan my

Charlie Company
2ND BN 75 Ranger Regt.

My Ranger brothers, Charlie Company, 2nd Bat, 75 Reg. I am standing front and center, behind the standard bearer.

Me, jumping into Thailand with the Thai Special
Forces, 1992.

next climb, hunched over a topographic map, plotting routes by flash-
light. At that point, most of my men would stop making eye contact
with me, not wanting to be roped into a stateside Eubank torture tour
immediately after finishing a U.S. Army-sponsored one.

I was still single, and in all these challenges and adventures, it seemed
there was always something missing. I would stand on top of mountains, gazing with wonder at the beauty, feeling the wind, but knowing something was missing. I was alone. I had always prided myself on
being independent, but I finally realized I didn't want to go through
life alone. So, to fulfill my next life goal, I found, pursued, and married
a beautiful girl, confident that relationships were another arena where
determination and toughness would be enough to succeed.

I was wrong, and our marriage ended within three years. I was
devastated, by the failure as much as anything else. I had been faithful
to her and thought I treated her well. What else could I have done?
Eventually, I realized what was wrong was me. I consistently put
myself first, then her, and Jesus after that. I was wrong even to marry
her with that attitude.

But I learned another lesson too—my feeling of incompleteness
wasn't something any person could fix; God and His way were the only
things that would help me feel complete. I always believed but also

Pete Dawson, Mike Stoneham, and I summit Denali (photo by Mike), 1998.

always seemed to hold some of myself back from Him. I believed, but I was not yet ready to really commit. I had a self-sufficient confidence that blinded me to my own weaknesses. I have always hated the idea of surrender and would never surrender. Whether in sports, climbing, or as a soldier, surrender was not an idea I would tolerate. But as I looked back at my life, I realized that I had surrendered many times: to selfishness, pride, and sin. It took failure in my life to see that I had surrendered many times to bad things and had not surrendered enough to good things—and had not fully surrendered to God. I had it backwards.

After the divorce was finalized, in shame and despair, I got on my knees, closed my eyes, and said, "Jesus, I am sorry. Show me the truth of this." Right away, I saw an image of the world with a small man (me) standing on it. There was the blue of the atmosphere and past that, the black of outer space. From that blackness, a jagged crack like a thunderbolt rent a chasm through the blue of the atmosphere, through the little man, through the earth and out the other side. The name of that chasm was divorce. Wow. Divorce was that big, that terrible. Just as angels sing when people come to the love of Jesus, maybe they cry when we divorce. Tears rolled down my face as I asked for forgiveness. I remembered the words of the missionary who had prayed for me: "Something will happen that will crush you, but you will not be broken." I was not broken. I could still love. A new love grew inside me for my ex-wife, and I prayed for her. Even if our marriage was over, we didn't have to be overcome by hate. (Years later, she asked me to baptize her children from her new marriage. It felt like a Christian soap opera, but we had reconciled, and I thanked her and God for that.)

As I worked through this failure and loss, my career progressed. And, undeservedly, I also met another girl, Karen Huesby. She was a special education teacher in Seattle, not far from where I was stationed at Fort Lewis. She was small, blond, a nonstop smiler and laugher, a radiant one like my mom, and also up for all the Eubank torture tours. Our first date was a challenging and technical climb up Mt. Shuksan in the North Cascades. The name "Karen" means "pure one," and she lived up to it. She had never dated and hated violence. A soldier was the last kind of guy she planned to marry. I pursued her with the same determination with which I did everything.

In the middle of spending all the time I could with Karen, exercising all the patience and faith I could muster, God also gave me another choice, this time about my vocation: I could stay in the Army, this time putting God first, or I could get out and, also putting God first, see what happened. I decided to leave. I was at the ten-year mark and left the Army as a major. At the time of my resignation from active duty, I was a captain slated for promotion to major, which I received while

Dad rides out on an elephant, accompanied by Nay Kaw, FBR team leader, and Karen soldier, Tha Da Der, Karen State, 2012.

in the reserves. I enrolled at Fuller Theological Seminary in Pasadena, California.

Now a seminary student, I continued trying to date Karen, pretty unsuccessfully. She still lived and worked in Seattle, but I was far away in Pasadena. In March of 1993, during spring break of my first year, I visited her in Seattle to see if our relationship was going anywhere. We had broken up in the fall, but then I visited her at Christmas, and we had started dating again. Now I wanted to see if she was really serious. We were at her apartment, and the discussion wasn't going well for me when a phone rang. Her roommate answered and said, "I think it was for you, Dave, but the line cut out."

I told Karen, "I'm not going to answer any phone calls. The only person I'll talk to is my dad." Dad was in Thailand and for him to call America would be a once-in-twenty-years event. "Unless it's my dad, have your roommate take a message, and I'll call them back."

About two minutes later, the phone rang again. Karen's roommate said, "Dave, it's your dad calling from Thailand."

"What?" I couldn't believe it. I picked up the phone and said, "Dad, what's going on?"

Karen's family visited us sometimes. Here, her mother, father, and two nieces come to a training in Shan State, 2010.

He told me about a visit he had from a Wa tribal leader from Burma who'd come to Chiang Mai, hoping to lead his people away from the drug trade and dependence on China. The leader saw my Green Beret picture and asked about me. Dad told him I was a soldier but was now preparing to be a missionary. The leader said, "We need him. We are a warrior people and the people will respect a soldier. But what we really need is God."

There on the phone, my dad said, "Dave, I think it's the leading of the Holy Spirit. You'll have to pray yourself, though, and see."

Right at that moment, I agreed with him. It was like a light suddenly came on and lit up my next step. I went back to the room and told Karen, "I'm going to Burma. I love you, and I'd like you to go with me as my wife. But I'll also understand if you don't feel like you want to marry me and don't want to do something like this. But I've got to go. That's how it is." This didn't seem to produce a sudden change of mind in her, so I thought, *This is the end of our relationship. I'll have to do some classic missionary thing, leave everything and go alone into Burma.* I took it as a challenge from God. I thought, *This is a test. I'm going to choose God first.* I packed up, ready to go back to school at Fuller and with Burma and the Wa now looming solidly in my future.

BURMA / MYANMAR

INDIA

Kachin

CHINA

BANGLADESH

Sagaing
Division

Chin

Shan

LAOS

Naypyidaw

Arakan

Karenni

THAILAND

Karen

Mon

Thaninthayi

Burma/Myanmar is Free Burma Rangers' primary area of operation.

FBR has 92 active teams in the states
highlighted in dark gray.

N

CHAPTER TWO

A Different Kind of Missionary

"Then you will know the truth and the truth will set you free."
—JOHN 8:32

Karen was working as a teacher, and as my spring break was coming to an end, hers was just starting. She had planned to spend the time with her parents, who lived in California not far from where I was going to school. Despite our uncertain relationship, she decided to ride down with me to visit her parents as I returned to school.

On the drive, we had a good time talking about what was going on at Fuller, and I sensed a change in her mood. She seemed lighter, playful, and maybe even romantic. *What's going on? I thought this was all over.*

In California, we stopped at Carmel to visit an Army friend of mine, John Nash, who had been my team sniper and communications sergeant in Special Forces. He wasn't home when we got there, at about eight o'clock at night, so I said, "Let's get some food, and I'll take you down to this beautiful beach I know about."

It's a little white-sand beach off the tourist path, and when we arrived, we were the only ones there. We started talking about our future again. By now, she was sitting on my lap, and I looked in her eyes and said again, "You know, I have to go, and I would like to marry you."

This time, the answer was different. She said, "Well, I don't want you to go alone, and I don't want you to go without me. And I don't want to be here without you."

"Okay," I replied. "Now I know what you don't want. What do you want? Will you marry me?"

"Yes," she said. Wow. No fireworks exploded behind us, and it felt like a negotiation for a used car (me), but it felt right too. We were married on the beach in Malibu just a few months later, on June 5, as our respective school years ended. We left one week later for Thailand, Burma, and the Wa.

We spent the summer in Burma, then returned to California where I continued with seminary. We spent summers in Burma for the next two years until, in December 1995, I finished seminary and was ordained. We formally moved to Thailand in March of 1996 to start our mission work. We had evangelism projects for the Wa. We supported a Wa hostel in northern Thailand and a Karen hostel in southern Thailand. We had outreaches in the jungles in central Thailand and did a little bit of cross-border work into Burma, where a military dictatorship was waging war against the many smaller ethnic groups who lived along the border.

It didn't take long before I started to get restless. One day, about four months after moving back to Thailand, I went for a run. Discontent was running through my head. *I don't think this missionary work is really for me. Everything we're doing is good. I can write a good letter about it, and it needs to be done. The people we help appreciate it and need it, but it's just not for me.* I thought of the quote I heard somewhere: "Don't ask what the world needs, ask what makes you come alive. Because what the world needs is people who have come alive."[4]

I was not coming alive.

The doubts flooded in. I shouldn't be a missionary. It was a nice, pious idea to serve God in a way I thought was the ultimate way. I thought maybe I'd be a little more spiritual, a little more holy by doing this for God.

I told myself maybe it was a false piety, trying to be good for God. Maybe I should go back to being a soldier. I knew how to do that. I could do it well, and now I could do it a lot better than before. This time, I'd put God first, my troops second, and me last. Before, sometimes I reversed that order. I'd do a lot better now as a soldier, and I could serve God that way. It was very naive and silly of me, thinking I could be a missionary.

I completed the run and was walking to the front gate of our property. I had basically decided to go back to the army and was feeling pretty motivated. *Man, I'm going to go back and be a soldier.*

As I walked up to the gate, more questions came. I knew it couldn't be that easy. I realized it was really about trusting God. Did God lead us here or not? Is God real or not? I stopped my questions right there.

I'd been through that battle before, and it went nowhere, except to God. I had felt God's love; that was a reality I knew from experience, not reasoning. For me, God existed. So, if God exists, I have to trust Him. If I trust Him, then I have to be able to praise God. If I say I trust God but can't be really thankful, I don't really trust Him.

I went through the gate, forcing myself to praise God. At the same time, another voice in my head was saying, *What kind of psychobabble is this, forcing myself to thank God?* With all these voices, I felt a little crazy, but no one could hear me, no one was around, so I forced myself: "Praise you, Lord." Every time a doubt came, I ignored it and said, "Thank you, God." When a feeling of being in the wrong place came, I said, "Thank you, Lord." I kept thanking God as I walked up to the house.

Within about an hour, I felt good. *Man,* I said to myself, *I feel great! I don't understand it, but I feel great and do trust God for everything.* That same day, my sister Laurie called with a new mission in mind.

"Dave," she said. "Let's go to Burma and visit Aung San Suu Kyi. She's just been released from house arrest." Laurie is my younger sister and we have a lot in common. A star athlete all through high school, she and I shared many adventures growing up, and later, she married my best friend, Pete Dawson, now a naval submarine officer. She became a champion for justice, and the government of Thailand's neighbor, Burma, was shamelessly brutal and oppressive. She wanted to get involved.

In 1987–1988, university students in Rangoon, the capital city, took to the streets to protest the government. The generals in power ruthlessly and brutally suppressed the protests, gunning down unarmed protestors and jailing their leaders. This was caught on camera and images of slender, bookish Burmese youths in blood-stained school uniforms went all over the world.

Western indignation resulted in sanctions and widespread calls for free and fair elections. In an effort to salvage their reputation and economic future, the generals, somewhat naively, held elections. Showing up to lead a victorious campaign for the opposition was someone they did not expect and had no idea how to handle: a slim, idealistic, Oxford-educated woman, Aung San Suu Kyi, the daughter of Aung San, the Burmese hero who had led the country out from the hated rule of the British. The protests had broken out while she was visiting her ailing mother in Rangoon, and she had elected to stay and help—even though she had a husband and two small sons back in Oxford.

My sister, Laurie, on an early mission, singing to Karenni IDPs, 2004.

Aung San Suu Kyi and her party, the National League for Democracy, won the election in a landslide. Rather than recognizing the results, the generals placed her under house arrest. In 1991, while imprisoned, she received the Nobel Peace Prize, an award that likely saved her life, though it did not win her freedom. The Orwellian status quo was more or less maintained in the country. Even so, constant political machinations signaled the uncertainty and violence just below the surface.

Now, in 1996, she was released, and Laurie wanted to visit her. Unfortunately, I had been blacklisted by the Burma government after my visits to the Wa area during seminary. The Burma Army warned me, not once but three times, that they would "take care of me" if I ever came back. A visa didn't seem likely, and should I get one, I figured they'd arrest me on arrival. Flying brazenly into Rangoon seemed like poking the giant in the eye.

We applied and were both awarded visas. Wow. The next risk was a bit bigger: arrest on arrival. Were we playing into their hands or was this God-willed? After a prayer on the beach at Hua Hin with Mom, Dad, and Karen, we felt "Go." Laurie left her two children, Sarah and Dave, with Karen, and we boarded a plane for Rangoon.

We were not arrested on arrival. Perhaps we overestimated the intelligence capacity of the Burmese military; perhaps we were on God's mission. While Suu Kyi was ostensibly "released" from house arrest, she still had very few freedoms. She couldn't actually leave her house, but she could speak to the people from her front gate on Saturdays and Sundays. We went to listen to her one day, along with the thousands of people who came regularly.

What impressed me that day was she was joking and laughing and had a radiant smile, as if everything was wonderful. How could she be so gracious and loving? Many of her friends and supporters were in prison or had been tortured, killed, or forced into exile. The people were oppressed and the whole country was in disarray. How could she be so full of love and lacking in bitterness? I looked around, my eyes shining. I thought, *This is wonderful. I'm looking at the process of a revolution led by a remarkably brave and loving lady.*

While thinking that, I turned and looked back at University Avenue, the street behind me. Military intelligence agents lined the street, and a couple of army trucks were parked there, likely full of machine guns in case the people got out of hand. City traffic went by beyond that, cars and buses full of people going about their daily lives—their eyes were not shining; rather, they were wide and full of fear. I felt these people were thinking, "What is Aung San Suu Kyi doing? Is she going to get us in trouble? I wish she'd be quiet."

This suddenly depressed me—although most people in Burma wanted change, they were too afraid, or too apathetic, to do anything about it. Even if Aung San Suu Kyi could lead the country to freedom, they would expect her to perform miracles within one or two years. If everything wasn't perfect, they'd blame her. I looked back at her. How could she give up her family, her freedom, her security, everything, to live in this constrained environment under house arrest? How could she do it for so many people who wouldn't even help her? I realized it must be because of love. She's like a mother who will always give love, and her best, to her son or her daughter, regardless their behavior. Because of love like that, Aung San Suu Kyi is able to keep going. Because she knows no matter what the people think, what they need is freedom. No matter what the people are willing to sacrifice, what they need is love and justice. And she's going to do her best to lead them there.

I was determined to meet her. I returned later to her gate, but she had been shuffled back inside the house and away from the people. As I looked around, a little man appeared and asked who I was. I introduced myself and told him I wanted to meet Aung San Suu Kyi. It turned out he was her cousin and had lost his previous job because of it, but now he was helping her. He gave me a phone number, and I returned to the hotel where Laurie was.

We stood together over the hotel phone. I dialed the number; I was sure it would be bugged and doubtful the call would go through. A woman's voice came on the line, "Hello?"

I said, "Hello. My name is David." As soon as the words were out, the line began to scream with static. I stopped talking, and the line went silent. She spoke and the static came again. When she stopped, it stopped. Someone was jamming our conversation. I hung up the phone. What a stupid thing to do, phoning when I knew the phones were bugged by military intelligence.

I looked at Laurie, and we prayed again, "Lord, please forgive us if our only reason to come here was adventure or self-aggrandizement or thinking we could play some important role in the freedom movement in Burma. Please forgive us, but we don't know what else to do. We felt we were supposed to come here, so we're going to call her again, Lord. If you want this to happen, we ask that you open the phone lines and let me speak to her. If we don't, if we're blocked, okay. We'll know we didn't come here to meet her." Laurie and I prayed this in Jesus's name, and I called again. This time, it worked: the voice came through clear as a bell, and we made an appointment for the next morning.

Laurie had to return to Thailand that day, unfortunately, but the next morning, I showed up at Aung San Suu Kyi's front gate, presented my passport, and was ushered into her meeting room. We had a one-on-one meeting for a full hour. I brought a Bible, the one I received at ordination, and gave it to her. I said, "I don't mean to be pushing a Bible on you, but this book has meant a lot to me and it's a story about God's relationship with humans and humans' relationship with God, and humans' relationships to one another. And it's helped me a lot, and I think there's good to be found here, true things."

She said, "The Bible. I read it every day. 'You will know the truth and the truth will set you free.'—that's my favorite verse. Thank you."

I also gave her my Special Forces crest, which is crossed arrows inside a scroll, and at the bottom it says, "De Oppresso Liber" ("Free the Oppressed"). And she said, "Oh, the things of war are sometimes beautiful."

I told her I really believed in "Free the Oppressed." She told me the country needed unity—between the Burmans and the Burmans, between the ethnic nationalities and the Burmans, and between the ethnic nationalities themselves. Burma is a country with over one hundred ethnic groups, which comprise 40–50 percent of the population and had suffered under the Burman ethnic majority since the end of World War II. She said the Burman majority had oppressed the ethnics in the past, they oppressed them in the present, and they would oppress them in the future. "That's our nature. But I know it's wrong. And I know it's wrong not because I'm a wonderful person, but because my mother taught me that all people are God's children. All people are the same. And so, we must strive to unite our country. This is one way you can help."

That motivated me. I didn't know how I would help, but I was ready.

Then I talked about prayer, and she said, "Yes, we need prayer. Please tell the pastors, here in Burma particularly, to pray for us and don't be afraid. They used to come to my house all the time, but now they're too afraid. Remind them, 'Perfect love casts out fear.' Please pray for us also."

As I got ready to leave, I remembered Elizabeth Elliot's words: "Obedience unto death." I said, "Aung San Suu Kyi, I can't do much, but I offer you everything I have, all one hundred and fifty pounds of me. It's not much, but I will be obedient unto the Lord until death."

"Oh, don't die," she said.

Despite my declaration, I agreed with that sentiment and said, with complete sincerity, "I don't plan to." Then I thanked her and left.

I returned to Thailand with a new sense of mission, a mission I liked: walk all around trying to help the ethnics unify and get people to pray for Burma. I thanked God for this. Then I started trying to figure out what that actually looked like. A Thai friend, Dr. Saisaree, who was also a friend of Suu Kyi's, suggested starting a "Day of Prayer for Burma." I thought it was a wonderful idea, so we did it—and it continues to this day.

I spent the next few months with Wright Dee, a Karen evangelist and former Karen National Union leader Dad had introduced me to. I wanted to organize a meeting among all the ethnic nationalities' leadership to hammer out a unified vision and goals.

By January 1997, seven months after my meeting with Suu Kyi, we were able to organize a meeting that included thirteen of the major ethnic minority groups in Burma. It was to last for a week. But just as

With Aung San Suu Kyi in her
home in Rangoon, 1996.

the meetings were starting, I became sick, diagnosed with malaria and
typhus at the same time. I asked God for strength and we moved forward with the meetings according to plan.

The meetings were held just inside the Burma border, in Mae Tha Ra
Hta. The ethnic representatives stayed together in bamboo houses and
there was real unity; they visited together after hours in their houses,
continuing discussions and sharing stories, smoking cheroots, and
chewing betel nut. We started each meeting with prayer. It was a silent
prayer, as there were Christian, Buddhist, and animist leaders present.
We said, "Take one minute, you can pray to God. If you're an atheist and
don't believe in any God, then it's a minute to reflect and think about
something outside your own situation, or your own tribe." Each night, I
visited every group and prayed with them. The sickness wiped me out,
and, weak and feverish, I had to stop between each house and pray for
strength to make it to the next one.

Eventually, they reached various agreements, including agreeing to
support Aung San Suu Kyi. This was important and a surprise because
Aung San Suu Kyi, before anything else, is a Burman. The ethnics don't
trust Burmans after all the abuse they've suffered. For them to say they
publicly supported her as the leader of Burma was an enormous com-
promise for many, but a wonderful thing. After it was all over, one of the

Buddhist delegates from the Pa-Oh tribe came to me and said, "Your God won. Your God was here. That is why everything was peaceful and in harmony and worked. We can feel the spirit and the power." My old Special Forces teammate, John Nash, who was out of the army and working as a freelance journalist, visited the meeting and wrote up the story for the *Bangkok Post*.

Working with these different ethnic groups, all of which were oppressed and attacked by the Burma Army, I learned more about the suffering of their people, many of whom were displaced inside their own homeland by the Burma Army. Just two weeks later, this suffering spilled over into Thailand, and my mission shifted once again—but it didn't just shift, it tightened and coalesced into something new, something it seemed my whole life had been preparing me for.

At the end of January, two weeks after the meetings, the Burma Army launched a major offensive right up to the Thai-Burma border, displacing more than five hundred thousand Karen, Karenni, and Shan people, killing many, and burning hundreds of villages. Multiple divisions of the Burma Army, along with twenty thousand prisoner porters carrying ammunition and supplies, swept the small ethnic forces before them.

The ethnic resistance armies were beaten back and dispersed in the face of that onslaught. Burma's military junta was heavily supported by the Chinese, who didn't want a democracy on their southern flank. They gave the Burma dictators weapons, ammunition, and military intelligence support. The Burma Army numbered over three hundred thousand men, while if you combined all the ethnic resistance armies, you might come up with fourteen thousand. The Wa were an exception—they had over twenty thousand soldiers—but they were also in a ceasefire with the Burma Army.

This offensive took place in an area where the ethnic resistance was only about eight thousand men spread over one thousand miles, taking on a few hundred thousand Burma Army soldiers. The ethnics were losing.

I had just finished meeting with the leaders of these people; they had shared their fears and their hopes with me. I saw how hard they worked to help their people, how willing and able they were to try to reach peaceful solutions. Now their people were being chased from their villages, slaughtered in their homeland. Refugees were streaming

Victims of a Burma Army massacre. Dooplaya, Karen State, 2002.

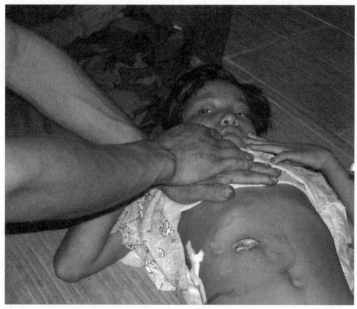

Eh Ywa Paw ("Flower Who Loves God"), nine-year-old girl shot by Burma Army after they killed her father and grandmother, Karen State, 2006.

across the border, and the Burma Army was even crossing into Thailand to attack them. I had to act.

I went south from Chiang Mai to a small border town named Bueng Klung, where there was a hostel we supported. I wanted to see what was happening there and how they'd been affected by the fighting. It was night when I got to Bueng Klung. The village was abandoned, and at the hostel, the only person I found was one kid I knew was an orphan, about twelve years old. I decided to stay at the hostel with him.

The hostel was two hundred meters from the Burma border and had a small mountain topped by a big rock outcropping jutting up about one hundred meters between it and the border. The Burma Army was just on the other side of the mountain. Their proximity wasn't conducive to relaxation. I was restless. While trying to sleep, I heard a rustling and scraping noise, then a sound like someone clearing his throat and grunting. I was feeling a little tense, but it seemed unlikely a unit of the Burma Army was stealthily sneaking up, making those noises.

But there was something there. I did not have a gun, but I had a machete. *I don't want to die lying on my back. If it's the Burma Army, I'll just make a run for it. If I can't get away, I guess I'll use this machete and then make a run for it.* I pulled the blade and carefully crept out of the abandoned hostel. There was almost a full moon, and I stayed in the shadow of the building. I looked hard into the moonlit shadows, machete at the ready; I wasn't feeling too heroic.

I heard the noise again. It was coming from a pigpen nearby. I hunched over, readied my machete, and slowly moved forward. What was it? I saw the last thing I expected: a pig someone forgot to let out. I smiled to myself, let the pig out, and went back to the hostel, where I rested a little easier for the rest of the night.

The next day, I met two Karen men who had fled from inside Burma and were living in the abandoned village. The three of us crawled to the top of the limestone outcropping. There was a cliff on the Burma side and a steep slope on the Thai side. I looked down, and there was the Burma Army. I could see about one hundred soldiers, but I knew there were two battalions, so I figured many more men were below me, just out of sight.

A little dirt track wound through the jungle below, and on that dirt track, in addition to the Burma Army soldiers, were Karen villagers. There was a refugee camp just inside Burma near this little outcropping,

but the Burma Army burned the camp and captured some of the refugees—men, women, and children. They were carrying large sacks of
rice, which the soldiers looted from the camp, deeper into Burma. The
soldiers loaded the men down with hundred-pound sacks, and they
were bent double, barely moving. Women were loaded with about half
that and were also struggling. It was the end of February, the beginning
of the dry season, and it was hot and dusty. For every eight or so Karen
people carrying loads, there were a couple of Burma Army soldiers
with guns. The column went on and on, a few hundred people carrying
loads, spread out in the dust under the hot sun.

I had no gun, but I did have the machete and some pen flares I'd
dug out of the truck this morning. A pen flare is something you shoot
in the air to make a bright light. If you shot someone with it at seven
meters or so, it would really hurt and might even kill. But it's certainly
not a conventional weapon to use in battle. The two Karen men who
had crawled up on the peak with me weren't soldiers. The fact was, we
weren't going to charge the column and free those people. We did what
we could, which was maneuver into a position on the rocks where I
could take some photos.

As I snapped pictures, I heard a gasp. I looked around. One of the
men who'd come with me had his forefinger curled between his teeth,
and was biting on it, hard, sobbing and trying not to make a noise that
would give away our position. He was watching his people, captured by
the enemy, and he didn't know what their fate would be. It looked very
bad. Many of them would likely die in the next couple of days—and we
couldn't do anything about it. Again, our lack of weapons impressed
itself on me. If we had three rifles, maybe we could do something, but
even so, we couldn't have saved all those people. As it was, we had nothing. I felt hopeless.

I prayed. I asked God, "What can we do?" I took more photos and
had an idea. I didn't know if it would help, but it was one way to make a
stand. Maybe the refugees would see it and feel hope, knowing someone
saw their situation.

There was an old bamboo pole with a Thai flag tied to it on the
ground. It marked the border at the top of this peak. I thought, *This
should go up so it will remind the Burma Army exactly where they should
stop.* They had already come into Thai territory quite a bit, including
into our hostel right before I arrived. I raised the Thai flag and tied it up.

That got the attention of the soldiers below, who looked up at us. I was mad. I yelled at them, "Hey, what are you doing? Let those people go!" Whatever they had been doing, they stopped and started shooting at me. The Karen guys took off—and when I say "took off," they were like monkeys. They scampered around the rock face, through a little notch, and were gone down the Thai side, where the slope was gentler. On this outcropping, there were some class four and five climbing moves, and a mistake could send you tumbling to your death.

I knew if I hurried too much, there was a better chance of me falling to my death than of getting shot. The Burma Army was at least one hundred meters away, and I hoped they weren't very good shots. I crawled along, taking my time, about as relaxed as could be while fleeing for my life. I got to the notch where the outcropping opened into the gentler slope and jumped through it, bullets winging over my head. As I scrambled through, the two Karen guys were there, laughing, and I laughed too. I remembered the words of Winston Churchill: "Nothing in life is so exhilarating as to be shot at without result."[5] Then we stumbled, leaped, and tumbled down the Thai side; we didn't want to be taken by the Burma Army, and they could easily come around that rock outcropping and capture us.

We made it back to the hostel, where my truck was still parked, packed with medical supplies. I decided I would carry as much as I could and walk on the Thai side of the border to a village called Lay Ton Ku, which was four or five hours south of Bueng Klung by foot. I had heard refugees fleeing the offensive had congregated there, many sick or injured.

I moved my truck to a safer place about two miles away, stopping by another abandoned house right next to a little trail into the jungle. As I parked, a Karen man walked out of the jungle, and when he saw me, he approached with a big grin. He was in combat fatigues with an equipment set fully loaded with magazines and hand grenades; he carried an M-16 rifle and a little cap perched on his head. He was fully kitted out for war. He had a big, bright, ruby-and-gold earring stuck in his ear. With his giant grin and flashing earring, he looked like a happy pirate.

He came up to me and said, in English, "Hello, my name is Eliya. I'm a medic. How can I help you?"

I thought, *Holy smokes, man. It's an angel from God! A pirate angel!* What I said was more practical: "I'm going to Lay Ton Ku. If you want to come and help me, great. I've got four backpacks of medicine and was going to try to carry two. You can help."

"No problem." He turned to the two Karen guys who had come with me and another passing refugee who also came from the jungle and said, "You, you, you. No need to run away. Are you men? You can run away another time. Right now, we've got to go help people. Pick up those backpacks. Let's go!"

They were mildly nonplussed but looked at each other and seemed to decide it was a good idea. So Eliya, three other refugees who had just fled Burma, and I, with all of my medical supplies, headed back into the jungle.

In Lay Ton Ku, we found 1,150 displaced people who'd fled to Thailand. They were scattered outside the village, sitting and lying on the ground, some injured, some sick. They had almost nothing. We started treating people and I began to see that Eliya was quite a medic. He had instant rapport with everybody. We stayed there for four days before crossing the border to see what the Burma Army was up to. Some people fleeing told us the Burma Army wasn't there but was operating about half a day away. That meant the area in which we were treating people on the Thai side was pretty safe. We treated people there and then walked back to Bueng Klung.

We got back to my truck by the little trail right at dusk. At the same time, out of the jungle walked four men carrying a man in a hammock slung from a bamboo pole. Three days before, he'd stepped on a land mine laid by the Burma Army. It blew most of one leg off, and his friends had carried him to Thailand. He was still alive, but his leg was gangrenous, and it stank. He was certainly going to lose it, and maybe his life. They asked me if I could evacuate him.

I said yes, and they said I should take him to the hospital in Umphang. It was about six hours of four-wheel driving, but maybe it would save his life. I agreed. They stuck two IVs in him and rigged him up in the back of my truck. His friend held him in place, and I realized I had to go right then. This mission was over.

I turned to Eliya, pulled out a Special Forces coin I had, and gave it to him. I said, "The motto of the Special Forces is 'De Oppresso Liber,' or 'Free the Oppressed,' and that's what you're doing in every way. I just want to thank you for what you've done, and I'd like to pray for you."

As I finished the prayer, he smiled, looked at me, and said, "Now I have to go find my wife and my son."

"Wife and son? I didn't even know you were married."

He said, "Yes, my wife and my son. They have been cut off by the attack of the Burma Army. There was no way I could find them and no way I could know where they were. But I did know where other suffering people were, and I knew my duty was to help them. I had to trust God. God will take care of my family. Now that I'm through with my mission of helping these people, I have to go find my family."

He picked up his M-16 and said, "Maybe next week I'll be dead"— and his laugh rang out through the jungle.

I looked at him, his teeth flashing white, his eyes merry and sparkling. The warm glow of the setting sun lit the sky above the already dark jungle. He turned around and walked off into the darkness. I knew I had met someone special, one of God's men of faith. I got in my truck and prayed again for him. Then I took the wounded man to the hospital.

The situation on the border was critical, and we started to ask how we could respond. That mission had been small, but it had helped. Eliya did find his wife and son, and later we met again and did more missions. I never had a plan other than to help the person in front of me. I would be glad, and they would be glad. That was how it started.

It gradually grew into a bigger response, even into a movement, for us and for the people under attack. We saw that while the dictators could destroy much and control much, no dictator can stop you from loving your people. No dictator can stop you from serving others. They can take your home, your weapons, your farm, your family—but no dictator can stop you from loving and serving if your heart chooses to. Even if you don't have a weapon or don't want to fight, you can do something. You don't have to sit in a refugee camp or a town waiting for someone stronger or better equipped. You can go in and give love and help the people.

We didn't respond with a strategy to defeat the Burma Army; we responded with a movement of love. It was asymmetrical warfare, fighting acts of hate with acts of love. We were surrendered to Jesus and love but would not surrender to oppression or injustice. We decided we would call ourselves the Free Burma Rangers. Being a former Army Ranger and a Texan, I liked the name. A Ranger is someone who will go anywhere, anytime, no matter how dangerous or difficult, to do something good. It was Eliya, along with another Karen leader, Htoo Htoo Lay, who came up with our motto:

> *Love each other.*
> *Unite and work for freedom, justice, and peace.*
> *Forgive and don't hate each other.*
> *Pray with faith, act with courage, never surrender.*

CHAPTER THREE

Animals in the Jungle–A Movement Begins

"Please, [when you tell our story] show us as people who haven't given up. Show us as people who love."

—SAW DEE GAY JUNIOR

MURDER AND RAPE

KACHIN STATE, BURMA: JANUARY 20, 2015

We were in Nam Lim Pa Village, Kachin State, when we got the news: two Kachin girls, missionaries from the Kachin Baptist Convention, had been raped and killed in a village not far from our location. Nam Lim Pa right then was mostly empty, as the residents we had visited the previous year had fled a few months before when the Burma Army attacked and occupied this village. While the Burma Army had since pulled back, it wasn't far off, and only a few villagers remained. Choosing not to run was a risky proposition; we had already held a memorial service for seven people who hadn't fled the initial attack. Their bodies had been found with signs of torture in hastily dug graves.

I was working at a table with a bench seat in a low-ceilinged, dirt-floored little shop that served noodles and sold snacks. Both tables and chairs were hard to come by in the jungle, so this shop was special. Our team included my family—Karen and our three children, Sahale, then fourteen; Suuzanne, twelve; and Peter, nine—and a few other teammates from Chiang Mai, including Micah, our Kachin coordinator, and Hosannah (or Hosie), who helped with general coordination as well as with organizing the Good Life Club (GLC).

Karen started the GLC to address the needs of the children in conflict zones; we would sing songs, do a Bible drama, give a health lesson, and hand out a bead bracelet with a Gospel message and a GLC shirt to

Maran Lu Ra and Tangbau Hkawn Nan Tsin, two Kachin girls raped and
murdered by the Burma Army, January 2015. (Photo courtesy of Kachin
Baptist Convention)

all the kids. There were also about thirty other Rangers from different
parts of Burma, who were now busy setting themselves up throughout
the abandoned village. Hammocks were going up, cooking fires were
being lit, and solar panels were being laid out to charge camera batteries and cell phones. As we rarely had a signal out here, phones weren't
supposed to take priority for power on missions, but they always got
charged somehow. This was how we first found out: via social media.
The story of the girls was spreading quickly.

As I typed away, answering emails and sorting photos, I heard a
buzz going through my team as they hustled around setting up camp.
Zau Seng came up to me, holding his phone out. "Thara ("Thara" means
teacher and is a form of respectful address in Karen language)—look." I
took the phone from his hand and looked at the screen: two women lay
sprawled side by side on a mess of colorful blankets and loose clothing.
They were both partially undressed, with their arms and legs splayed out
unnaturally. Their faces were bloodied, and their fingers were bloodied
and broken. A long thick piece of firewood, covered in blood on one
end, lay next to them—leaving no doubt about the cause of death.

I closed my eyes as sorrow from deep within began to rise. Rage rose
with it.

I wanted to cry. I thought of them and their families. I thought of my daughters, my wife, my sisters. I opened my eyes and looked again at the brutal image on the tiny screen.

My team shared what they knew: the girls were named Maran Lu Ra, age twenty, and Tangbau Hkawn Nan Tsin, twenty-one. They were from Kachin State's capital, Myitkyina, and had been sent by the Kachin Baptist Convention (KBC) as volunteer missionaries to teach about God's love to the people in northern Burma along the Shweli River and the Kachin-Shan state border. The KBC sends volunteers out by twos every year into areas of need. The rape occurred in the KBC church compound in Kawng Hka Village, Muse District, northern Shan State, which was just south of us. On the night of January 19, 2015, Burma Army soldiers entered the church grounds where the girls were sleeping, raped them, and beat them to death.

Villagers nearby heard the girls screaming, and when they went to check, they saw Burma Army boot prints and the bodies of the dead girls. The church members went to the Burma police, but they took no action.

We were so close, and yet we could not stop it. This is why we were here, why we'd been coming for some twenty years—but the people's suffering had not ceased, nor had the brutality of the regime lessened. We came to stand for freedom and justice with those who suffered, but freedom and justice were elusive. I gathered the team and showed them the picture of the two girls, brutally murdered in their beds. I made everyone look. I told them, "This is what the enemy does. This is why we are here, because the world must know this is happening." They stood in silence.

I knew what I felt: hate. I knew what I believed: hate was wrong. Right then, my feelings and beliefs were not matching. I often told people, "Our hearts change all the time, and if you must choose between your heart and your duty, choose duty." I needed help. I dropped to my knees in front of the team and said, "Dear God, I am so sorry about these girls. I confess I hate the Burma Army, and I want to kill them. But I will obey you. I give up hate and revenge. Please help me and our team to do your will in this. Please help the girls' families and all of us. In Jesus's name I pray. Amen."

We sent out the report that night. It was all we could do. This was evil, and evil had to be stopped. But how? What we could do we would, and I drove our team on.

THE LONGEST WAR: SHORT HISTORY OF THE ETHNICS' FIGHT FOR FREEDOM IN BURMA

My first mission with Eliya in 1997 was the beginning of FBR, and it started with the Karen people. It says in the Bible, "We love because He first loved us" (1 John 4:19). These words describe how it's been with God and me. It is also how it was with Eliya and the Karen people and me. They loved me first. I love them too, but they loved me first. They brought me along like a small child. I was in their hands, and my love for them gave me peace no matter what happened.

The Karen are a people whose homeland stretches from the delta area of south-central Burma to straddle the border with Thailand. This arbitrary line between countries has made all the difference for those who live there. In Thailand, they are mostly farmers, living in small villages carved out of the jungle. Many still live in bamboo houses in little villages tucked away in Thailand's national parks. Their life seems almost idyllic, peaceful, and agrarian.

In Burma, the Karen have been fighting a brutal civil war since 1949, when the British officially left. On January 4 of that year, Burma first gained independence. But the ensuing government was largely formed by and for the majority Burman nationality and left out the ethnic nationalities. Christian Karen officers in the national army of Burma were replaced with Burman Buddhists. Christian churches, mostly Karen, were seen as vestiges of British influence and were attacked. Within three months of independence, the new nation was embroiled in civil war on multiple fronts.

Though engaging in all-out attacks against the ethnic peoples, the original Burman government was nominally democratic. But in 1962, General Ne Win and the military overthrew it, installing a military junta in its place. Now it was not just ethnic minorities under attack, but the majority Burmans were facing oppression as well. Ne Win left no hope for a federal system. Fighting in the country increased as more of the ethnic nationalities organized to resist the brutal, oppressive tactics of the military, whose goal was not just to control but to "Burmanize" the entire country.

Since then, there has been a succession of Burman dictators, leading what they called "the Burmese way of socialism." They implemented a ruthless "four-cuts" strategy designed to cut off the ethnic armed groups from food, funds, intelligence, and recruits. On the ground, it looked like full-on attacks on villagers and forced relocations out of ethnic areas where the ethnic forces operated. Thousands of villages were destroyed or relocated, and thousands of civilians were raped, tortured, and killed.

By 1988, the military was divided as to who should lead, the economy was in shambles, the ethnics still had not been defeated, and there was a student uprising.

These protests vaulted Aung San Suu Kyi to fame, if not power. In the face of international condemnation, the military merely reshuffled itself, changed the name of its party, and carried on as it had, trampling human rights in contested ethnic areas and overseeing an Orwellian regime in areas it fully controlled. The generals offered conditional ceasefires to many of the weaker ethnic armed forces, while concentrating their fighting forces on the most determined opponents, including the Karen people.

Suu Kyi and her party, the National League for Democracy (NLD), did not give up, and finally, in new elections decades later in 2010, they were again elected and became part of the government. However, in the meantime, the military rewrote the constitution, guaranteeing themselves power and ensuring Suu Kyi could not be president or prime minister. Eventually, bowing to popular pressure, she was allowed to take the role of state counselor and the NLD and Burma military began to share control of the government. This led to ceasefire talks with the ethnic armed groups and some ceasefire agreements. However, in spite of agreements, the Burma Army continues its attacks.

At over seventy years, Burma has the longest running civil war in the world. The Karen, along with other ethnic groups, continue to struggle for human rights, justice, and self-determination. The Burman majority makes up about 60 percent of Burma's population and the ethnic groups, of which the Karen are the largest, make up the rest. Even now, the Burma military not only attacks the ethnic groups, it oppresses its own Burman people. People continue to suffer murder, rape, burning of villages, and displacement. Over one million Rohingya people have been displaced to Bangladesh, with seven thousand killed and three thousand raped. Also, in Arakan State, the Burma Army is attacking the Arakan people, displacing more than sixty thousand in 2019. Attacks are ongoing against the Kachin, Ta'ang, and northern Shan, causing one hundred thousand or more people to flee into the jungle. Even in cease-fire areas such as Karen State (as of the writing of this book), the Burma Army is attacking and displacing people in order to build fortifications, roads, and project their power. Since 1997, when FBR began, over two million people have been displaced in Burma.

Back in 1997, when I met Eliya walking out of the jungle, he was walking in the footsteps of generations of Karen resistance fighters. When I threw two heavy backpacks of medicine on my back and turned my steps toward the jungle that hid villagers and the Burma Army, I was walking on the same path: forty-eight years of Karen medics, soldiers, farmers, mothers, and fathers who never gave up. They had not just sur-vived. They were thriving and living with grace. In so many cases, they were not bitter, they did not hate, they did not complain, and they loved.

The twenty-five-year-old son of one leader of the Karen resistance, Dee Gay, told me this soon after I began working with the Karen: "We don't fight because we hate. We don't fight because we think it's a holy war. We fight because it is the only way to protect our land and our fam-ilies and our wives and our children and our homes. And yes, we know that the Burmese are also the children of God. It's tragic. It's terrible to fight them. But we have no choice. They won't talk. They just come and they burn and kill and torture and rape. So we have to fight."

This is what I mean when I say they brought me along like I was a small child. I took pictures and videos to help them tell their stories. But they taught me much of forgiveness, of loving your enemy, and of faith. And I never forgot Dee Gay's request: "Please, show us as people who haven't given up. Show us as people who love."

At the beginning, our first team was just five men, like a split team in Special Forces. But this was a Special Forces team of hobbits. "When is second breakfast, when is third breakfast"—they always made me laugh. The ethnics laughed at everything, including themselves—they seemed to me the humblest men in the world. Life was a joy to be lived, dangers were to be faced together, and there was room for everyone.

We all had animal names and called ourselves "the Animals." I was the foreigner Mad Dog, and Eliya, who continued to do missions with me as a medic, was the Karen Mad Dog. After our first meeting, he'd found his family and moved them to a safer place on the Thai side and was trying to start a clinic to help the refugees who were there. At our second meeting, which was unexpected, he was able to meet Karen too. I gave him some supplies and money for his clinic, and he looked at me and said, "I have nothing to give you."

Then he pulled a silver ring off his finger and handed it to me. I'm not much of a jewelry guy—when my wedding ring was lost while I was swimming a flooded river on the way to a Karenni refugee camp, I didn't replace it—but I put on this ring to use as my wedding ring. My wife is very understanding. She smiled and said, "Sure, that counts."

Eliya and I were like brothers. He's a wild man: a laughing soldier-medic and a champion Karen kickboxer, a good singer, guitar player, dancer, wrestler, soccer player—actually he's good at any sport. He's gifted with his hands, speaks five languages, and he can cook. He's always full of energy and laughs at danger—mortal danger, like when the Burma Army blocked us on three sides, and we couldn't go out the fourth because they had that under observation. He looked over at me, grinned, and chuckled, as if to say, "This is fun."

His dad was a pastor, and Eliya was a Christian, sort of—he prayed when he was in trouble but not too much otherwise. I had started praying all the time, often aloud, after seeing how God led me when I asked. I'm about ten years older than Eliya, so he looked at me as a little more experienced, and one day he asked, "Do you always pray like this? Do you always pray all the time? Did you always do that?"

I said, "No, not always. It used to be just when I was in trouble." I guessed I hadn't been in trouble that much because I certainly hadn't prayed often before. "But," I told him, "Now I believe God cares about everything we do, and there's nothing too small or too big for God. It's better to ask. I think the first thing we should always do is pray, the second is think, and the third is act."

So Eliya started to pray more. I could see a difference in him, in some of his wild-man ways that were wild but also not good. He started realizing that about himself and took steps to change. We grew closer.

Eliya was always cool in action, slow to fight, quick to make friends but ready for the worst; he was good at fighting and healing. He was also wise. If ever I said anything that was not loving, he would say, "Thara, God doesn't like that. We have to love each other." He is God's gift to me to save my life, help raise our children, build FBR, and keep me close to God. He was the first Ranger.

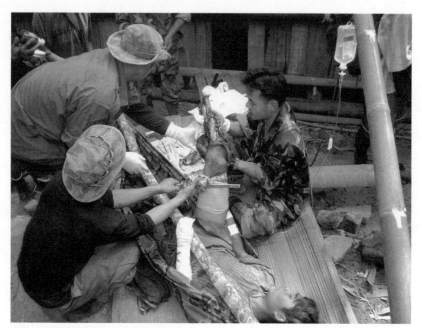

Eliya, Winston, and S4D treat a man who stepped on a landmine, Burma, 2004.

Bird was the next ranger, a small, bouncy, chirpy guy, strong as a Sherpa, who was smiling all the time and happy with everyone. His name was Toe Bee Bay, which means "robin," but we just called him Bird. When Bird joined our team, he was Buddhist and didn't believe in God. He had a real servant's heart, though. He'd get up first thing in the morning, if we weren't moving right away, and go to the fire and make coffee and bring me a hot cup. Being on the team, he started becoming interested in God. He began to pray, and Jesus came to him in a vision more than once. He cut off his spirit bands and became a full-on evangelist. Once, in the middle of a long, all-night walk, he told me, "You know, my heart is so full of God right now, and I want to share it with everyone. I want to let the whole world know how much God loves us, how much God can give us a great life and make us straight." That's Bird. He was our human rights documenter, photographer, and reporter.

Monkey was our pastor, though he started out as an atheist. His experience was less mystical than Bird's but also powerful. I asked him to go to a training that was going to be in English in Chiang Mai. He was a refugee in a Karenni camp on the border and was too intimidated to go. But he also didn't want to say no to me. I told him to trust

God and go. Rather than say no, he decided to do exactly that—the going part, at least. He marched into the airport at Mae Hong Son to catch a flight to Chiang Mai, fully believing that, as an undocumented refugee, he'd be turned away and possibly detained. To his utter surprise and some chagrin, the policeman only said, "You'd better hurry or you'll miss the plane!"

He started to think about God more seriously after that. He began to read and share the Bible and became downright pastoral, giving comfort and praying with people. He was also our videographer and he was very good at that. But his main job was being our team pastor. He's Karenni, small, quiet, and very humble but tough. If you asked him how he's so strong, he'd say, "Anything that is strong comes from God." He's also a very funny guy with the low-key kind of humor that always slips a joke in when you're not expecting it. He's thoughtful and, like a good chaplain, helps keep our team on an even keel.

Another person on our core team was Mucu, or "Kathay Y'Wa" in Karen—which translates literally as "the horse that carried Jesus." We just called him "Donkey." He was a Karenni soldier for twenty years, a tough guy who fought many battles and killed many people. He started watching us before he was on our team and he criticized us—we weren't tough enough for him. At the same time, he wondered why the lives of our team members were the way they were: full of joy.

One day, while still a soldier, he went back to the front line from the refugee camp and ran into the Burma Army, unexpectedly, by himself. He told us the story later: "We all started shooting at once. My weapon jammed when I was only four feet away. There were about six of them, and I turned and ran. I knew I was going to die. Right then, I called out to God and said, 'God if you save me, I'll follow you.' The bullets went all around me, underneath me, beside me, over my head but, unbelievably, none of them hit me. That was the turning point in my relationship with God, and I knew I needed to follow Him." He joined our team. He was our security guy, an assistant medic, and a pastor.

Paw Htoo was the second FBR woman, after my wife Karen. Paw Htoo and her husband were running away from the Burma Army when they were caught; he was bayoneted to death in front of her by the soldiers who had caught them, and she was arrested. She was pregnant when she was captured and gave birth in prison. After she was released,

Monkey carries Suuzanne on an early mission.

she escaped to the Karen defensive lines and joined us. She was a nurse and a brave, beautiful, and humble woman.

Htoo Htoo Lay was our great advocate and sponsor. He was the second-highest leader in the Karen National Union (KNU). He was educated in Rangoon, trained as a lawyer and worked on the side as a pastor. When he realized how much his Karen people were suffering in their homeland at the border, he moved there and joined the resistance. He was mostly deaf from a mortar that exploded near him during a fire-fight. He would start each morning around 5 a.m., singing hymns at the top of his voice and sweeping the floor of his house. His heart broke for the suffering of his people, and he was always pushing for more action to help, more action to fight the Burmese, more action to make change. He hated politics and bureaucracy. We became close friends.

At first, FBR was like a volunteer fire department: we all had other jobs, and we did those when there were no new attacks or between mis-sions. Then the Burma Army would move into another area, hundreds of villagers would be on the run, and we would come together to help them. I would go with the team and the other medics and soldiers from the KNU. We would bring medicine and treat people, and I took pho-tos and conducted interviews. I'd fire these reports out to everyone I could—the U.S. State Department, my military contacts, any journalists or lobbying groups I knew were interested in human rights issues, as well as our donors, who were supporting us to buy medicine, food, and cameras so we could help more people.

On these missions, I learned the mettle of the Karen, and we became a true team. One time, on an early mission with Eliya, we were trapped by the Burma Army, pinned against a riverbank by a column of advancing Burma Army troops. It was night, and they knew we had just crossed. They were coming to kill us. There were five of us: Eliya, Monkey, Bird, a Karenni soldier, and me. We were unarmed except for hunting knives. We crouched behind some bushes, hoping they would pass by and not see us. Just then, a boat came up the river behind us with a spotlight. It was looking for us, too, and there would be no way to avoid the light without being exposed to the advancing troops.

It was terrifying, and I pulled my knife out and began to pray. I looked over at Eliya as he also pulled his long knife out. The moonlight glinted off the blade and then off his teeth as he laughed quietly. I saw a relaxed and fearless determination that said, "We may die, but many of them will too." I had the same determination but definitely was not feeling relaxed. We all tensed for the attack, and I prayed again, "Lord, I know this is a selfish and fearful prayer, but please turn them back so we do not need to kill them and so we don't need to die. In Jesus's name I pray."

Then the boat was even with us, the floodlight sweeping the area close to where we crouched. As we tensed to spring out and attack the troops in front of us, the boat hit an obstacle and was knocked back, throwing the man with the floodlight off balance and sending the beam of light shooting straight up. The driver overreacted and gunned the engine, and the boat lurched past us before the light could shine back where we were. This was our chance, and we took it, sprinting away into the darkness.

Another time, we were in Karen State, trying to evacuate ninety-six men, women, and children who had survived a Burma Army massacre. The Burma Army surrounded us with four battalions and was closing in on our column of wide-eyed and terrified children and their mothers, with desperate fathers crouched under the trees. We were trying to figure a way out. There were none of the usual Karen smiles or laughing, only fear and the feeling of imminent disaster.

Eliya crept up to me, smiling through betel nut-stained teeth. He was strumming his M-16 like a guitar and softly sang to the huddled

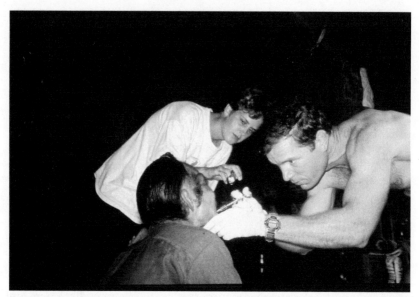

Doing dental work on a Karen patient in Lay Ton Ku, Thailand, assisted by Amy (Davisson) Galetzka, FBR's first volunteer, 1999.

people, "Don't worry about tomorrow, just do really good today, the Lord is right beside you to guide you all the way. Have faith hope and charity, that's how to live successfully. How do I know? The Bible tells me so." His eyes sparkled as he finished, and the tension eased. We all smiled, prayed again, then found a narrow way through the encircling Burma Army.

We were doing missions like this regularly. The fighting was constant, and thousands of villagers were being displaced. With Htoo Htoo Lay's encouragement, the KNU soon asked us to train full-time teams who could respond to Burma Army attacks in different areas at the same time. In 2001, in Lay Wah camp just on the Burma side of the border, we held our first relief team training. The KNU picked teams to send, and we trained them, supported their missions, and published their reports. They still belonged to the KNU and coordinated missions with their leaders. The KNU was happy to do this; we didn't assume any authority over the teams, so they were still KNU people. The Karen leaders knew our only agenda was to help their people as long as they wanted us to.

It was during this time Karen and I decided to start our family. Our first child, Sahale, was born in Alaska on August 23, 2000. We had already planned to be there that summer, having fallen in love with the beauty and wildness of Alaska. We had climbed Denali (Mount

McKinley) and it felt like the kind of place we wanted to return to when we visited America and so we were happy for our first child to be born there. In 2002, Suuzanne was born in Thailand. And in 2005, Peter was born, also in Thailand. When Sahale was born, our Karen friends kept with our tradition of animal names and called her the "White Monkey." This meant, also according to Karen custom, my name changed: no longer was I Mad Dog—I was now "Father of the White Monkey," or "Tha U Wah Ah Pah," and Karen became "Mother of the White Monkey," or "Tha U Wah Ah Mo" (TUWAP and TUWAM for short). Suuzanne was named "Baby Bear" for her wild and happy personality, and Peter became "Baby Tiger." The children grew up in the jungles of Burma, carried by Karen and me and the Animals, which is what we continued to call our team of ethnic Rangers. Peter was three weeks old when Karen first carried him into Burma. We had to walk three nights to get to our camp, moving only in darkness and mostly off trails to avoid the Burma Army. Karen carried him in front of her so he could nurse and, in the darkest areas, would have one hand on my pack as we moved without lights.

The kids were a new element to our mission. They brought new risks and raised many questions about our mission from our family, friends, and supporters—though not from those we went to help. Bringing them was certainly not something we took lightly. We decided to do missions as a family only after prayer and discussion. Karen, of course, felt the risks most acutely, certainly more so than anyone questioning her decision. In 2003, before the birth of Peter, she wrote the following letter to answer those questions:

> ...I am preparing to take my children again to a remote location in Burma. There we will be training young leaders who will conduct relief missions to people fleeing attacks of the Burma Army. I wanted to put down my thoughts and reasons for this trip in case something happened to us and people said, "What was she thinking, doing this?" As a mother, I deeply love my children. They are a joy and fulfillment in my life. Nurturing and educating them is my passion, as I give them experiences and truths that will be tools for the rest of their lives.
>
> Even before I became a mother, I was committed to working with Dave together as a team. As we began our family, I enthusiastically put my all into motherhood to raise our children to

love God and others, and to travel with us in our work. Our children love the people they meet and have many "aunts" and "uncles" in Thailand and Burma. To them, we are all one big family. They have been greatly blessed by their time in villages, in refugee camps and with internally displaced people (IDP— someone who has fled their home but not crossed an international border, as opposed to refugees, who have fled their country) in Burma. Many there have said that they also were encouraged that we brought our "heart's treasures" to visit them.

Although there are risks, I am excited by the wonderful opportunity for Sahale and Suuzanne to continue to experience the great love and fellowship that comes on our trips with friends inside Burma. I have been touched again and again by the deep love shown in time and energy on our behalf, and I earnestly hope that by seeking the simplicity, generosity and hospitality given to us in these remote areas, my children will naturally treat others this way as they grow up. I see this as a significant investment of eternal values. I hope we show the people we meet that they are of great worth. As a family, we want to give back some of the love and encouragement they have given us. I also hope we can affirm that there is a joy and peace regardless of circumstances and that the hardships they endure can be redeemed by God's love. I believe in the reality of abundant life for everyone. Jesus has promised this, and I hold on to that hope. As a family, we love to be together, and we go as part of the larger family of God's children.

As God opened the doors to this ministry, I feel he has given me peace in many ways. At the beginning of our work, I felt God say to me, "Karen, you and I have always been close. If Dave were taken away from you, would we still be as close, or would you be angry with me and turn away?" I was reminded that Dave, and all the people in my life, are gifts, not givens, and that the most important relationship in my life must be with God first. Even in sorrows or disasters, I believe that God is sovereign over all that happens and is the only steadfast anchor in the joys and trials of life. Later, a dear friend told me that the most significant prayer she offers as a mother each day is "I give my children back to you, Lord." Whether I think I am living in "safety" or not, thanking God for his wonderful provision keeps me grounded.

Lastly, I asked a great Karen leader, who is also a lawyer and lay pastor with many dangerous experiences, how he prayed for his own protection. He told me that he does not pray for safety.

Instead he said, "I pray that I am in the right place at the right time, doing the will of God. It is not my business to worry about my safety and I leave the number of my days on earth up to him. In the end, I hope to hear him say to me, 'Welcome! And well done my good and faithful servant!'"

In our ministry with the Internally Displaced People of Burma, I have focused on children. We started the Good Life Club with the theme of "abundant life" from John 10:10. In this verse Jesus says: "The thief comes to kill and destroy but I have come that they may have life and have it abundantly." This is Jesus's promise and it is even more meaningful in contrast to the "thief" who comes to kill and destroy. In our work, we are faced with people under great oppression and crisis. Is abundant life possible for them? Many of those suffering have strong faith that instructs and inspires me. Does their faith in Jesus give them an overflowing, exceptionally good life amidst their fear and misery?

We do not go with many answers, but we go knowing the power of love and hope. I am earnestly seeking this abundant life, to be a testimony of it for those we meet, and also to learn more about it from people who seem to have nothing that the world values, but who live in riches of love that I long to understand and share. I want this for my children also. I thank God that we can go as a family and with the love and joy that God gives, which makes our own lives abundant.

All three children grew up this way and had the blessing of hundreds of ethnic uncles and aunts taking care of them. In addition to the eternal values in Karen's letter, they also learned to hunt, fish, and move in the jungle. We had them on packhorses from an early age. They became skilled equestrians and performed songs as they stood on their horses' backs. Suuzanne taught her favorite horse to lay down on command. They became competent in difficult situations as a result of living a frontier life, and it translated into competence in recreation as well, when we visited the U.S. They were climbing by the time they were three years old, and Peter summited both the Grand Teton and Mount Rainier when he was six—the youngest person to summit those mountains. They love to compete in rodeos and even win some, though they have no formal training and have to borrow horses. They've also skydived and learned to surf.

Karen carries Peter with Sahale, Suuzanne, Hosannah, and Doh Say near Doh Heh Der, northern Karen State, 2007.

Karen leads a GLC program in front of the posts of a house burned down by the Burma Army. Cat, Eliya's wife, is on the far left, Paw Htoo and Daisy are to the right of Karen, and Kiryn (Johnson) Trask is on the far right. Karen State, 2006.

We love climbing, from the Himalayas to Alaska. Here the family summits Mt. Rainier, WA, with Chris Sinclair, Micah Beckwith, Hosannah Valentine, and Dr. John and Christa Shaw, who helped start our Jungle School of Medicine, 2013.

Peter, six, and sisters Sahale, eleven, and Suu, nine, on summit of Grand Teton, 18 July 2012. That year, Peter was the youngest to summit both the Grand and Mt. Rainier.

Peter rides steers in Cody, WY, 2017. (Copyright: Cody Enterprise Journal)

Suu rides barrels in Cody, WY, 2018. (copyright: Cody Enterprise Journal)

Sahale rides barrels in Cody, WY, 2018. (copyright: Cody Enterprise Journal).

Peter (along with Sahale and Suu) skydiving tandem in Czech Republic, 2012. (copyright: Jump-Tandem CZ).

This has helped them learn other lessons as well, including that no matter how skilled and brave they are, they still need help. In America, this meant generous people lending the girls competition horses to race barrels, and for Peter, it meant steer- and bull-riding gear. Nevertheless, the biggest lesson they have learned is a personal reliance on God and on those who love them. "Daddy, we're not just a family. We are a team," Suuzanne said to me once, when we were infiltrating the Nuba Mountains of Sudan on a relief mission. She was eight. We had been invited to help the Nuban people of Sudan, and while on this relief mission, we were bombed every day. We hid in caves with the Nuban families until the planes left. The leader of the Nuba resistance said, "Thank you for bringing your family to be with our families in need. We can see that because you brought your children, you love us and do not want anything from us."

Someone once asked me if people ever criticize us for bringing our family into dangerous areas. "Only those in safety, not anyone in those areas," was my answer. We go as a family because we love being together, we feel this is God's best way for us, it is the best life we can offer our children—they are very competent kids—and because there are families in need, and Karen and our children can help them. We go as a family, but never blindly and only after prayer, discussion, and advice from our team, supporters, and those we go to serve.

Suu and Peter with a python they will eat, southern Karen State, 2011.

Suuzanne rides with her monkey near Doh Thay Der, Karen State, 2012.

Sahale with her monkey, and Suu, ford a river in Burma, 2010.

Me with Htoo Htoo Lay, the Karen leader who helped us start FBR, 2009.

On a Burma mission in 2007; Chit Pay, our mule man, is on the right.

CHAPTER FOUR

A New Door Open—The Movement Grows

"Our role is to help the people and shine a light in a dark place and give love."

—MONKEY

As our family grew, the relief team training did as well. Before long, other ethnic groups heard about what we were doing and asked us to train their people also. Within a few years, in addition to the Karen people, we were training Shan, Karenni, Arakan, Lahu, Chin, and Mon teams. Later, we trained Kachin, Padaung, Ta'ang, Pa-Oh, and Naga teams. These are all distinct ethnic groups, with their own languages and traditions. The Naga, Chin, and Kachin are predominantly Christian. The Karen, Karenni, Padaung and Lahu are a mix of Christian, Buddhist, and animist while the Mon, Shan, Ta'ang, Pa-Oh and Arakan are mostly Buddhist. All are struggling for freedom from the Burman majority.

To help support these growing operations, we also had a growing staff of volunteers. At first it was just Karen and me, running around and doing missions with the ethnic guys. As we grew, more of the ethnics committed more time with us, and we began to have a few foreign volunteers help us. Shannon Allison, my old Army buddy, came on missions with us when he could take time off from his dental practice in Louisiana. Johnny Galetzka came on missions between his geological survey work trips, and helped with some of our early satellite communications systems. And in 1999, Amy Davisson, a young American woman just out of college, came to work with us as our first full-time volunteer. As we grew, more would come, some for a few months, some for years.

Our main training moved deeper into Karen State, hidden away in a little valley with a beautiful, boulder-strewn stream running through it. The site was chosen by our friend, General Baw Kyaw Heh, who was one of the most effective commanders of the Karen. For the first few years, we would have to come a couple weeks before the actual training to clear the jungle brush overgrowing the place between trainings. Our team erected bamboo houses for my family, the instructors, and the classroom, and the students made their own shelters. A Karen leader nicknamed "The Fox" christened it Tha U Wah camp after Sahale, the White Monkey.

We also conducted trainings in Shan State, north of Karen State. On the west side of Burma, we trained teams across the border in India. When the Burma Army broke the ceasefire with the Kachin far to the north, we did several trainings up there. But Tha U Wah camp became the heart of our operations in Burma. Along with the relief team training, we started the Jungle School of Medicine, which is both a school and clinic located in our camp. The school was founded by FBR's Karen medics and two physicians, one of whom was Dr. John Shaw. It provides a one-year training program for our medics, significantly improving

New foreign volunteers came too. Here, Nathan Collins and Jesse Cusic, perform for the villagers on a relief mission, Toungoo District, Karen State, 2010.

With Micah Beckwith, Jesse Cusic and Lyle Wilder, enjoying dried fish for Christmas Eve dinner, Saw Wah Der, Toungoo, Karen State, 2008.

their capacity, while the clinic gives us a permanent health care presence in the local community.

As we've grown and continue to operate in war, questions about our role have come up. The line we walk is a fine one, between conventional relief and development, and unconventional frontline operations. For me, the stronger pull is always to be more involved in the action. This is my personality and training. In these situations, we have always prayed and discussed, and listened especially to our ethnic teams. In the end, we are visitors in their land.

The question of our role was especially challenged and thereby clarified on one relief mission in 2009. We were in northern Karen State where the Burma Army displaced over two thousand people from the Ler Mu Plaw valley, killing, raping, and burning their homes. We split our team into two groups, with one going to take care of the people who were displaced while the other, led by a squad of five Karen soldiers, went to document what had happened. I was in the documentation group, and we were on a hill above Ler Mu Plaw Village, filming the blackened stumps of what once were homes, and over two hundred Burma Army soldiers below us. Two Karen villagers came with us, and one of them started to cry as we looked at what was once his home.

After we finished filming, the Karen soldiers with us could not contain themselves any longer and fired on the Burma Army troops. The Burma Army instantly returned fire with rifles and machine guns, and we all got behind any cover we could find. I started filming again. I was taking photos when a Burma Army machine gun below me shot rounds into the rock I was behind, throwing chips into my chest and face and narrowly missing me. "That's it," I said, with a feeling like when my kids have gone too far. It wasn't emotional, just a firm, "This must stop." I pulled out my pistol and emptied it at the machine gunner. One other Karen ranger we called Taxi, next to me, was also returning fire, along with the five Karen soldiers. The machine gun stopped, but other fire came, intensely, and we pulled out. None of us were hit.

We were at mid-slope of the mountain, running up as fast as we could for the pass at the top because there was another Burma Army unit to our left, also heading in that direction to cut us off. We had to get to the pass before they did. We were on steep ground, with bad footing, but the Karen scampered up it like deer. As I was trying to keep up, grabbing rocks and roots and trying to accelerate, something brown flashed beside me. I caught my balance and looked: it was a barking deer we'd flushed. A shot rang out, bang! One of the Karen, in mid-stride, had seen the deer, swiveled, and killed it with one shot.

The Burma Army was still shooting at us, and the soldier leapt down the side of the hill, grabbed the deer, threw it over his shoulder, and took off running back up the hill, with a smile on his face. It was pure survival instincts in action. *Man, I'm glad these guys are on my side.*

We got back to the rest of our team and talked about the incident and the fact we'd fought the Burmese. We prayed together, and I said, "If it is not our role, we should not fight the Burmese. But if it is our role, we should not be stopped by fear of the Burmese soldiers, or by fear our supporters will stop supporting us. One day, we will see God face-to-face and have to answer to him. If we haven't fought and tried to defend people, God might ask, 'Why didn't you?' And if our answer is that we were afraid people would blame us and stop supporting us, that will be a sad meeting. But if we do fight and God asks us 'Did I tell you to do this?' And we have to say, 'No, we just thought we should'—that will be a sad meeting also. So the question is, what does God want us to do?"

There were more than seventy Rangers assembled from eight ethnic groups, including our headquarters team. Nate and Jesse, two of our full-time volunteer staff, were there along with long-time friend and supporter John Moore, and Steve Gumaer of Partners Relief and

Development, who is also a good friend. "What is our role?" I asked the whole group.

Rangers began to respond, and then Eliya spoke up. "Look at these displaced people. They have no homes. They're out of food and medicine, and some are begging. I've never seen Karen people beg. You white people don't understand. It's not about fighting the Burma Army. We want to kill them, but more than that: we want to remove the stain of them—we will eat their excrement and drink their piss—to remove the stain of them from our land."

His eyes flashed; I could tell those words were wrenched from a place deep inside him that could feel every moment of decades of oppression. *Wow,* I thought. *Maybe we'll change, right here.* I asked, "Who agrees with Eliya? Please raise your hand." Everyone, including me, raised our hand.

And then I said, "Anything else?"

After responses from a few other Rangers, Monkey spoke up, measured and quiet. "Eliya is right. The Burma Army does evil things and must be stopped. Our people need to be free. What is our role in this? Our role is to help the people and shine a light in a dark place and give love. It is not to stop the Burma Army. It is to show love."

Again, I asked, "Who agrees with Monkey?"—and everyone, including Eliya and me, raised a hand.

Then I said, "So, even though it is right to fight the Burma Army because of what they do, the Free Burma Rangers will not become a militia with that duty. We will stand with the people and not run if they cannot run. And if we get trapped, it is up to each individual, as they feel God leads them, whether they defend themselves and the others or not, but we will not leave them." We agreed to abide by this unless three things happened: one, our leadership and their wives felt God tell them it was time to change; two, our close supporters felt the same way; and three, we were given three hundred new weapons to fight with. The first two were spiritual and relational tests, the last was a physical one. As of the writing of this book, we have not changed our role, become a militia or gone on the offensive. We have, from time to time, defended ourselves and the people we are serving. Our role remains the same: to give love and help and put a light on the situation.

We've trained more than five hundred teams who have conducted thousands of relief missions throughout Burma. We've provided medical care or other relief for more than one million people. But when I think about our work in Burma and what we have to show for it, I think the relationships we've built are more important. More than buildings or infrastructure, we've built relationships, we've encouraged them among others, and we've seen God change people's hearts through their relationship with Him.

We had one ex-Burma Army soldier come to our training; at the end, he asked to be baptized. He confessed to terrible things he'd been required to do as a soldier, such as killing pregnant women and babies. He said he was sorry and asked forgiveness from everyone at our camp; he didn't know if they'd forgive him or not. But they forgave him. After his baptism he came out of the water beaming, and into the open arms of the Rangers there, who all embraced him.

The Burma Army, however, did not change. Attacks against the Karen, Karenni, Shan, and others continued. In 2011, they broke a seventeen-year ceasefire with the Kachin in the north. We began doing missions there, which is why we were there that day in January of 2015.

KACHIN AND SHAN STATE MISSION, 2015

We sent the report out about the rape and murder of the two girls by the Burma Army and prepared to continue the mission. But before we left Nam Lim Pa, we had a memorial service to conduct.

When the Burma Army first came to this village two years ago, nearly everyone fled. Only seven people stayed; one was a twenty-year-old disabled man named Brang Aung. He had a stroke at a young age and was partially crippled. When his mother and sister left, he told them he would stay because he "didn't think the Burma Army would bother someone like me." The Burma Army occupied the village on November 17. It wasn't until December 31, when his mother and sister heard the soldiers had left, when they felt safe to return. They went to their house, which was ransacked and looted, but they could not find Brang Aung. His sister told us the story, describing how she went down to a neighbor's house to look. She said, "I saw a suspicious pile of dirt in the garden; we dug it up and saw my brother—he had been killed. When I saw his body, I fell down unconscious." His right arm was cut off at the shoulder and the soldiers also cut off his right calf.

That attack happened in November of 2013, and we came to the village in January of 2014. The villagers had already fled again because the

Burma Army was still nearby. We discovered Brang Aung's body, along with several others, buried in the hasty graves their families were able to carve out before they ran away again. We reburied them and held a memorial service but didn't know who they were. Now we were able to meet Brang Aung's mother and sister and hear their story and let them talk about him. We prayed with them, recorded their evidence, and sent it all out. Then we had one more memorial service, this time with a name to remember and lift to God.

Next, we headed southeast, to northern Shan State. It was a complicated area, where multiple ethnic groups struggled under Burma Army oppression and each other. They were caught between the power of their own government, the power of neighboring China, and the profitability of the opium trade. The previous year we came here with the Ta'ang National Liberation Army (TNLA), the local security force for the Ta'ang people, and with elements of the Kachin Independence Army and Shan State Army North. In this area were Ta'ang, Shan, and Kachin people, as well as Chinese opium farmers.

Opium production in that area was enforced by Burma Army-backed ethnic Chinese militias. The Burma government profited from opium production and provided tacit support for the on-the-ground forces running the drug trade. The opium farmers were wretchedly poor. Many became addicted to the drug.

The local Ta'ang, Shan, and Kachin ethnic people, knowing the destructiveness of the drug and understanding clearly it was one more avenue of control and exploitation for the Burma Army, had a policy of opium eradication. During the previous year's mission to the Pang Say area, we made unlikely friends with an ethnic Chinese family of opium farmers.

They lived under the eyes of the militia controlling them. We had approached their small settlement on a little hill with caution, not knowing what they would do. They were afraid and suspicious. But our team, including Karen and the kids, made friends pretty quickly. We gave them the GLC bracelets we handed out at kids' programs that have beads in five colors to tell a story of hope and encouragement. There was a mom there, a grandmother, and the mom's brother. Her husband was away because their son was arrested by the Burma Army and her husband was trying to get him out of jail. That night, we slept at their house on the hill, overlooking their opium fields, which were lush green and frosted with white, blossoming poppies, nearly ready for harvest.

The next morning, some of the team climbed a mountain above the village to take photos of the overwatching militia camp. When we returned to the village, new TNLA soldiers had arrived with a different mission than ours: drug eradication. They had long sticks in their hands, and with their weapons slung over their shoulders, they waded into the lush green fields of poppies and started knocking down and destroying the opium plants. One of their officers stood to the side, organizing them, ensuring they stayed methodical and didn't miss anything. The family hadn't been warned but soon realized what was happening; the mom ran down the hill, crying and pleading. This was their crop for the year; their livelihood was being destroyed before their eyes.

Sahale, Suu, and Peter came yelling, "Dad, Mom, they're destroying the family's opium, stop them!" Opium farmers don't usually generate a lot of sympathy, but we found ourselves in the strange position of being sympathetic, not with opium-growing, but with the family.

The crying mother got no sympathy from the Ta'ang officer and ran back up the hill, her anguished wails carrying over the fields. We looked on helplessly. We agreed with opium eradication, but we were watching the lives of new friends being destroyed. Opium was the primary way to rise above subsistence farming, but it put the growers under the control of ruthless and violent men and on the wrong side of the law, whatever that meant in this lawless country.

Inside her house, the woman sobbed. Karen sat with her, but she wouldn't even look at her. The brother stalked off, away from the house. Our team watched the soldiers destroy the field without joining in. They soon finished and marched off down the hill. Karen was still trying to comfort the lady and getting nowhere. Everyone was tense, and our security guys and ethnic team soon had us packing up. They were ready to head out.

The mom's sobbing finally began to slow. She explained haltingly through a translator that they had needed the money from the fields to help get their son out of jail. Now she didn't know what would happen to him. We prayed with her and gave her some cash to buy food to survive. We told her we agreed with drug eradication, but we thought it had to come with a substitution program. We told her we loved her and, more importantly, God loved her and could offer her a new way. Then we headed on to the next village.

A year later, we wanted to go back and see that family again. We did not know what to expect. We were told the opium farmers hated the TNLA and would not like us either as we traveled with them. It wasn't easy to get to their place. The TNLA wasn't sure they wanted to bring us, given tensions with the farmers and the movements of the Burma Army, which was maneuvering in the area. We had to walk far out of the way to get around them.

We prayed and wanted to go, to give love and help in any way we could, and report on the Burma government's exploitation of the opium trade. We pushed the local leaders and security to take us. They eventually agreed, and after about two weeks of walking, sometimes twenty to thirty miles in a day, we arrived. When we topped out on the hill where the village sat, the mom came out to meet us, bearing coffee and sweets. This was unexpected, and we were overcome by her graciousness and generosity despite what had happened the year before. We could hardly communicate because of language differences, but we felt love and affection bonding us. They thanked us for the help the previous year. They told us they had stopped growing opium, and their lives improved as they grew beans and raised cattle, which we had also seen other households do as an alternative to opium in the area.

We gave them more funds to help with food as they transitioned away from opium, and prayed with them. "Please pray for my son," the mother said. "He is still in prison." Karen gave the family more GLC bracelets and a Gospel book in Chinese. This was a better-than-expected reunion, and we left smiling and wanting to see each other again. As unlikely as it seemed to us, these were friends for life, and seeing them again was the highlight of our mission.

We had to head back. It was a good mission: we had a wonderful reunion with the Chinese family and made new friends. It was good experience for our new Kachin, Shan, and Ta'ang teams. We were able to document forced labor in Kachin State while we were at Nam Lim Pa, in addition to sending out the report about the two raped and murdered girls. But it had taken us many days to get here, circling around the Burma Army, avoiding roads, crossing mountain passes. We needed to be back in Thailand by early March for our annual meetings. Because the Burma Army was in blocking positions and looking for us, we had a lot of walking ahead.

It was February 4, 2015. We were at the beginning of our walk back, about nineteen days out. By midafternoon, we arrived at the village where we would sleep that night. It rained during the walk, which wasn't normal for that time of year. We slipped and slid down steep dirt trails and were happy to find a bathing stream while it was still daylight. We settled into the house where we would sleep, and I found some hot water for coffee and a good spot to do an evening of admin—mostly answering emails.

In the meantime, Micah, our headquarters Kachin coordinator, an American missionary kid who grew up in Thailand, started working on communications—"commo"—for me. Out here, we were off the grid and carried a satellite receiver to send and receive basic email. This helped us get out real-time reports, as well as stay on top of everything in other parts of our work. Our satellite communication (satcom) system cost six dollars per megabyte for internet use, so we limited it as much as possible. I did all my work offline through an email server rather than a browser and only turned the satcom system on to send and receive email. As I settled into a good spot to work, Micah brought up my computer. He had downloaded all the new messages I'd received since the previous night and sent everything I typed out while offline.

I scrolled through to see if there was anything "hot." Everything was pretty quiet in Burma, except for here. I saw a message from Victor Marx: "FBR in Kurdistan?" Victor was a good friend and a world-class martial artist, man of God, and gifted counselor. He and his wife, Eileen, started an organization called All Things Possible (ATP) Ministries that helped kids in prison in the U.S.

He'd visited our training camp in Burma once and helped teach hand-to-hand combat, shared his testimony, and helped train our chaplains. He demonstrated and taught disarming techniques, quickly subduing any attacker. He did all this with humility, humor, and respect for everyone. As he taught, he told the Rangers: "Never take someone's dignity away; treat all with respect." The young Rangers were in awe of this blinding-fast, gentle-but-tough guy. Victor also shared his story of abuse as a child and how, as a young Marine, Jesus changed his life and gave him a new start. Seven Rangers asked to be baptized after he shared what Jesus did for him. He taught me better knife-fighting

A ranger is baptized by Victor Marx, Jeff Sutton, and Karen pastor, Edmund, at our training camp in Burma, 2014.

techniques and, most of all, how to better love and serve God and people. We became good friends.

Victor's email read: "Dave, please come and help the Kurds in Kurdistan, Iraq, where ISIS is attacking people. Be here in seven days. I will pay for it."

I knew what was happening in Iraq and Syria. We saw on the news the brutal ascendency of ISIS, and in 2014, we went to speak in Waco, Texas, at World Mandate, a missions conference sponsored by Antioch Church, where Francis Chan was the main speaker. There we met Iraqi Christians who talked about what ISIS was doing to the Christians and others. It was a terrible situation, but we hadn't felt a call to go there. Our main work was in Burma, and our hands were full. We took two relief missions to Sudan in 2014 to train teams in the Nuba Mountains. The Nubans had been under daily attack by the Sudanese Armed Forces. Now there was a ceasefire, so we had not gone back. We were also invited to Nigeria and to Ukraine—but we weren't chasing conflicts and needed more confirmation.

When I saw Victor's message, I laughed out loud. This was a surprise. I said, "Hey, look at this: we just got an invitation from Victor to go to Iraq to help the Kurds. We have to be there in seven days!"

That would be impossible unless a lot of things changed. We'd walked nineteen days, sometimes covering more than twenty miles a day, up and down mountains, just to get here. The straight-line distance to the border was only about eighty miles of walking, but the Burma Army was in our way and looking for us. For any of us to get to Iraq in seven days, the Burma Army would have to move out of our way, we would have to walk thirty miles a day, then it would take two days of driving to get to an airport. The idea was laughable, really—but I was learning to listen while I laughed.

Later that evening, I read the message to our whole team and asked for prayer. Monkey led us as we offered this up to God. I asked the team what they thought. "If God opens the way, we should try," was the consensus.

Okay, we would keep praying and see what happened. The next morning, as we were getting ready for the day's movement, we got a message from the Ta'ang resistance, who were watching the Burma Army. "All three Burma Army battalions in front of us are moving." They told us it looked like they were following the same route we had taken to get around them a few weeks ago, like they were following us. That left a channel open for us to go through.

The Ta'ang said, "If you go right now and walk fast, you can get through the gap before they realize it."

We prayed again and felt, "Go for it." We moved out. For three days, we hiked up steep trails, along ridges, and over mountaintops, the beauty of Shan State stretching before us. We passed opium fields under the control of local militias loyal to the Burma Army. We moved all day and into each night, only resting a few hours before moving on. By the end of the third day, we penetrated the gap left by the Burma Army when they turned to follow our old trail.

Even with this new gap opened, the Burma Army wasn't far. As we dropped into a populated valley, with fields, fences, and scattered homes in the distance, our forward guides gestured for us to move faster. They wanted us to run. We took off, everyone shuffling along under their rucks across the field. We reached the other side and hit a road. There was a convoy of old flatbed Kachin logging trucks sitting there idling. We were going to get a ride. The trucks were slowly starting to pull out, gears grinding, big tires churning the dust on the rutted dirt road. Our team was about fifty people, and they were swarming the trucks like ants, tossing their bags up on the planked truck beds, hauling each other up the sides. After all the walking we'd done, everyone was excited for a ride.

"What's going on?" I asked Naw Seng, our Kachin coordinator.

"Burma Army is moving again," he said. "They just left this road. Now all these trucks, they want to go. We go with them."

I could see the map of this area in my head. This road had been blocked for weeks. It was why we walked so far coming in. These trucks also got jammed up behind the Burma Army. If this road was opened, it was a straight shot back to the border where we'd started. Going this way with trucks, we could be there in two days.

We wound up and down more mountains and came to a river too deep for the trucks to cross. But, to our amazement, a local crew was already there, just finishing a log bridge. We crossed and kept going, eating up the miles. As we neared the border, we got news the Burma Army was preparing to attack a village near us, so we stopped. If there was an attack, we would have to go back and help and we would not go to Kurdistan. We prayed and immediately got a message that the Burma Army had turned back. We kept going.

We made it to the border, and my family and I crossed without incident. Our plan was for Peter and me to go on this initial trip. Micah, Hosie, and our ethnic team members would finish the mission in Kachin and Shan states, and Karen, Sahale, and Suu were committed to hosting a group of visitors and family in Chiang Mai.

As the Kurdish immigration official stamped my passport and I walked through into the high-ceilinged baggage claim area of the Erbil airport, I shook my head in amazement and thought of the last week. Miles of jungle were a blur of walking, running, and roaring trucks. Within seven days, we had passed through the Burma Army, crossed multiple borders without incident, and landed in Erbil, Kurdistan. For us, it was a miracle. "Impossible" is a human word, not a God word. We had asked God a question. God had given us an answer. *What would it mean?* I wondered. I knew this was the beginning of something but I did not know what.

CHAPTER FIVE

Give Up Your Own Way– An Invitation to the Kurds

"You know what people need most? They need healing for their souls."

—Dr. Nezar, minister of health, Dohuk, Kurdistan, northern Iraq, to Dave in February 2015

God wants a relationship of love with each of us. How we respond has something to do with the kind of person we choose to be.

The first choice is the natural man who does whatever his impulses drive him to do. He does not care about society, laws or morality. He is selfish and only appears to conform to others when it suits his purpose. Under pressure, he will seek only to save himself.

The second is the social man who generally does the right thing morally and legally, wants to be good, and be well thought of, tries to obey laws and to help others. When under pressure, he will save himself and his family and friends, but not more than that. He is moral until it costs too much.

The third man is the idealistic man. He is highly moral and under pressure will not give in. He is willing to sacrifice anything, including his life, for what he believes is right. However, he can be unbending in ideals and in the end can be misled by pride and inflexibility.

The fourth, or spiritual, man looks like the idealist except there is always room left for God to lead in unexpected ways. He has an open mind and heart to God's leading that enables him not to be trapped by rigid ideals or dogma. This man is led by faith that God loves him and others, knows what is best and will lead him in every situation. This man also tempers his ideals with scripture, the counsel of others and a realization of his own limitations. Trust in God allows him to be flexible in every situation—not flexible in personal or social morals but flexible to his own role. As he lives a life of love, justice and mercy, he can afford to lose because he knows that the things of the world are fatal but not final. When he fails, he asks forgiveness, makes necessary restitution and tries again. The spiritual man is obedient until death, even the death of his concept of right or wrong.

—DAVE EUBANK, 2007 GLOBAL DAY OF PRAYER
FOR *BURMA MAGAZINE*

In February 2015, ISIS was near the peak of its success. They held territory stretching from Raqqa, Syria, up to the Turkish border, and across the Iraq border nearly to Baghdad, with smaller pockets scattered throughout Syria—some forty thousand square miles, or an area roughly the size of Switzerland. With roots in Anbar Province of Iraq, they took advantage of the unrest in Syria to build their strength and launched from there in 2014, taking the world by surprise and quickly sweeping across eastern Syrian into Iraq. They scored perhaps their biggest victory by taking the largest city in northern Iraq, Mosul, in June 2014.

From there, they made officially known the scope of their ambition: they were not just conquering land and people; they were establishing a caliphate. Abu Bakr Al Baghdadi declared himself the ruler of Muslims everywhere. He was the supreme leader, and their war was a holy one.

This pronouncement, given in the flush of a victory which delivered into their hands all the money in the banks of the city, U.S. weapons and military equipment from the nearby Iraqi Army bases, a path south toward Baghdad, and lucrative oil fields—this message brought tens of thousands of Muslims to join the caliphate from all over the world. Baghdadi told them it was their duty, and they came. They came to fight and not just for land or money or a leader—but to fight for God. It's estimated some forty thousand fighters from eighty countries flocked to Iraq and Syria to fight for ISIS.

The battle wasn't restricted to the Middle East. ISIS encouraged jihad anywhere there were enemies of Islam—that is, anyone who didn't subscribe to their brand of extreme ideology. Other Muslims were targets nearly as much as anyone else. They didn't want only to conquer territory; they wanted to win hearts and souls—and if they couldn't, they wanted to destroy them. Absolute brutality and fear went hand-in-hand. Terrorist attacks were instigated across the globe. ISIS shocked and terrified with brutal and staged executions—murders recorded and disseminated on media platforms, reaching into the farthest corners of the world.

For example, February 15, 2015, was the day in Kachin State when I received the invitation email from Victor. At the same time, ISIS released a video that was seen around the world. In it were twenty-one Coptic Christians, Egyptian men they had kidnapped in January. The captive men were shown walking on a rocky beach, identically dressed in orange jumpsuits and handcuffs. They were not blindfolded. Beside each man walked another man, an ISIS member; these were also dressed alike, in black with black masks on. The captors forced each of the captured men to kneel with his back toward the sea, his eyes toward the camera. Then each ISIS member cut off the head of his captive.

Their ideology was stark, legalistic, and they took it to its severest extreme. They were true idealists. The world would struggle to not let them set the terms of the battle, that is, to not respond with hate and violence to equal theirs, or fear.

I did not know what we could do in Kurdistan. It was not the jungle; it was desert. Everyone there drove trucks; no one walked. I knew no one there and didn't speak the language. I'd never deployed to the Middle East when I was in the military. But there was a great fight against evil there, so maybe we did have a part.

The Kurds are a people I heard compared to the Karen of Burma. They are the largest ethnic group in the world without its own country, with thirty million people spread between Iraq, Iran, Turkey, and Syria. In each of those countries, they've been oppressed and abused, and in each country, they have fought for freedom and, sometimes, simply for survival. In Iraq, Saddam Hussein tried to wipe them out, killing thousands and sending millions fleeing to Iran. In the wake of that attempted genocide, which the U.S. helped to stop by establishing a no-fly zone over Kurdistan, the Iraqi Kurds now have a semiautonomous state in Iraq.

Many Kurds are Muslim, but they are fiercely patriotic, and many told me they are Kurds first and Muslims second. There is an independent, wild feeling about them that made me think of my family's roots in Texas and the Wild West. I quickly grew to love them.

And it was the Kurds who first stopped ISIS. ISIS stormed through Mosul and out the other side, racing toward Kirkuk and the valuable oil fields long contested between the Kurds and Iraqis. With the Iraqi Army having fled, it was a race between ISIS and the Kurds to secure them. And it wasn't just the oil fields, but all of Kurdistan. Erbil, the capital of Iraqi Kurdistan, is just ninety minutes from Mosul.

With the oncoming threat of ISIS, the Kurds rose up. The Kurdish armed forces are called the Peshmerga (which literally translates to, "one who faces death") and they are famed fighters—but in this fight for the existence of Kurdistan, more men were needed. A significant home guard was called up, and men of all ages responded: university students and shopkeepers, businessmen and farmers, laborers and drivers. Signs began popping up throughout Kurdistan: "We are all Peshmerga."

With the help of coalition airpower, they succeeded. The Peshmerga fought ISIS on four fronts: Sinjar to the west of Mosul; just short of Dohuk, northeast of Mosul; at the city of Bardarash, east of Mosul; and east of Makmour, to the southeast of Mosul. ISIS did not take Kirkuk with its valuable oil fields. They came within twenty-three kilometers of Erbil but could get no closer.

Only in Sinjar, to the west, did the Kurds fail—at first. Sinjar is the home of the Yezidi people, an ethno-religious group who practice Yezidism, which is ancient mix of Zoroastrianism, and, later, Islam and Christianity. They are not a large group, and almost all of them live in villages in or around the Sinjar Mountains, with the city of Sinjar containing a mix of around sixty thousand Yezidis, Christians, and Muslims. They are mostly farmers and herdsmen and generally a peaceful people. The militants of ISIS considered the Yezidis to be Satan worshippers, the worst kind of heretic. They were marked by ISIS for destruction.

As ISIS approached Sinjar from both Syria to the west and Tal Afar and Mosul to the east, the Peshmerga retreated. The Iraqi Army, too, reeling from the loss of Mosul, could do nothing to help. The Yezidis had no official armed groups. Even before ISIS, they had pressed to be able to arm themselves, knowing the threats inherent in their region, but were refused. The Sinjar area was contested between the Iraqis and Kurds and neither wanted another armed group there. This policy proved disastrous for the Yezidis.

August 3, 2014, is a day burned forever on the hearts of Yezidis—the day ISIS came. They came suddenly, storming in on pickup trucks with mounted machine guns. They rolled into the first villages of the Sinjar area in the early morning hours. People were just getting up. ISIS came in shooting and met little resistance. Some people they killed immediately, like the men in Kocho Village: four hundred men were shot or beheaded in that one village. ISIS lined up the men and boys and made them hold up their arms; hair in the armpit meant you were a man and you were killed. No hair got young boys transferred to a training camp. Old women were shot and dumped in mass graves. Younger women and girls were rounded up to be sold as slaves to ISIS families. As ISIS moved from village to village, they destroyed them, blowing up and flattening the houses.

As news of the attack spread through these Yezidi communities, so did the panic. Everyone started fleeing. They threw as many of their belongings as would fit into cars, trucks, on tractors, and took off. Any relative—sister or daughter or son or husband out somewhere else, staying at a friend's or in the field, were left behind. There was no time to find them. Those leaving family behind could only hope their loved ones would find their own way out. Soon, long lines of overloaded vehicles were crawling along the roads. ISIS came from two directions, and there was nowhere to go but up the mountain, so up they went. It was a bottleneck, a single, narrow, winding, paved road overlooking the plains stretching to Syria. ISIS chased them up the mountain, firing with rockets and small arms. When ISIS overtook a car, they'd pull everyone out and shoot them right there. The side of the road was soon littered with bodies and burned-out vehicles, people's belongings strewn on the ground around the wreckage.

Through the chaos, the Yezidis realized they'd been abandoned— no one was coming to help. At the top of the mountain, two brothers, Hassan and Hussein, acquired a ZSU 23mm twin barrel antiaircraft gun from fleeing troops. It was mounted on a Ford F-350 pickup truck and, together with every Yezidi there who could fight, they manned the high ground where the narrow road topped out and turned the gun on ISIS as they came up, destroying ISIS vehicles and killing all ISIS attackers who tried to approach on foot. The mountain, rough, full of deep, dry gullies, barren of trees and water, rocky, and dusty, was crawling with people. Lines of fleeing people trudged through hidden ravines, families hunkered down under rock overhangs, shushed their children and animals, tried to disappear. Some fifty thousand people escaped to the mountain that August morning. At the top, the battle raged, and the pushback was enough to stop ISIS from overrunning the whole mountain. A refuge of sorts was established.

However, ISIS was able to surround the mountain and laid siege to the men, women, and children stranded there and looking for water, shade, and food. It was a desperate situation, one that soon had the attention of the world. Babies and the elderly died of thirst and exposure. Temperatures in northern Iraq in August regularly top 120 degrees Fahrenheit. The Iraqi Air Force began dropping in supplies, and so did the U.S. and western coalition. On August 7, President Obama announced the U.S. would begin air strikes on ISIS, fearing a genocide of the Yezidi people would happen if they didn't.

In the meantime, the Kurdish People's Party of Turkey, or the PKK as they were called, came and helped the Yezidis hold the mountain, along with the Kurdish People's Protection Units, or YPG, of Syria. The PKK was an outlawed party that had been fighting a low-grade civil war against the Turks since 1984, in response to years of Turkish oppression. The leader of the PKK, Abdullah Öcalan, was captured and jailed in 1999. The PKK was considered terrorists by Turkey but they were tough and disciplined fighters. On August 9, with help from U.S. air strikes, they fought through the ISIS lines on the northwest side of the mountain and began a massive evacuation of the trapped Yezidi families into Syria.

An exodus began off the mountain. Around forty thousand people walked for twenty kilometers, crossing into Syria and then back into the ISIS-free part of Dohuk Province in Kurdistan. Still, around ten thousand people remained. ISIS soon fought the PKK off and closed the gap, surrounding the mountain once again. But the majority of the people escaped. It is estimated that in the initial attack, some five thousand men, women, and children were killed or died of exposure and another ten thousand went missing.

In December 2014, the north side of the mountain was cleared of ISIS, and by February 2015, they were pushed completely off the mountain, though they still held most of the city and villages to the south. By now, the Peshmerga were back and fighting the ground battle to retake Sinjar, while the coalition hammered ISIS from the air. The people who stayed on the mountain, about eight thousand of them by then, were living in tents just below the top. The Peshmerga and PKK shared the mountaintop in separate compounds, uneasy allies who were only united in fighting ISIS.

This was the situation in February 2015 when I arrived.

Peter and I landed in Erbil, the capital of Iraqi Kurdistan. It's one of the oldest continuously occupied cities in the world, being the site of human settlements since about 5000 BC. At the center of the city, an ancient citadel sits on a small hill, and below it is the old market. Many of the government buildings are in this older part of the city, while the bigger, more modern buildings are at the edge. At the end of February, it was cold, raining in the plains and snowing in the mountains. In the lowlands, everything was starting to turn green, and I was a little surprised at how beautiful it was.

We linked up with Victor and, right away, were in meetings. We met with some Christian members of the Kurdish parliament that first day, and the following day, we met with the defense minister of the Kurdistan Regional Government (KRG). The way these meetings normally work is you get ushered into a large office that will have a big desk against one wall, while the other three walls are lined with sofas. Everyone sits down, and it feels very proper. The Kurds like ceremony and are always dressed up and perfectly groomed, every hair in place. Someone brings in small cups of heavily sweetened tea for everyone. If the meeting goes long, sometimes coffee will follow.

As we finished the meeting with the defense minister, Mustafa, he looked at Peter. Peter was nine years old at the time. He wore an oversized FBR shirt and carried his Karen bag with him everywhere—these are colorful bags the Karen people weave by hand in the jungle. In his bag, he usually had at least one knife, a camera, a headlamp, spare batteries, and a lightweight Gore-Tex jacket. The defense minister looked at him and said, "Who's this boy?"

I said, "That's my son."

"You brought your son here? This is a war zone."

This was a standard question Karen and I were used to answering, "You bring your kids to war zones?" Most of the time, it wasn't really even a question but more a judgment, like, "What are you thinking, bringing your kids to war zones? Don't you care about them?"

I told him, "Yes, but there are lots of kids here—everyone who lives here has kids here, and their kids are just as important as mine. And we care. I want to help, and I love my kids and want them to be with me. And they're helpful too. This is how we do things—as a family."

The minister was from a people who had been fighting for their lives for generations, and he said, "You brought your son, your most precious thing. I give you my most precious thing, my country." Wow. We spent a whole meeting trying to get access and there it was. Yet, this was also typical—people living in the midst of danger rarely criticize our choice to stay together as a family, even when it is dangerous; they usually see it as a sign that we are "all in" with them.

Victor grinned and said, half-joking: "Can we have that in writing?"

The defense minister was not joking and affirmed, "Yes, you can go anywhere you want."

Where we wanted to go was Sinjar. It wasn't easy, even with the defense minister behind us. The ISIS siege of the mountain had just recently been broken, and there was one gap you could get through, but access was unsure and restricted.

After that meeting, we drove to the city of Dohuk to meet the minister of health for the Dohuk Governorate, Dr. Nezar. Dohuk is on the way to Sinjar and is a Kurdish city tucked between two bare, rocky mountain ranges, the Bekhair to the north and the Zaiwa to the south. It's a strategic point for trade between Turkey, Syria, and Iraq. It also became a refuge for thousands of Christians and Yezidis fleeing ISIS. The KRG did a great job taking in these people ISIS specifically targeted.

In Dohuk, we met with Dr. Nezar and his staff. They were helping oversee the health care in the refugee camps and emergency services for Peshmerga soldiers and IDPs on Sinjar Mountain. Victor and his team were very interested in helping in the camps, working with Yezidi people and especially with the women and children, who were incredibly traumatized by ISIS.

Dr. Nezar is Muslim, an educated, soft-spoken, and gentle man. He met us in his office, spoke perfect English, took time to get to know us, and was helpful. At the beginning of the meeting, I asked if I could pray with him. When I finished, he looked up and said, "You know what people need most? They need healing for their souls." I thought, *This guy is not normal. Thank God I can meet him.*

As we were talking, Victor was on the phone talking with his team; it looked like they weren't going to be able to get up to Sinjar, but that was still where I wanted to go. Sinjar was the front line, and that was where our team needed to go, where we were most valuable—not in the refugee camp.

I told Dr. Nezar, "I'd still like to go to Sinjar with my son."

He said, "With your son? Oh—you are serious. Okay." He thought for a minute and then said, "Tomorrow one of my ambulances is going up. You can ride with them."

Wow. I was grateful. He'd barely met us and definitely didn't have to do that. I said thank you, we prayed again, and our group left. It was starting to get late by then. Our meetings were over. All Kurdish offices usually close by three in the afternoon, and it was well past that. That was fine with me. I decided to get a workout in—on the mountain that rose steeply from the edge of town. It had a giant Kurdish flag painted just below the ridge. It was dark by now, and raining, but I had a good scramble up and down. Standing on the ridge, at the top, looking down on the lights of Dohuk, I was grateful to be there. I saw, as I did so often in Burma, how life and joy could go on, even with an evil like ISIS only miles away.

The next morning, we were back at Dr. Nezar's office to meet the ambulance and found out it was going to be a bigger deal than just one ambulance. ISIS had had the mountain surrounded in siege since August and there had been serious fighting there, with many different groups working uneasily together to push ISIS out. The mountain was only recently liberated, and all those groups, including the PKK, Turkish Kurds, the KDP (Kurdish Democratic Party, the current ruling group), PUK (Patriotic Union of Kurdistan), and Goran—rival Iraqi Kurdish political parties, and different Yezidi factions, were going to visit the site of the victory. ISIS continued to hold most of the city, but there was a lot of symbolic power in this trip to the top of the mountain, and these groups were jockeying for power in the newly liberated area.

Instead of jumping into the back of a single ambulance, we joined a convoy of seventy Land Cruisers, along with gun jeeps and pickup trucks with mounted machine guns full of Peshmerga in the back. The road to the mountain was a small, two-lane highway paralleling the Syrian border; the drive turned into a breakneck race, with all the vehicles tearing along at over 120 kmph, racing each other. Sometimes, they'd be four abreast on the tiny road, trying to edge each other out. I thought, *These guys are crazy. They've got enough enemies; who wants to die in a car wreck?*

It was only later I realized all these different parties were racing each other to be the first to get up to the newly liberated mountain—sort of like the race to plant the flag on the North Pole. They all wanted credit for the victory.

As we approached the mountains, which rose dramatically out of flat desert, we started to pass completely leveled villages. Houses were crumbled, cars were twisted metal carcasses, and big, overturned tractor-trailer trucks lined the road. ISIS was not intent on just conquering—they wanted to destroy. Nearly all the villages near the base of the mountain suffered ISIS's carnage. The road to the top winds through bare rocky ravines, with the mountain plateauing in a few places and opening into hidden valleys where farmers and sheepherders had settled. ISIS hadn't reached here, and the farms and villages we passed were almost idyllic in contrast to the devastation we'd just driven through.

Just below the top of the mountain were the IDP camps. Though many thousands of people were able to escape in August, when the PKK and coalition air strikes temporarily broke the siege, many also stayed, either because they didn't want to leave their land or because they were unable or too afraid to make the trek to the Syrian border. Now these people were living in tents in the cold and mud, but with the siege broken, they were, at last, able to get supplies.

From the top of the mountain, we could look down and see the town of Sinjar and the battle taking place below, marked by billows of smoke from air strikes and the sound of distant concussions. I talked with some of the people who fled to the mountain and heard their stories. I wasn't the only visitor with the delegation—there was also a Norwegian pastor named Per Ove who would become a friend. We were there just a few hours and then drove back down. I was with the KDP delegation—the controlling party of the Kurdish government—and on the way back, we stopped at a Peshmerga fort. They had a big bonfire going and were celebrating the liberation of the mountain. I was standing next to the fire with Peter, and there was a woman standing next to me, professional-looking and engaging. The Kurds are, in general, pretty moderate in their practice of Islam, and Kurdish women have more freedom than in many other places. But still, this lady, here at the fort, standing around

Early family photo, with Dave, Laurie, Ruthanne, Suwannee, Allan, and all their pets in Thailand, 1972.

The early team. Back, R-L: me, Muku, Shannon, Monkey, Winston, Eliya, Bird. Front, R-L: Green Monkey, Fox, Paw Htoo, Le Baw, with other team members, 2001.

We baptize a former Burma Army soldier who joined our training and then asked us to baptize him, 2013.

The kids perform for villagers in Burma as Jesse Lee, Hosannah, Dave Dawson, and FBR teams look on, 2015.

Graduation of new FBR teams at Tah U Wah training camp, Burma.

My family in Badush, west of Mosul, with our team Humvee, 2017.

Sahale walks by a burning shack and opium field on a mission in northern Shan State, 2015.

A Kurdish tank fires during the battle of Bashiqa, October 2016.

Iraqi soldiers help with children's program in Mosul, December 2016.

Karen general Baw Kyaw Heh, and me, near Tha Da Der, 2006.

Karen medic Slowly with Aisha in the Humvee right after she was shot and while we are waiting for rescue, Musharrifah, May 4, 2017.

Me, treating Lt. Hussein after he is shot six times by ISIS. I was hit in the left arm in the same attack. Tammuz 17, May 18, 2017.

The few survivors of an ISIS massacre. Demoa is on the left, with a child who was killed before we could get there, Near Shifa Hospital, W. Mosul, June 2, 2017.

Our team running back to safety with the little girl and two men, trying to stay ahead of the tank and out of ISIS fire, Near Shifa Hospital, W. Mosul, June 2, 2017.

With Demoa, eight months after her rescue, 2018.

Karen medic, Eliya, with Mohammed and Shaheen, in Sahaji, February 2017.

Shaheen comforts a wounded Iraqi soldier, one hour before he himself is shot, May 4, 2017.

Me with Demoa after the rescue, Near Shifa Hospital, W. Mosul, June 2, 2017.

the fire with all these men after viewing the front lines, was most definitely in the minority.

I introduced myself and asked, "Who are you?"

She said her name was Hiva Mirkam and she was a member of parliament. We started talking, and I found out her family fled Iraq during the war with Saddam Hussein and the Ba'athists, who implemented a concentrated Arabization campaign in Kurdistan during the late '70s. Hiva and her family lived for years in a refugee camp in Iran and returned to Kurdistan as the KDP and its leader, Massoud Barzani, began to ascend again, partly by helping the Iranians in the Iran-Iraq war of the '80s. After that war, Saddam was still in power and took his revenge on the Kurds and the KDP, attempting to wipe them out in the infamous Al Anfal campaign that included large-scale use of chemical weapons.

In 1990, Saddam invaded Kuwait and the first Gulf War ensued. George H. W. Bush encouraged the various dissidents in Iraq, including the Kurds, to overthrow Saddam; as a result, there were many small, underfunded, and under-armed uprisings. However, without the expected outside support from a western coalition, Saddam was able to suppress those groups and did so brutally. The U.S. did, however, enforce no-fly zones over various parts of Iraq, including Kurdistan, and that gave the Kurds some breathing room. A civil war between rival Kurdish factions was the immediate result, but by 1997, there was some measure of stability in the semiautonomous region, and it began to pursue a policy of maximum economic growth, encouraging foreign investment and becoming one of the most stable and functional regions in the Middle East.

Through this violent and brutal history, Hiva managed to become one of the first women in politics in Barzani's Kurdistan. She had overcome much, and her stories ranged from relatively small advances, like becoming one of the first women to drive a car in Erbil, to joining parliament. Eventually, I asked her if she was married and she sort of stiffened up and said sharply, "No. I don't need a man." I was taken aback at first but realized she wasn't speaking from an anti-man ideology; she'd been hurt. She suffered but did not let herself be defined by that—rather, she grew strong through it. We became friends, and later, it was a joy to have her meet Karen and my daughters.

Later that night, the convoy continued back to Dohuk.

I had one other connection in Kurdistan besides Victor, a woman named Tera Dahl, a staffer for Minnesota congresswoman Michele Bachmann. I first met Tera in D.C. during a Burma briefing; she was Bachmann's adviser on various foreign policy matters with an emphasis on humanitarian relief and a focus on the Middle East and counterterrorism issues. Tera visited us in Burma briefly; she thought the unifying qualities of FBR training she saw in Burma might be effective in Kurdistan as well.

She connected me to a man named Farhang Afandi, the son of a retired defense minister, General Hamid Afandi. Farhang was studying in Canada and Hamid was peacefully retired when ISIS attacked. As they pushed to within twenty-three kilometers of Erbil, and it looked like they might take Kurdistan, Hamid joined those Kurds who chose to fight. He came out of retirement at the age of eighty-one to help bolster the Peshmerga. Farhang left Canada and returned home to help his father and his people. Farhang was in his early thirties, spoke English perfectly, and was passionate for his people. He was also very smart and clear-eyed about the reality of their position and their strengths and weaknesses. For men like Hamid and Farhang, ISIS was just the most recent enemy in their history of battling for survival and recognition as a people. Tera gave me Farhang's number, and when we got back to Dohuk after Sinjar, I gave him a call.

His father was in charge of one of the most important sectors in the Kurds' line of defense, Sector 7, which was located near the city of Bashiqa, just thirty-five kilometers from Mosul and about one hour from Erbil. The frontline positions there ran along the edge of the Nineveh plains, running along a series of ridge lines above the plains; at night, you could see the lights of Mosul in the distance. Hamid and his men were right in ISIS's backyard. I called Farhang and told him I wanted to visit the front line. He said, "Yes, come on!"

We drove southwest about an hour from Dohuk. It's quite a striking area, beautiful in a sort of stark, ancient way. In February, everything was greening up after the winter rains, and fields filled with new wheat stretched away toward Mosul. Hamid Afandi's headquarters was a little cluster of tents and buildings at the base of a mountain, called Mt. Alfaf, that rises about one thousand meters on the northern edge of the Nineveh plains. About two-thirds of the way up the mountain is a Syriac Orthodox monastery built around 450 AD called Mar Mattai.

We met with General Afandi in a wall tent with a gravel floor. He wore traditional Kurdish garb: pants, with baggy legs gathered at the ankles, and belted at the waist. The jacket can be buttoned but is often worn open with a white shirt underneath. We were served the requisite tea, and I explained who we were. The general listened politely. At the end of the meeting, I asked if I could pray. He looked surprised but said yes. As I began to pray, I felt God tell me, "Get on your knees and pray." *What? They'll think I'm a Christian nutcase,* I thought. But I knew that voice and had a choice: be afraid of what men may think or obey God. I got on my knees and prayed. When I got up, the general looked me in the eye and said, "You believe in God and fear Him like we do. We can see that, and we trust you. Go wherever you want."

On the way to the front, we decided to first go up to the monastery on the mountain. The Peshmerga had stopped ISIS just below this monastery, and the people from several Christian villages below had fled there for refuge when it looked like their homes might be overrun. The Syriac Orthodox brothers who lived there cared for the IDPs and were determined to stay, even if ISIS came all the way. One of them, Father Joseph, told me, "If ISIS made it here, we would do as our master Jesus leads us. We would tell the ISIS troops that Jesus loves them and would not run." These monks inspired me; they were humble and quiet but solid and full of courage and love.

We walked back down to meet Farhang at his father's headquarters, and he took us to a frontline post just a couple of kilometers away. The Kurds' primary positions were created from dirt berms reinforced with sandbags. The soldiers were generally set up in abandoned houses where they could sleep and cook. Many of these were damaged from the initial ISIS attack. We looked out toward Mosul from their position, pulled out binoculars, and looked for activity—there wasn't much happening, a bit of intermittent shooting back and forth but mostly quiet. Then my group started shaking hands with all the soldiers, preparing to leave.

I had this feeling, though, that I should stay. I wasn't here to be a tourist; the front line was where our work was, and it felt wrong to just shake hands and leave. The men manning this position were putting their lives on the line. Their families and homes were not far away, and many of them weren't actually soldiers—yet here they stayed, in destroyed houses, cold at night, hot in the day, boring when it wasn't life-threatening.

I told Farhang, "I'm going to sleep here tonight. Pete and I would like to stay."

He said, "What? You're gonna stay here? Man, it's dangerous."

"Yeah, but your people are here. This is what we're used to." And he agreed. I was a little surprised. *Man, we're not in America. These guys understand.*

As everyone got in the cars to leave, one of Victor's security team, retired Ranger and Delta Force Sergeant Major Greg Birch, leaned over to me and said, "Major Kookie Man—don't do anything stupid-er." He grinned, and I laughed with him.

"Roger, Sergeant Major!"

They drove off, and I got to know the officer in command of that post, a man named Major Nabaz. He gave us a tour around his section of the front. Pete still had his Karen bag over his shoulder and was running around with his video camera out, hoping to get pictures of ISIS. The soldiers wanted to let him shoot a light machine gun and an AK-47. I said okay, and Pete did, afterward pronouncing, "Dad, that was cool!" We again pulled out binoculars and scanned the plains below for movement. There was intermittent shooting and shelling, but nothing hit close to us.

The sun set and dusk came. One of the soldiers brought around a tray full of small steaming paper cups full of hot, sweet tea. Peter and I drank it and looked out over the desert. War is full of waiting, and I felt what I recognized as the lull of waiting start to seep through me like the warmth of the tea. Then suddenly, there was a high-pitched crack and a bullet sang through the air over our heads. Immediately, there was another, then a burst of machine-gun fire hit below our position. A Peshmerga truck-mounted machine gun opened fire on our left, suppressing the shooters. Everyone jerked to the alert and moved to their positions, yelling at each other to get ready. Before I could shove Peter down to what I knew was a covered position, he had his camera out and was recording as he ran, staying low along the edge of the dirt/sandbag position. "Under fire, gotta find cover," he said into the camera as he held it up over his head to get a better angle. He got into the only bunker on the perimeter and kept filming.

Pete is only nine years old, and he responds to fire like a veteran, I thought. I knew his life experience to that point prepared him well, and I was proud of him. In our American history, I remembered Kit Carson who, at the age of twelve, drove his own mule team deep into the wilderness. Today, like Peter, there were still kids facing and meeting real challenges. "Nice job, Pete!" I yelled at him as I moved to get a better view of what was happening.

It turned out to not be much. A little bit of sniper fire and some machine gun bursts as it got dark, but then all grew quiet again. I started thinking about how we would spend the night. I was going to sleep right there next to the sandbags and started looking for the safest place for Peter. I found where the bulldozer that dug out the position had made a little hole behind the line. There were sandbags around it, and I put Peter there. I told him, "If we get hit, you stay right here, and stay low. If things get bad, I'll come and get you."

Later that night, with Peter tucked into his little foxhole, sound asleep, I was up talking with Major Nabaz. Though his English was pretty limited—and my Kurdish nonexistent—I soon understood they'd intercepted a radio transmission that ISIS was going to hit our position at midnight. Uh-oh. I prayed, and Major Nabaz got his unit on full alert. Midnight came and went, with all of us peering out into the night, on edge and ready. No attack came.

They started picking up ISIS communications again and caught two commanders arguing: "Where are you?" "Where you are supposed to be." "Where is that?" "I hear you there." "No, I'm here!" "What is wrong with you? You should be here." "I think we are lost." It was comical. Still, there was no attack.

We stayed up most of the night, listening, and ready to repel an attack, but ISIS couldn't get it together. Around 4 a.m., it seemed the two ISIS units successfully linked up. Once again, everyone stepped up their alert level, but then, it turned out a third element was also supposed to be part of the attack and was lost. Finally, at 6 a.m. it was starting to get light, and the ISIS commander got on the radio and said, "You guys are all idiots! Now we've got to cancel. If we attack in daylight, the U.S. airplanes will bomb us." There was never an attack, just a little bit of shooting.

After dawn, the Peshmerga guys started to relax and head off to sleep. I stood, looking over the sandbags, out across the Nineveh plains, as the sun came up. What was I doing here? I thought about the previous night: what would I have done had an attack come? I could have helped a little, maybe, but not much. I came because I thought God wanted it—He made an opportunity, and I took it. So, I started talking to Him. "God," I said. "I don't speak Arabic or Kurdish. We're just a small NGO. This is a mechanized country. It's not the jungle. We're pretty good in Burma because there's not really anyone else there. But here, they're professionals. They don't waste their time. I don't have much to offer here. But if you want me to come, I'll come. What do you want me to do?"

I felt God respond, "Give up your own way. Give up the Free Burma Ranger way, and just come help these people."

I had used the Free Burma Ranger way a long time. I liked it, and it seemed to work. This felt like being pulled from the middle of a construction project by your dad and told, "Stop working on this house and go across the street. There's an old lady over there. For the next month, do whatever she tells you." I was going to give up my own way. I had no idea what that would look like, so I asked God how to pray. The answer I got was this: Pray that ISIS is stopped, that Kurdistan is free, and that all enemies become friends. I prayed those things while trying to imagine our role.

It didn't seem to make much sense. But, as I thought about it, neither did Burma when we first started. We were small, just moving and responding to constant attacks. Now, we'd grown and built up an organization, and Burma had also quieted a little. We had time to look around and listen to the cries of our neighbors, so to speak. We were invited to Iraq and, as I thought about our history in Burma, I knew our scope of operations wasn't going to be the deciding factor here, either. I started in Burma with the idea if I could help one person, they'd be happy, and I'd be happy—that was how we could start here too.

I didn't know what it would look like. I didn't know who we would help, or how. I didn't know how we would pay for it. I did know there was a great need here. I knew ISIS was a great evil that had somehow seized the hearts and minds of millions—some in a brotherhood of brutality and violence, and many others in a convulsion of fear that could only end in hatred. I felt God say to give up my own way and just help the people. I only had a few ways in mind of helping people. If we came back, where would God lead us?

CHAPTER SIX

The Wild West: "We Are All Peshmerga"

"I am the second Jonah. I didn't want to come, but God wanted me to. I am here and I am happy!"

—ELIYA

MARCH 2015

It was warm on the deck at my house. Beyond the deck, the afternoon sun slanted through humid air, making the water of the pond in front of the house look inviting. The leaves on the trees just beyond the deck were still, unstirred by any breeze. I stood next to a large whiteboard on which I'd drawn a loose rendering of ISIS and Kurdish positions in Kurdistan. In front of me, sitting in chairs, sprawled on the floor, or standing to stay awake were about fifty of our primary leaders and coordinators from Burma, along with some foreign volunteers and visitors.

"And so, I feel God is calling us there. We will need medics and cameramen. I would like to bring our leaders..." I turned and looked at them: "...Eliya and Monkey, for this first trip. But I don't know if we should go there! We need God to tell us for sure. Please pray about it and we will make a plan tomorrow." Everyone nodded slowly. I mostly had their attention, though it was always hard to stay awake this time of day. A few eyes were wandering toward the soccer field. "Okay. I think it's time for sports." The meeting broke up as everyone ran to get soccer shoes—or take a nap.

Peter and I had returned to Thailand just in time for our yearly FBR meetings in March. At these meetings, FBR's ethnic leaders from all over Burma come together with the headquarters office staff. We meet, pray, go over the past year, discuss our plans and, at the end of each day, play sports. The leaders don't usually have opportunity to hear what's going on in parts of the country other than their own, or what FBR is doing in other places. Our headquarters team is a mix of volunteers from different countries and joins the group to hear updates, make plans, and strategize how to better support the teams in the field.

This timing was important. If we were going to go somewhere new, I wanted the support and needed the prayers of all of our team. This new mission would depend on the right medics and cameramen from our ethnic teams.

After talking and praying about the new mission, we agreed to go forward if we could get the money. We are donor-supported, so we never know exactly how much money we'll have but have been doing this long enough we have a pretty good idea from year to year. Then, because we're responding to attacks and crises, we don't plan too strictly how we're going to spend our money.

We also don't ask for money. We pray for the help we need. We tell stories, share the needs we see, and thank those who help. We want to always trust God to provide what is needed to do what He wants. If someone asks if they can help, we say yes! But we don't want money we're not supposed to have.

For this next mission, we needed a fair amount to come in. We agreed we shouldn't use our general funds because those were all donated for Burma projects. This mission was new, not something our supporters knew much about. The Kurdish trip would have to get designated funding. We set the minimum at $60,000 to be able to be of use but decided if $30,000 came in by the time we had to leave, we would go, trusting God had brought us that far and would provide the rest in good time. The first $30,000 was to cover plane tickets to get a team over there, vehicles, food, and medical supplies. If $30,000 came in specifically designated for Kurdistan, we could do it and also feel confident we were in God's will. In the meantime, we started preparing.

Three members of our ethnic headquarters team, Eliya, Monkey, and Ray Kaw, agreed to go. Ray Kaw was a Karen long-time Ranger, a skilled medic who was with us on an earlier mission to Sudan and helped to start the Jungle School of Medicine. He was quiet, highly skilled, gentle, cheerful, and tough. This gave us two medics and one videographer.

The rest of the team would be my family of five; Micah, who was also our Kachin coordinator and was part of the initial decision to go to Kurdistan; Jesse, our overall operations coordinator, an arborist and skydiver from Tennessee who had been with us for eight years;

Hosannah (Hosie), who had been with us for nine years and helped with general administration as well as the GLC program, reporting, and mission coordination (she had also been on the Kachin mission when we had prayed about coming here); Jonathan, who was new to us but not to this kind of work and was a young, super-fit climber who worked for a Bible translation group and went on solo trips into Papua New Guinea to make language maps; and Paul Bradley, a missionary and former Navy Seabee who helped us part time with training chaplains when he wasn't doing his main job with an organization called Cadence.

At the last minute, I also invited Justin, who had worked on and off with us for a couple years and wasn't one of our normal coordinators. He was a former Marine who had enlisted after 9/11 to help people but became disillusioned with how the war played out on the ground. He was badly wounded in action in Fallujah in 2004, and now he was in Thailand, working on a bachelor's degree in religion on the GI Bill and helping us part-time. He wanted a chance to go back again to help people. I wouldn't normally invite someone without lots of FBR experience and who wasn't a Christian—Justin was agnostic—on a new mission like this, but I prayed with him and felt it was right. He would eventually save my life twice in battle.

We planned to go in three groups: Jesse and Paul would be the advance party to start getting things set up, sort out vehicles, communications, places to stay, and other logistics; then my family and I would go to meet leaders, make friends, and get the necessary permissions; Jonathan would come with us and help Jesse and Paul. Finally, the Karen guys, Hosannah, Justin, and Micah would come when everything was ready to kick off.

Those were our plans. A lot of things had to happen before any of this would take place.

We prayed for funds and got almost the entire amount before our advance group was scheduled to go. The day before they were supposed to leave, we were still three hundred dollars short. I called some of our donors, any of whom could have covered that amount easily, and asked for prayer. I told them they should not give the needed funds, as I wanted to be sure God wanted us to go to Kurdistan. If God wanted us to go, the funds would come. The next day, the day we were to leave, Mike Potter, a retired teacher from the red-dirt hills of Oklahoma who started a second career over here after retirement, came by the house and said, "I felt God wanted me to give you something. Here's one thousand dollars."

We left that night.

Another thing we needed was visas. For Americans, it was no problem: we got thirty days on arrival. But for the Karen guys, the process was an unknown—to all of us, including the people issuing them. A few phone calls to nearby Iraqi embassies (the nearest was Malaysia) resulted in conversations like: "You want to get visa for who? What country?" Burma! Then lots of talk in the background. "Where?" Myanmar! More talk. "The country is called what?" Burma, or Myanmar! "Oh, Myanmar. Okay…" Apparently, people with Burmese passports didn't travel to Iraq frequently. It turned out that Kurdistan's semiautonomous status meant we didn't have to get Iraqi visas, which was why it was easy for us Americans. Tera Dahl eventually helped us with the Burmese guys, submitting the applications in person at the KRG office in Washington, D.C.

Ray Kaw and Monkey received their visas in good time, but Eliya's was delayed. Eliya was having second thoughts about going and when he didn't get a visa, he thought he wouldn't have to. I felt Eliya was supposed to be on this trip and had the team buy him a ticket anyway. When they went to his home, twelve hours from Chiang Mai, to pick him up, he actually hid for a while, hoping they would leave without him. But he had promised; Monkey talked to him, and he realized he had to follow through, so he came to Chiang Mai, laughing at himself, but still not sure he'd have to go. The morning before the last group was supposed to leave, they called the D.C. office, and the official hung up on them. Something was blocking Eliya—and he was glad. "I told you, I'm not supposed to come," he said, laughing.

Now we were scrambling on the Kurdistan side to try to get him special permission. We figured we had made enough friends that it was possible, eventually. In the meantime, we had to get him on the plane. We told Hosie and Micah to stick with the plan, don't change any tickets, but bring Eliya along until you get absolutely stopped. We also sent out an email to all our friends to pray.

At the airport in Bangkok, they took with them all the papers they could muster, including filled-out visa applications, the correct visas for Ray Kaw and Monkey, FBR materials, letters of invitation (from ourselves), other forms in Kurdish from their government website that we filled out at random. The ticketing agents were skeptical, asked questions, and knew about as much as we did about Kurdish visas; Hosie and Micah talked, told stories, listened to stories, and somehow Eliya was eventually issued a boarding pass—with the result that, when he landed in Erbil without any visa, he was promptly detained and moved to the deportation area of the airport.

I called everyone I knew and eventually reached Farhang, whom Peter and I had met on our first trip to Kurdistan. He called the interior minister, who personally went to the airport and gave Eliya permission to enter Kurdistan. Eliya met us on the front line, and his laugh rang out as he said, "I am the second Jonah. I didn't want to come, but God wanted me to. I am here, and I am happy!" It was perfect: God called Jonah to tell the people of Nineveh about Him, and Jonah fled. God chased him down, and when Jonah finally obeyed, the entire city of Nineveh was converted. We could only hope Eliya might have the same effect in Nineveh on our own mission.

The Kurds became for us like the Karen people were. They opened their doors and welcomed us. They let us live with them on the front lines; they invited us into their homes, and we met their families. They opened their country to us. Unlike the Karen, they have a well-established bureaucracy, which they helped us thread our way through. General Hamid Afandi assisted us a lot—he reminded me of my father. As we made our plans, he told us, "People come to help us, but they do not talk about God. You talk about God, and that is special to us. We depend on God. We can never forget you came to help us. You are welcome here." He was eighty-three. At the end of our meetings, he would say, "Thank you for coming to help us. We will never forget you!" Then, a few minutes later, he would ask with a smile, "Now what was your name?"

Our Karen team members connected especially closely with the Kurds, with a bond of love and understanding born of a common experience of oppression.

We spent the first few weeks of that mission in General Afandi's sector. We presented a ten-week plan to him and the KRG, to train their people like we do FBR teams in Burma. They were interested but said there was no way they could spare that many men for that long from the front lines. There, the front line remained generally static, but there was sporadic fighting every day. The distance between the Peshmerga and

ISIS lines fluctuated, ranging from approximately four hundred meters in some areas to two kilometers in others.

Here, the untended fields of wild grass and wheat between the lines were regularly burned by ISIS and the Peshmerga to reduce cover. The fires sometimes reached great heights and sent massive plumes of smoke into the air. The smoke from ISIS positions, as opposed to the Peshmerga's, was often thick and black. One Peshmerga lieutenant told us the dark smoke came from burning tires, and ISIS created the black smoke to intimidate the Kurdish people and to obscure their ground movements from coalition air surveillance.

Forward of the Peshmerga line were floodlights illuminating the field and highlighting enemy movement. Night was the most common time for ISIS attacks. Behind the lights were trenches for stopping the armored Humvees and other armored vehicles ISIS was using. ISIS had taken Ramadi shortly before we got to Kurdistan, and they had captured a fresh supply of vehicles. The Peshmerga were ill-equipped to stop the ISIS mechanized assaults and it was mostly coalition airpower that stopped ISIS vehicles before they could push through the thin Peshmerga lines.

The Peshmerga numbers were few. Most of the line was reinforced with new, part-time volunteers; they were men of all ages, bakers, nurses, merchants, carpenters, farmers—all normal civilians—who answered the call to help defend their homes. The better-trained, full-time Peshmerga were positioned all along the line to train the new troops for the fight. However, none were trained as medics, and their only medical plan was evacuation.

Together with General Afandi and the officers on the line, we came up with an alternative training plan. We would do three four-day training modules at different positions right on the front lines. This meant the men wouldn't have to leave their posts; we would go to them. We cut our training down to focus on combat first aid, casualty evacuation, videography and reporting, land navigation and GPS use, and some rappelling and room-clearing techniques. We had to remind ourselves we were there to serve the people and their needs. Listening was critical if we were to understand what they needed.

Our team stayed in a village called Merki at the base of Mar Mattai monastery where I visited on the first trip, with the nearest town being Bardarash, about ten kilometers away. Most of the families in Merki were still gone, the teachers were all gone, and everyone was in a sort of limbo with ISIS just two kilometers away. We stayed in the village school compound, which had buildings on three sides and a two-meter wall with a metal gate on the fourth. We called it our Alamo and pulled our own security when necessary. I didn't ask the Peshmerga about security. I actually never ask about security when going to a new area. To do so would imply we don't trust the people who asked us to help and we are afraid. Both of those can break trust.

The people still in the village welcomed us, bringing tubs of home-made sheep yogurt and rice dishes and hanging around to visit. Eliya and Ray Kaw had dental and medical patients right away. Every day, we ran up the trail to the monastery for our workout, and we made friends with the abbot, Father Joseph, whom I had met on my first trip. He was as determined to stay as ever.

We also felt it was the place we should be. We met a Kurdish Christian woman who was a pharmacist, relief worker, and evangelist. She said, "God uses us, and we each build just a small cube, but these small cubes are the building blocks of God's Kingdom and He uses us all." I had asked God what we could do, how a small group from the Burma jungle could help here. Meeting these people, being welcomed by them as part of God's family, and being invited to build something with love encouraged us that we were in the right place. Every day, as we looked out across the Nineveh plains toward Mosul, toward the ISIS lines, I prayed as I was led before: that ISIS would be stopped, the Kurds would be free, and the hearts of the enemy would change to follow Jesus.

We did GLC programs in the village on the weekends and trainings during the week. Our translator was a man named Bahaa. He was a Christian Arab we met in Erbil, where he'd fled with his family. When we were up the mountain at the monastery, he could just see his village in the distance, still controlled by ISIS. One day, he was our translator as we interviewed a family from the village. They described how ISIS came within four hundred meters of them before being stopped. Later, he told us, "This village is a miracle. I—I have a little jealousy. ISIS didn't stop before they got to my village." Translating for us was not easy for him—we were asking him to return to the front line. He'd already escaped once, and going back toward the enemy was not something he wanted to do. He stayed with us for just a couple of weeks before deciding to go back to Erbil.

ISIS launched daily sniper, machine gun, and mortar attacks on the mountain position above Bashiqa. Along with the Peshmerga of Kurdistan, northern Iraq, a contingent of Kurds from Iran, the PAK (Parti Azadi Kurdistan or Kurdish Freedom Party) also manned the bunkers and trenches of the front line. The PAK were fighting for freedom in Iran when ISIS attacked, and they came over to help their fellow Kurds. They were highly disciplined, idealistic, and tough. One night, after we finished medical and video training for the PAK and Peshmerga, ISIS attacked our position, opening up on us with machine guns from positions just below ours. The line came alive, men yelling orders, jumping on their weapons, firing up the ISIS positions below. All thoughts of evening tea and cigarettes were temporarily abandoned.

Amidst the shooting and yelling, the PAK drove a machine gun-mounted Toyota up to the line. They wrestled two giant speakers onto the bed of the truck below the machine gun and turned on the Peshmerga fight song, full blast. "Peshmerga, Peshmerga...." blared over the battle, punctuated with the ear-splitting staccato of heavy machine-gun fire. Everyone on the line joined in, shooting and singing. The pitch-black night was lit up by streaks of orange, red, and white flame coming out of the muzzles of the machine guns; the flashes and explosions briefly illuminated the faces of the soldiers as red tracers painted lines down to the ISIS bunkers and fighting positions. Kurdish voices were raised in song over it all. *What a moment,* I thought. *What a people.*

Everyone was smiling, laughing, cheering, and shooting. They were happy warriors and taking it to ISIS with style. The troops fired all the weapons they had in support of the machine guns, and the music blared on. It was a festive fight. Our side took no casualties, but ISIS seemed to be badly pummeled, and their attack died down. Gradually, the shooting and music from our side tapered off and then stopped. The men stood around shaking hands and laughing. We had won for the night, and our hearts were light.

After Bahaa left, our next translator was also a Christian, a man named Michael. He stayed with us for one week but was not ready for the next part of our mission: moving to Sinjar. After we finished the three four-day trainings in General Afandi's sector, our plan was to go to Sinjar. I knew the need there was great—in the Mar Mattai area, the villagers had not actually lost their homes and the front line was relatively static, for now. On Sinjar, more than eight thousand people were living in tents on the mountainside and there was daily fighting in the city.

We were sad to leave our friends at Merki. During our time there, Karen and Hosie visited their homes and had laughter-filled tea-drinking sessions with the women. Once, they joined as the women and men gathered the sheep in for the evening, the strong mom of the family catching the milking ewes in a wrestler's grapple as they were herded by the men. Later, the women shared cookies and tea from a picnic basket in the back of the farmers' ancient pickup truck. The day we drove out, we shook hands all around, gave out FBR shirts, took a photo, and promised we'd be back.

From Merki, we went to Dohuk. One of the officers we befriended during our trainings, Captain Mohammed, was from Dohuk and opened his home to us. He had a daughter a little older than Peter, two sons a little younger, and a smiling, welcoming, hospitable wife named Speda. Their house was not huge, with three bedrooms, but they welcomed our whole group of fourteen people to eat and sleep there. The first night we arrived, it wasn't until about 9 p.m., but they laid out a huge meal for us and later we all slept, spread out all over all their floors and in their kids' bedrooms. It was another example of Kurdish hospitality.

We also met with Dr. Nezar again and I introduced him to my family. He looked each one of my kids in the eye and asked them how they felt about being there—but in a kind way, not as a challenge. He told us we could stay with his medics on top of the mountain, where there was a tent clinic that served both the Yezidi IDPs on the north side and any wounded or sick Peshmerga fighters evacuated from the south side. We also met up with Tera Dahl, who came to join us for a few days and helped us find a new translator named Joey. He was a young guy who had had plans for university until ISIS came. His real name wasn't Joey, but he told us his favorite show was *Friends*, which has a main character named Joey, so that's what his friends called him. He'd spent the night before we met him watching *Friends* reruns to review his English.

Shannon Allison, my Army Special Forces dentist friend, also joined us for Sinjar. Shannon and I had known each other since we were cadets and were both selected for the Marshall Awards, which had us attend a seminar at Virginia Military Institute. I had gotten bored and slipped out for a run. As I had settled into my stride, I noticed another runner going my direction on the other side of the street. I picked up my pace a bit to pass him, and he did likewise. He also seemed to follow me. I kicked it up another notch, and he matched me. By the time I got back to the class site, we had finished a blazing ten-kilometer run. I went up to him and asked, "Who are you?"

"I'm a cadet skipping the meetings, just like you," he said, then his laugh cackled out, one of those laughs you can't help but join. He wasn't tall, but he was big and broad, solid muscle. We've been friends since. Shannon was one of the original FBR members and the first foreign member besides my wife and me. He was with me on many of the early missions in Burma, trained Eliya and many of our medics in dentistry, and treated hundreds of patients. He had gone with us to Sudan and wasn't going to be left out of this, either.

With our bigger team, we headed to Sinjar. Captain Mohammed was just getting off his duty hours at the Merki front line and decided to come with us, which was great because he helped us through all the checkpoints along the way. We were not a normal group to be going to Sinjar—women, kids, Americans, no big NGO (non-governmental organization), and no armored cars or security contingent. Checkpoint soldiers had no category for us, just lots of questions. Actually, in this part of Kurdistan, there were very few NGOs; we were right next to the wild border of Syria, where ISIS came from and the fighting in Sinjar was still heavy. The closer we got, the more it felt like an apocalyptic no-man's land, abandoned and destroyed.

We had just cleared the checkpoint at the Sahala bridge and were on the road where it parallels the Syrian border. Suddenly, a man on a horse galloped across from the Syria side. Peshmerga troops in a roadside outpost opened fire with their AK-47s, and the horse and man raced past us. We all jerked our vehicles to the side of the road, and I jumped out to see if we could help. Captain Mohammed poked his head out the door and yelled at me, "Mr. David! Don't worry, they will get him. He is a smuggler from Syria, very bad." The horse and man tore off back toward Syria with bullets zipping by them. They got away, and we felt like we had wandered into the Wild West, but with AKs instead of six-shooters.

As we wound up the north side of Sinjar Mountain, we passed the Yezidi IDP camps spread out on a plateau just below the mountaintop. At the peak of the fighting, ISIS had nearly made it to the top of the mountain and would probably have wiped out all the Yezidi people had they succeeded. On the top, the PKK, the Kurdish separatist group

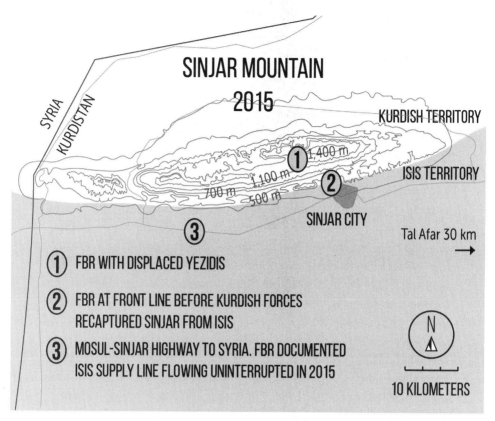

SINJAR MOUNTAIN
2015

SYRIA
KURDISTAN

KURDISH TERRITORY

1,400 m
1,100 m
700 m
500 m

ISIS TERRITORY

SINJAR CITY

Tal Afar 30 km →

1 FBR WITH DISPLACED YEZIDIS

2 FBR AT FRONT LINE BEFORE KURDISH FORCES RECAPTURED SINJAR FROM ISIS

3 MOSUL-SINJAR HIGHWAY TO SYRIA. FBR DOCUMENTED ISIS SUPPLY LINE FLOWING UNINTERRUPTED IN 2015

N

10 KILOMETERS

from Turkey labeled terrorist by both Turkey and the U.S., had multiple positions, one at an old missile launch site Saddam Hussein used. Other positions included an old walled fortress with towers, over which they flew their yellow and green flags with a single star in the middle.

Between these fortifications, there was a KDP Peshmerga base as well as a PUK Peshmerga base; the KDP and PUK were rival parties of the Iraqi Kurds, with the KDP winning the most recent elections. Three giant cell towers loomed over all this, easily visible from the bottom of the mountain. Between the PKK fort and a KDP Peshmerga base, a MASH-like field hospital tent was set up, with a couple of CONEX-box-type buildings serving as a kitchen and bedrooms for the Peshmerga medics sent there by Dr. Nezar.

That's where we set up camp. The mountain was rough and rocky, with scattered scrub brush and thistles. There were three to four of Dr. Nezar's 122 ambulance unit medics up there at all times. They rotated out every ten days or so. There was a cook, a young Yezidi man from

Sinjar who escaped the ISIS massacres and worked for the medical team. And there was a full-time nurse. You could tell right away she wasn't a normal lady: she wore camouflage fatigues with a Peshmerga patch on her arm, makeup, and gold earrings. She welcomed the group with a smile, but also watched us at first with wary eyes. I had met her on our first trip, and when she recognized us and got a big hug from Peter, she relaxed and smiled broadly, saying, "I remember this boy. Thank you for coming back. Welcome!"

Her name was Khansa. She was Kurdish, originally from Syria. She had come to Sinjar just after ISIS attacked and was on top of the mountain through the battle, under fire, and helped care for the thousands of fleeing and desperate Yezidis. She hadn't left the mountain since then. She had been recognized by Massoud Barzani, the president of Kurdistan, for her bravery and service. He gifted her with a little CONEX house for herself back behind the clinic. She would become a good friend.

We also made friends with the medics and the cook. The medics were all Kurds, with families down in Dohuk. Their time on the mountain was a real expedition for them, like a camping trip. They were concerned and slightly uncomprehending of our comfort level with camping: no beds, no bathrooms, sleeping outside. The cook was Yezidi, and his family had been chased out of Sinjar. He was a young, laughing, fun-loving guy.

Sometimes, at the end of the day, we'd all go out and play football in the road in front of the clinic as the sun set; he'd join us, and sometimes the medics would stop being dignified long enough to also run around for a while. Throwing and catching aren't natural here since everyone grows up playing soccer—it's the same in Burma. Later on, in combat situations with locals tossing hand grenades, this awkwardness could prove dangerous. But up here on Sinjar Mountain, with a golden sunset lighting up our games and our team of Americans, Karen, Yezidis, and Kurds running around trying to figure out American football, it was all comedy and joy.

But the fighting was close and the sounds of mortar rounds, rockets, and air strikes in the town of Sinjar below us could be heard regularly from this clinic site. If we went over the crest of the hill to the south, we could see the fight below. As we began work in the IDP camps just below us, we soon began to realize the scope of the disaster that had befallen the Yezidis. It seemed everyone had a story of loss and pain.

One story struck me the most, from a man who was providing security for the IDPs. He was a Yezidi IDP himself. He told us that when ISIS attacked his hometown of Sinjar, he was away, and his mother, father and one-year-old baby were captured. He was distraught but said, "What can I do? My baby, along with thousands of others, is being held far from Sinjar, deep in ISIS-controlled territory. There, they live like slaves. The boys are trained and brainwashed to grow up to join ISIS, and the girls are used for sex. If I go and try to break through ISIS lines to get her back, I will be killed quickly. Then my family will have no father, my wife, no husband, and my baby will still be captured."

His eyes glistened with tears as he spoke; he said his only hope was in God. I had no response except to hug him and tell him God did care and his hope was real. I prayed right then with him that God would give us a miracle and his baby would be returned to him that month.

At that same GLC program, we talked to a woman who also fled ISIS from the Sinjar area. Her brother and nephew were killed by ISIS as they tried to recover food from their homes for their families. She began to cry, asking, "When will we be able to go home? Only God can help us, but will He?"

These were just a few of the thousands of stories of human misery, injustice, and lives lost. They reinforced our feeling that we should be there and made me more determined to add my voice to the appeal for help.

When we later drove down the winding switchbacks on the south side of the mountain to the city, where ISIS was and where the fighting was, we were retracing the steps of the Yezidis, who had fled the town less than a year earlier. Littering the side of the road were the scattered clothes of families who were executed, their bodies in shallow graves under piles of rocks. On the roadside were their burned-out cars, clothes, and possessions they lost as they fled ISIS and were gunned down by them. It was heart-rending. Below us, we could see smoke rising from the impacts of mortar shells and cannon rounds.

On the first trip, ISIS controlled most of the city and all the road networks east, west, and south of the city. With control over those roads, they had an open supply, transport, and power projection line connecting Iraq and Syria. We drove down to the edge of the city to the headquarters of Peshmerga General Ezadine Sado, the officer in charge of the Sinjar battle. He was a tall man with ramrod-straight posture and a small pencil mustache. As our smaller frontlines group walked into his headquarters, he looked at us with some confusion. Through Joey, we explained we had come to give medical and dental treatment as well as training.

He said, "Welcome. You can go up to the ridge there where we have positions overlooking the city." He pointed to a low ridge running east to west behind the city at the foot of Sinjar Mountain. Flanking the city, the ridge formed a defensive line with ISIS in positions directly below.

We drove up a steep rocky road on the back side of the ridge, and as we neared the crest, we could hear gunfire and see mortars impacting the surrounding area. Peshmerga troops were scurrying between positions but, dominating the scene as we pulled in, was a big man with a huge handlebar mustache operating a machine gun mounted on the back of a Toyota pickup. He wore a white shirt and a cowboy hat and was laughing as he fired away at ISIS. We got out of our trucks and, crouching to avoid incoming fire, ran up to the berm.

The man on the gun stopped firing and came over to greet us. "Welcome, welcome," he said smiling. "Who are you?"

Joey, our new *Friends*-loving translator, unpacked himself from a vehicle, where he had folded himself as deeply as possible when we got into range of ISIS fire, and came over to translate for me. "Hello, I am David," I told him. "I am here with my team and my family—they are up on the mountain with the IDPs...." I pointed up the hill behind me. "We're from Burma, but we're here because we heard about your situation and want to help and God told us we should come."

"I am Edo," he said as he shook my hand. He told me his family was also up on the hill. He was Yezidi and was a commander in one of the new Yezidi militia groups that had sprung up in defense of their people after the ISIS attacks. He had two sons there with him, strong, handsome guys in full fatigues, with big mustaches, and friendly smiles. They stood silently on either side of their father. "Wow, what a family!" I said. "You guys are strong!" I gripped his shoulder, and his sons tensed. "How can we help you?"

They needed everything, but mostly their freedom and security. Later we met his family up on the hill. They had their own little settlement away from the main body of IDPs, on a windswept ridge on the south side of the mountain, looking straight down at the city. They were a stoic and independent people. Later, they invited us to their place

With our Yezidi friend Edo and Kurdish Captain Mohammed, Sinjar front, 2015.

and served our whole group a big meal in a long wall tent. Edo had two more sons besides the two with him on the front line and several daughters as well.

We were able to do GLC programs for their group, and Edo quickly became a good friend. He gave us a big tent and, later in the battle, an AK-47. He welcomed us to be with them wherever they were positioned on the front line.

We moved back and forth between the front line and the top of the mountain. On top of Sinjar Mountain, we worked closely with the 122 Ambulance Unit; Eliya and Ray Kaw treated patients, while our dentist, Dr. Shannon, performed over four hundred dental procedures. We treated IDPs as well as wounded Peshmerga troops. The rest of the team did GLC programs and interviewed people who had lost family members and all they owned. Micah, Jonathan, and Justin helped with medical and information training and the running of the mission.

I only brought part of the team down to the front lines at Sinjar City, leaving Hosie, Karen, and the kids on top. The Peshmerga controlled only 10 percent of the city, and ISIS was attacking every day with mortar, rocket, machine-gun, and sniper fire. Every day, there were casualties. We treated the wounded, performed dental treatments, and trained the Peshmerga as we had at the Bashiqa position. At night, the attacks intensified as ISIS pushed forward with ground assaults. During the day, between attacks, we trained as we could, and at night, we slept when possible. When there was too much fighting for sleep, we prayed and stood with the Peshmerga and Yezidi volunteers as they defended themselves.

One night, we were on the west flank of the Peshmerga line, on a small hilltop at the base of a finger ridge that ascended behind us to the main ridge forming the secondary defensive line behind us. We had been up on that line when we first met Edo. Our position projected out into the edge of the city. ISIS was in a line of houses one hundred meters away to our front, and to our right was a field with a small outbuilding.

To our left was a Peshmerga position in what remained of an ancient citadel. We called it "the castle," but not much of it was still standing. ISIS-held buildings were just fifty meters away, and the castle was pounded day and night by small arms, machine guns, and mortar fire. We had been there earlier in the day and been under fire the entire time. There was no way to give a good training there, but we could see the bravery and tenacity of the men defending the spot. We prayed with them and left some tourniquets and medical supplies.

Our current position on the right flank was protected by a dirt berm and a series of bunkers set into the berm with machine gun crews all along the line. On the right, the position curved back to the base of the mountain. On this curve were three small positions with no overhead cover. In fact, overhead cover was very rare in any Peshmerga positions. We finished training for that day amidst sporadic fire from ISIS and were invited into a tent behind one of the bunkers. We would sleep there and move to another area to train the next day.

The Peshmerga shared their dinner with us, a Kurdish specialty called dolma, a savory rice and meat combo stuffed in vegetables. We rarely went hungry on the front. As we were beginning to eat, Justin said, "We don't have any weapons. What'll we do if ISIS attacks tonight?" Micah had a 9mm Glock pistol loaned to us by friends in Erbil, but that was one pistol for nine people.

"Don't worry," I said. "If God wants us to have guns, He'll give them to us." Though the tent was dark, I was pretty sure I could feel Justin roll his eyes.

Just then, Captain Mohammed crawled into the tent. "Tonight, maybe ISIS will attack us here. Here, Mr. David, take my pistol just in case. I have my rifle." He handed me a 9mm Walther with two extra magazines.

Shannon laughed and said, "Don't worry. Nothing ever happens when I'm here."

At that moment, an ISIS mortar crashed into our perimeter, quickly followed by another, and machine guns opened up at us from the front. We all looked at each other. No dinner for now. I said a quick prayer, and we crawled out of the tent to face the attack.

CHAPTER SEVEN

Daoud Shingali and the Falcon– The Gathering Storm

"If I die, my mother will *&%$ kill me!"

—SHAHEEN

ISIS was hammering the front part of our position, and we already had a casualty. "Drag him back to where we can treat him," I yelled, and Eliya and Jonathan ran through gunfire to carry the wounded man off the line. Bullets were smacking into the sandbags and berm in front of us, and we stayed low as shrapnel from exploding mortar rounds flew by us. I looked over the berm to my right and saw at least five muzzle flashes from ISIS fighters firing AK-47s as they maneuvered onto our flank. A shell exploded overhead, and in the flash, I saw Justin, crouched, taking photos. He gave me a big, relaxed grin.

Most of the fire was hitting our front positions. On the right side, there were only four Peshmerga firing back from three small positions. ISIS was now within fifty meters and moving in deliberately spaced rushes at us. I prayed, "Lord, is this is the time for me to defend?" I felt "yes." I stood up and emptied my pistol at the closing fighters.

A Peshmerga lying next to me tugged at my pant legs, "Mister, get down, you die." I crouched and changed magazines as bullets hit nearby, then fired again on the closest fighters. The ISIS attack on this side faltered, and the fighters fell back. Just then, the Peshmerga's only armored personnel carrier (APC) pulled up into the middle of the fight.

It was sent to evacuate the wounded. Unknown to me, it also carried General Ezadine. Eliya, Jonathan, and I ran up with the wounded soldier and pushed him inside. Eliya jumped in with him to continue treatment while Jonathan ran back to help others. I tried to close the heavy armored door, but it would not budge. Bullets were hitting the vehicle close to my head, and I prayed, "Lord help me close this door!" I felt along the underside of the door, found the locking mechanism and, releasing it, was able to close the door. The APC rumbled off into the night like some kind of mechanical rhinoceros, bullets striking its side.

I ran back to the berm just as a machine gun opened up on our flank. I had one more magazine for the pistol and started to shoot again when a Peshmerga handed me his rifle. I tried to look through the optics, but with no night vision, I could see nothing. The ISIS machine gun found its range and began to chew up the sandbags next to me as I struggled with the scope of the rifle. I took aim as best I could and returned fire. Tracers streaked out of the barrel—tracers! I could aim after all! I put rounds right on the machine gun. After about fifteen shots, fire from there ceased.

Our right flank was now under less pressure, and I turned to our front. The Kurds had a machine gun-mounted Toyota truck parked up next to the berm, but the gunner had been shot, and no one dared get up on the exposed truck to take his place. ISIS bullets from heavy machine guns in the buildings to our front were hitting the position with deadly effect. Just then, out of the darkness, a man strode up, shouting. It was General Ezadine—he had come in with the APC and dismounted to rally his men to hold off the attack.

He saw the empty gun, yelled out some angry Kurdish words, and mounted the truck bed to take the gunner's position. He cleared a jam and, between shouts and admonishments, began firing the heavy 12.7mm Dushka. There was so much enemy fire, I expected to see his head explode any moment. *What a brave man, what a general!* His shooting rallied his men, and a steady rate of fire from the Peshmerga halted the ISIS advance. Their attack began to dwindle.

The Peshmerga called for air support from the coalition, and a few minutes later, a jet fighter dropped a bomb to our right front, where ISIS was attempting to marshal its troops for another assault. A huge explosion shook the ground as the bomb went off with a great ball of red fire. That was the end of the ISIS offensive that night.

The next day, we were at Edo's position again, and I gave the pistol back to Captain Mohammed. I didn't want to hang onto anything God did not want me to have.

During this mission, we photographed a steady stream of trucks resupplying ISIS between Syria, Kurdistan, and Iraq. There was a main highway running through Sinjar and hundreds of trucks used it each day, some heading west to ISIS-controlled areas of Syria, and some coming east from Syria on their way through Sinjar and on to Mosul, Ramadi, and other cities ISIS had captured. While the coalition air-power was in heavy use in the city of Sinjar, they were leaving this strategic thoroughfare untouched for some reason. People asked us, "Why are those trucks allowed to pass freely?"

Everyone was grateful for coalition air strikes, and the people loved America and all the countries helping them. They thanked us again and again and affirmed it was their own Kurdish duty to defeat ISIS and rebuild their land. But they couldn't understand why the use of air was so limited and why ISIS was able to move vehicles and trucks freely. We wondered the same thing.

Throughout this mission, my prayer was, "Lord, help me share your love and the Gospel of Jesus. I do not know how to do that the right way here." Most of the people we were helping, training, and working with were Muslims and Yezidis. We prayed with everyone we met and often found we were united in love and a common purpose. I added the prayer that all could go home to my regular three prayers: 1) ISIS be stopped, 2) Kurdistan would be free, and 3) the hearts of the enemies would change.

It seemed to me most of what we did on that first mission was feel and show love. As we walked, worked, ate, treated, helped, and took cover together, the people we met shared all they had with us. Many told us: "You became close to us. You lived with us and let us get close to you. There is no barrier of any kind between us. We know you love us. We love you and consider you as our people. Thank you for coming here to stand with us. We ask God to bless you and all who sent you." As we left after that first mission, I knew this was right. We would be back.

That summer in 2015, in the U.S., we were given the opportunity to speak in Washington D.C. We testified alongside a young Yezidi woman named Bazi who was captured by ISIS in August 2014 from Sinjar City; she was sold to an ISIS recruit and was held and raped for five months in Syria before escaping. She described the rapes and murders of hundreds of people. Her powerful testimony brought many to tears. She appealed for help for the more than three thousand other girls who are still held captive. With my family, I briefed several congressmen, State Department, and military officials. I passed on the thanks of the Kurds and Yezidis for the U.S. help and air strikes, but I also described how, for some reason, those air strikes were missing or avoiding strategic ISIS supply routes. People were surprised. Congress, and others I met in D.C. knew nothing about it. They promised to look into it. One week after our briefing, U.S. air strikes took out those roads and supply routes.

Our next mission was in October and November 2015. This time, I took a smaller team, and we spent most of the mission in Sinjar, where they were fighting to take back the city. My nephew, Dave Dawson, was with us for the first time, and Micah came back. I brought my son Peter along again. Joseph, a Karen medic, and Zau Seng, a Kachin videographer, were the ethnic contingent.

We were not able to convince any of our previous translators to come with us, so Victor put us in touch with another guy he met during his work in the camps. His name was Shaheen, and he was Yezidi. His family was in a refugee camp outside Dohuk, and their village near Sinjar was still occupied by ISIS. Shaheen let us know his name meant "falcon," but when I first met him, it was not the animal name I would have chosen for him. He was small, thin, and chain-smoked. His English was great, and he did a great job as a translator, but I got to hear a lot of profanity-laced cynical opinions and complaints from him too. He was in no way a soldier and even told me one day, "I'm a coward. I don't want to get near the fighting. I hate it. That is for stupid people."

I told him we weren't the U.N. or the U.S. Army, and we couldn't pay him much, but we were there to help the people. On our first trip back down to the front line of Sinjar City, he refused to go. "No way," he said. "I am a coward and will not go."

I prayed and replied, "You've been complaining every day that people do not help your people here in Sinjar. You've complained to me that America is of no help. Now, here we are, ready to help, and you refuse to go. I need you to go with us to translate. This is the time for you to choose to be a man and act in love. To be brave. You need to stop being a coward. I'm sure God wants you to act in love and help!" I paused. "You can change your life. You and your people need our medics to help. I will pray with you, and you tell me what God says to you."

I took his hand, closed my eyes, and prayed. I looked at him. "What did God tell you to do?"

He looked at me sheepishly. "God told me to go with you." Then he grinned and said, "This is terrible! If I get $#&%*@! killed, my mother will kill me!"

Down to the besieged city we went, and he became braver. He stuck with us and became a close friend and an invaluable guide to the people, cultures, and politics of the area. He was brilliant, and I learned much from him. I asked him once, "What is the difference between Yezidis and Christians?"

He said, "One hair." And between Islam and Yezidi? He replied, "One mountain." He was a poet and had been studying Arabic at the university when ISIS attacked and disrupted his education. He was devastated by the horrors of what had happened to his people, and it was his drive for justice, I think, that kept him with us at first.

We mostly lived on the front line. ISIS was not giving up Sinjar easily, and we were regularly under mortar and machine-gun fire. While we were there, Jiří Šitler, an old friend we first met when he was Czech ambassador to Thailand, visited us. He had been on missions with us before and was very funny, brave, and also very smart. He joked all the time, yet even his jokes were educational. He was transferred from Thailand and, at that time, was the Czech ambassador to Romania.

He was the most unusual diplomat I knew, staying with us at the front line, braving the mortar and machine-gun fire.

He made us laugh and managed to befriend anyone he met. He had been part of the resistance against communism in the Czech Republic, and when it fell, he was appointed the ambassador to Thailand by Václav Havel, the new leader of a free Czech Republic.

With the amount of fighting in Sinjar, I decided it would be better to keep my nephew, Dave, with Peter at the top of the mountain. We would go up and join them and take care of civilians every two or three days. Sometimes, I brought them down to visit us, and on one occasion, four mortars landed all around us as we were sending them back up the mountain. When the firing stopped, I asked Peter, "How was that?"

"Not very fun, Dad, but I'm okay. I think it's better to not be in the middle of the mortars." Peter is very practical and unflappable.

That mission lasted until the second week of November 2015. Just before we left, a congressional delegation showed up in Erbil, with representatives Steve King and Dana Rohrabacher. We met with them and Peshmerga General Hazar. We were able to keep making friends in the KRG. We got enough encouragement from the leaders we knew to decide we should plan another, bigger mission and keep pushing for a full training. I emailed reports out and told our team back in Thailand to start planning another mission for January and February. This would be a bigger mission, with Karen and the kids and a GLC crew.

We returned home to Thailand and Burma for a relief team training and follow-on relief mission in Karen State. In October 2015, the government of Burma signed a ceasefire with several of the major ethnic groups, and in many parts of the country, things were quiet; there was still little trust in the government, especially considering the ongoing fighting and displacement occurring in Kachin and northern Shan states. But we felt that the teams on the ground and the headquarters team in Chiang Mai were doing a great job, and this freed us up to return to Kurdistan.

Just after we left Kurdistan in November, the final push for Sinjar took place and the city was taken back from ISIS. On November 13, 2015, it was retaken without a fight, as ISIS had fled in the days prior after heavy bombardment by coalition air forces. Multiple groups, including the KRG Peshmerga, the PKK from Turkey, the YPG from Syria, the YBS (Yezidi affiliate of YPG), and the HPE—the Yezidi force Edo was part of—participated in the takeover and now vied for control of the city. ISIS lost the city but still held a line two miles outside it, and the fighting continued.

We returned in January 2016. The other sectors in Kurdistan continued to be static, so we went straight back to Sinjar. Our plan was to set up camp on the mountain, leaving Karen, the kids, and the ladies up there like before and bringing the guys back down to the city and the new front line, which was now two miles outside the city. We arrived at the top of the mountain around midnight in the middle of a storm. There was light snow and a whipping seventy-mile-an-hour wind. The clinic had been upgraded from a MASH-style five-by-ten-meter army wall tent to a concrete structure, ten by twenty-five meters, with an examination room, a pharmacy, an office, and a central bay with capacity to hold about twenty beds. There was also a shower and toilet. We unloaded in the middle of the storm, moving supplies inside the clinic. I could hear Eliya's laugh ring out as we struggled to set up our tents in the wind outside. This would be more winter than we'd seen in Iraq yet. We woke to several inches of snow outside our tents and our Burma guys, bundled from head to toe, stomping around to keep warm.

We followed our plan at first, with the guys heading down to the new front line, now on the south side of Sinjar City. Our first trip down, we toured what had been, on our previous trips, occupied by ISIS. The city was about 80 percent destroyed by a combination of ISIS rockets and mortars in their initial attack, follow-up destruction by ISIS targeting primarily Christian and Yezidi neighborhoods, and then coalition air strikes in the battle to oust the militant fighters. Much of the city was still mined, and we walked around carefully; ISIS dug tunnels in many places, and we also took care as we explored those. They could be mined or even manned.

Very few families had returned because ISIS was still nearby and also because of the disputes among the groups who took over the city. No cleanup had been done; the recent occupation was still fresh and the tragedy still raw. The smell of unburied bodies came from the rubble of destroyed buildings. In places, piles of clothes, with human bones nearby, lay untouched since the day the victims were gunned down by ISIS. On one street, overlooking the city park, we found a baby onesie with a bullet hole in it. During this initial exploration, we saw some families had moved back, so we soon brought our whole group down.

It was just a couple months after the liberation of the city, and while ISIS was not far off, they seemed to be on the defensive. The urgency was less than it was before. In some ways and places, it felt like the aftermath. Now we were looking into the eyes of people who knew the worst had happened to them. We interviewed survivors: one girl who had escaped after eleven months of being held and passed around as a slave for ISIS fighters; a man whose family had been captured then ransomed and was in Germany, where there is a large Kurdish and Yezidi population. Yet it was not the aftermath. Thousands were still held, and we talked to many people who were still hoping against hope they would see their children, wives, brothers or sisters alive again one day. Many knew just enough to know, whether their loved ones were alive or dead, the worst had probably happened to them.

The grief of the people we met hid behind duty, hid behind their fight. It battled hope and weighed upon them sometimes like a betrayal. Our first night all together in Sinjar City, we were given an abandoned house to stay in, not far from Peshmerga headquarters.

Unlike much of the city, the house was intact. Our Peshmerga guides knew we wanted to tell the stories of their people and brought in a soldier whose wife had been captured, along with his children, one two years old and one two months old. He entered the room with dutiful alacrity and stood at attention, ready to help. We asked him to tell us about his family—and the struggle began playing over his face: the fear, the effort at self-control, and the limbo between hope and despair. Shaheen was our translator and was the same as before: chain-smoking, cynical, joking. But as he relayed these details, I saw a tear slide down his face.

Soon the man had told us all there was to tell. His name was Nezar Samuel, and I asked him if I could pray. He nodded yes. I took his hand, and in that eyes-closed moment of appeal to God, grief won. The dutiful soldier's face collapsed for a moment, and he raised his eyes to the ceiling in agony—but not certainty—that the worst had happened to his young wife and children. After I finished the prayer, he disappeared out the door and into the night. The next day, he was the guard at the local Peshmerga headquarters, busily and stoically guiding us to the office we needed to visit.

As the liberators took back land outside the city, they began to discover mass graves. At one of these sites were the remains of seventy-eight women who had been captured, taken out of the city, and shot. Another contained the remains of fifty men. More and more of these sites were found.

One bright, sunny day, we brought our whole group, including my family, to visit several of these gravesites. The first one was out in the desert to the south of the city. The wind whipped across the barren land, and we walked into it, the sun hard and bright but not warming. We came to the grave, marked by some sticks stuck upright in the ground. Around the sticks, clothes and shoes were scattered randomly. We approached and gradually the bones came into focus: human bones, lying in the clothes they were wearing the day they were gunned down. Spent shell casings were scattered around from the bullets that ended their lives. Here, we were told, around thirty people were buried. Shaheen told us, "After ISIS captured the city, they separated the people. These are the people not useful to ISIS."

At another site, Shannon, our dentist, picked up two skulls, one adult and one child, and pointed out the evidence that both had been bashed in the mouth with something like the butt of a rifle before they were killed. Eighty-one people were buried there. Another site by the side of the road came with a story of rescue from a man who stopped to talk to us as he drove by. These people nearly escaped. They were on the other side of the mountain from Sinjar but were caught on the road, and ISIS fighters began executing them on the spot. The people of a nearby village we could just see in the distance realized what was happening, and the village men rushed out and drove ISIS away. Still, more than seventy people were killed.

At one spot, where a makeshift barrier had been set up with four sticks and red fabric strung between, a man in jeans and a blazer sat on the ground, heedless of the dirt and bushes. "This, this is where my wife's family is buried," he said. "Her uncle, everybody—these are their bones, scattered here, left for the animals and the weather, and anything. When she found out, she went crazy...It is like no one cares that these bones are left here, not taken care of. No one cares." The spot he was sitting on was where ISIS tired of carrying a disabled man and shot him. In the distance, a group of eighteen, including his wife's family, was killed. There were two more groups, but no one knew where they were buried. Two survivors of this mass execution were able to supply details.

At that time, more than twenty mass graves had been discovered in the Sinjar area. But thousands of people were still missing, and ISIS still controlled many villages. The man told us, "I want people to come and see with their own eyes. This is something people cannot believe unless they see it with their own eyes."

We too thought the world needed to know. Sahale and her friend, Elle Arnold, who had taken a semester of university off to join us on this trip, made a video called "Not Alone: American Girls Speak Out." We shared our footage and the stories we were collecting with all who were interested.

Interest grew in our Middle East work, and we received more support this time, from Victor Marx and his organization, from Reload Love (another nonprofit run by Lenya Heitzig and Jen Santiago), and others, and we had enough money to buy relief supplies. Most of the families who had fled Sinjar were still living in tents on the mountain. We were able to buy thousands of warm clothing items: jackets, gloves, socks, and hats. We did ten GLC programs in the big mountain IDP camps, in Edo's mountaintop village, and down in the city.

Not far from the house we stayed in, we met a family who had moved back to their home and reopened their family business: breadmaking.

Peter looks at the remains of Yezidis killed in an ISIS massacre and buried in a mass grave outside Sinjar, 2016.

They were supplying the Peshmerga with bread every day. Shaheen and another local man named Ezadine, a former dental hygienist who became one of our translators, coordinated with them, and they opened their compound for a GLC program.

After we met them, with typical Yezidi hospitality they invited our whole group to sleep in their home. The father's name was Faisal; he always wore slacks and a button-up white shirt, open at the neck. He had a full mustache, as did most Yezidi men, and gray hair. He met me with a strong handshake, a mild smile, and patient eyes. His wife was a round, bustling, hospitable woman, always demanding we stay for dinner. They had an eighteen-year-old daughter who helped throw together some of the best food I've eaten in Kurdistan. And they had several sons and grandchildren. When they broke out their family photo albums for us to see, we found out ISIS had kidnapped the wife of one of his sons. They didn't know where she was.

I knew he wasn't a normal man. His city was in ruins, his family was scattered, and their future was unknown; yet his eyes were full of peace, and his home and family were full of joy. He reminded me of the man of peace in Psalm 37, and I told him so. This home became one of our favorite places to visit; my kids would do school sitting on the sofas lining the walls of their living room, and Karen and Hosie would try to learn Kurdish cooking secrets in their kitchen.

We stayed in Sinjar a few weeks, training and treating soldiers on the front line. With the city taken and ISIS pushed back into the desert, it was quieter here than it had been before. Even as the fight moved to other fronts, Sinjar took a special place in my heart. The people's suffering and their courage and kindness in the midst of it had touched me and we had made life-long friends here. The local people called Sinjar "Shingal" and I took this as my local name. From then on, when in the Middle East, I would introduce myself as "Daoud Shingali" ("David of Sinjar").

After this, we went back to the front near Merki Village and the monastery, where our team had spent the first mission. Captain Mohammed rejoined us and invited us to stay at his outpost there, where he was part of the local general's headquarters element. His commanding officer, General Bahram, had his command post set up right on the front line overlooking the town of Bashiqa, which ISIS had occupied in 2014. He welcomed our whole group, and we set up in a cinder block bunker and tents.

This Bashiqa position would become another home away from home in Kurdistan, and General Bahram, one of our closest friends. The dining hall was a long tent with several long tables lined up and a TV suspended from the roof at one end. Below the TV was a diorama of that section of the front line. The floor was gravel, and red plastic chairs lined the wall. Karen and the kids spent hours there, doing school. We used it for administration work, setting up printers and computers. The soldiers on post became friends and were always bringing in tea and chocolates when they knew our group was there.

The winding gravel road to this position made for good running, and on cold mornings, as the Peshmerga soldiers woke up and stood outside their bunkers, stamping their feet to stay warm, our whole group would go run, heading away from the ISIS lines and back toward the main road and the mountain where the monastery was. On this first visit, we stayed here a few days then went back to Sinjar.

In Sinjar, ISIS threw a new twist into the fight: chemical weapons. On February 11, they launched several mortar rounds into Sinjar packed with an unknown chemical, later proven to be sulfur mustard gas. Then, on February 25, they launched another one with rockets. In total, 287 soldiers were sickened and evacuated off the front line. We were there for both attacks and joined by Chuck Holton, a former U.S. Army Ranger and correspondent for the Christian Broadcasting Network (CBN). He helped us get this news out. One of the rockets landed just ten meters in front of Faisal's bread shop, with shrapnel shattering the front window. One of his sons was wounded.

Was this going to be a new weapon to contend with? Knowing ISIS's ruthlessness, it wasn't a threat we took lightly.

The week after the second chemical attack, in the first week of March 2016, we returned to Thailand for our March meetings and to report to our team there and the ethnic leaders. But in May, we resumed our position on the same front lines, which continued to be static. We trained Peshmerga and Yezidi soldiers, mostly in combat first aid, treated people as needed and deepened our relationships with our friends there. Shaheen was our primary translator and a good friend, despite his crankiness. While he could be making one hundred to two hundred dollars per day working with the U.N. or big news agencies, he came and worked with us for fifty dollars a day. Ezadine helped us when we were in Sinjar but had another job coordinating health relief into Sinjar, so he went back and forth.

We really needed another steady person for when we split into two groups, so we hired a young guy named Dlo to assist Shaheen. Dlo's older brother, Omar, worked for the Peshmerga intelligence near Merki, and we became friends with Omar after going through his checkpoint multiple times. He once invited us to his house for dinner and that was when we met Dlo, who asked us for a job. We hired him on a temporary basis; his English wasn't great, but he was local and knew the area and people well. He would become a key part of our team.

During our February mission, I started thinking and praying about going into Syria. That was where ISIS had started; the fighting there was heavy, and the suffering of the people was great, while in Kurdistan everything was pretty quiet for the time being.

I got in touch with a journalist friend who was there, to see if he thought we could be useful. He put me in touch with his "fixer" named Bashir. In our last week in Kurdistan, Bashir secretly crossed the border near Sinjar and came to meet us at the clinic on the mountain. He showed up wearing a polka-dot bow tie with round red-framed glasses.

He was neither a James Bond nor a Rambo, but, as I got to know him, I would watch a movie about his life any day.

He was an operator: he said the journalist had told him FBR worked on the front lines and was needed in Syria but that we were "really Christian and prayed a lot." It turned out Bashir was a Christian too, but in the environment of the YPG, he kept that under the radar. He told us that when he heard we were Christians, his heart started to beat faster, and he thought, "Maybe this can be the beginning of change in Syria, of God's Holy Spirit moving like a mighty river of change...."

I listened to this story and replied, "Let's be clear: FBR is not a river, or even a trickle. We're just a tiny drop."

Bashir looked at me seriously, then smiled. "Dave, we are all only little drops of water, but when we are part of God's rain, and when we fall together, we become part of God's river." We loved him right away but didn't have time right then to go to Syria, so we sent him with relief supplies back over the border.

On this mission, in May and June 2016, just six of us—my family and Eliya—were able to get to Syria. We treated the wounded at the front lines, and during one battle, Eliya worked side-by-side with a U.S.

Near Sinjar with Bashir, our Syrian coordinator, and Nezar Samuel, who shared his story about losing his wife and two children to ISIS. They are now reunited, 2016.

Army Special Forces medic named Jonathan Johnson to save the lives of families shot by ISIS as they fled. Bashir proved to be a very effective guide: we also gave food to desperate IDPs, visited Kobani, and helped over one thousand orphans—all in about five days.

When we finished the Syria mission, I felt we should postpone our planned trip to the U.S. and go right back to Syria. I asked our team to pray and, when we all asked God together for His answer, my family and team all said, "Keep going to America." I did not agree but did not have any conviction that God told me to go back to Syria. So, I acquiesced and said, "I do want to go to Syria now but am not sure of God's will in that, so I submit to you all."

We had just enough time for some fun before we left Kurdistan: a climb. We drove to Soran, a Kurdish city near the Iranian border where our friends General Bahram and Major Nabaz were from. We visited them, but our main objective was Mount Halgurd, the highest mountain in Iraq, rising to around twelve thousand feet. With minimal climbing gear, we chose a harder route with a lot of snow and ice. I used Eliya's machete as a makeshift ice ax, cutting steps into some of the steep ice we encountered. I had a rope, and we belayed each other up the tougher parts.

Our next mission was in September 2016. This was after a summer in the U.S where we reconnected with our supporters who help us do this work. In between meetings and speaking at churches we were also blessed by our friends with many good climbs, surfing trips and horses for the kids to compete with in rodeo. We came back well reinforced.

On this September mission, we did much the same thing, including a slightly longer trip to Syria with eight people. This time, I was allowed to bring Monkey and Shannon in addition to my family and Eliya. In Syria, we got down to the front line and saw that ISIS and the Free Syrian Army (FSA) were often the same thing, and the FSA were often being used by the Turks as a proxy force. While we were in Syria, the rest of the team continued training on the front lines near Bashiqa. By then, we had trained more than one thousand Peshmerga and Yezidi soldiers.

There were beginning to be more rumors of the long-planned offensive to push ISIS out of Iraq, and while we were in Syria, the Peshmerga near Bashiqa picked up some families fleeing Mosul. Our team gave medical help and interviewed them.

Those families had left Mosul on the evening of October 1, 2016, nine people slipping through the dusk to the outskirts of the city and into the empty darkness to the northeast. They were on foot, two women carrying babies, one small child, and four men. Some thirty kilometers away, at the Peshmerga command post above Bashiqa, those guarding the line got the word: nine people coming toward you from Mosul.

As well as they could, the Peshmerga tracked them. At a certain point, two of the men broke away and headed back toward Mosul, now sitting restlessly under the threat of the impending counterattack. Three weeks before, coalition air support had dropped leaflets over the city advising people to flee if they could and to stay away from ISIS, because there would be no mercy shown when the attack began. Some were heeding the advice, and just the week before, a group of twenty people—men, women, and children—were received at General Bahram's headquarters and sent on to Erbil for processing.

The small group of October 1 was intercepted early in the morning of October 2 after walking most of the night. By then, there were only seven people. The Peshmerga soldiers brought them to the command post and began the process of clearing them to continue—also feeding them breakfast.

The family had just finished eating when our team was given the go-ahead to talk with them. One of the men was with his family, a wife, and two children. The other woman with a baby had a husband already in Erbil. The second man sat silently to the side while the father answered most of the questions.

They had left Mosul because things were getting very bad; now there was no food. They heard on the radio the offensive would happen on October 19. They decided to go. It was not so hard, as there had been decreased presence of ISIS lately. But they knew if they left their house, they would lose it. Before ISIS, they had a normal and good life. After ISIS, things gradually became worse. Now civil society was in shambles: there was no health care, no education system, very little information from the outside world, no food in the markets—and no freedom. The women were afraid to walk alone on the streets—ISIS made the threat that anyone they caught out without a male relative would be punished.

More ominously, before Mosul had been a city of many different kinds of people and religions: Christians, Muslims, Yezidis, and others living together. Now the others were gone. This Muslim family didn't know where they were or what happened to them; they had no stories of executions in the street or any of the brutality for which ISIS was infamous. There was just a quiet disappearance. They thought many of the Christians ran away but did not know any details. Their story was one of the slow disappearances of all the things that make a life. Finally, this family decided to escape before they too were "disappeared."

As the Peshmerga hurried them toward the car that would take them to Erbil and an uncertain future, our team gave each of the three children a GLC bracelet as a reminder they weren't alone and God has a plan for them. Toh, a Karen medic, treated the smallest baby, who was coughing uncontrollably. They got in a small white car, trailed by an armored truck, and headed off.

We had promised the Kurds we would stand with them when the fighting kicked off, but still, there were only rumors of an imminent attack. I knew, while the fight to push ISIS out could start tomorrow, it could also be months away. There were a lot of factors at play. We had committed to speak at a missions conference in Alaska in the last week of October, followed by six weeks of speaking across the U.S. We decided we couldn't live based on rumors and stuck with that plan. Our team left Erbil on October 15, 2016—my family and I to the U.S. and everyone else back to Thailand.

Just a few days later, the fighting began in Bashiqa area. The Iraqi Army had been slowly fighting their way north from Ramadi and Fallujah, but the Kurds had been on hold until the coalition, including the Iraqis, reached them and gave the go-ahead.

When ISIS first attacked, the Kurds had defended and moved farther into territory Iraq wanted to control. The Iraqi government was afraid the Kurds might take more land if they fought off ISIS independently. Now, the battle had reached the outskirts of Mosul and the Kurds were again part of the overall strategy. The town of Bashiqa was the biggest prize on that northeast front, and it sat right below General Bahram's command post. On October 19, the Peshmerga, after years of sitting on their line, fending off attacks from ISIS, finally went on the offensive.

In Alaska, I was getting updates all the time from the people on the ground there. This was it, and I had promised I would be there with them. I had prayed for nearly two years that ISIS would be pushed back and the Kurds would be free. That battle was starting. I felt I needed to go back. But I had also made promises here in the U.S. I talked to my family and the churches in Alaska, I prayed about it, consulted our team back in Thailand—we all decided I should go back after finishing all my Alaska speaking commitments. Karen and the kids would finish the rest of the U.S. tour.

Just four days after arriving in Alaska, I got on a plane and headed back to Erbil. It was October 20, 2016, almost exactly twenty months since that day in February when I first landed in Erbil with Peter, straight out of Kachin State. The battle was just beginning.

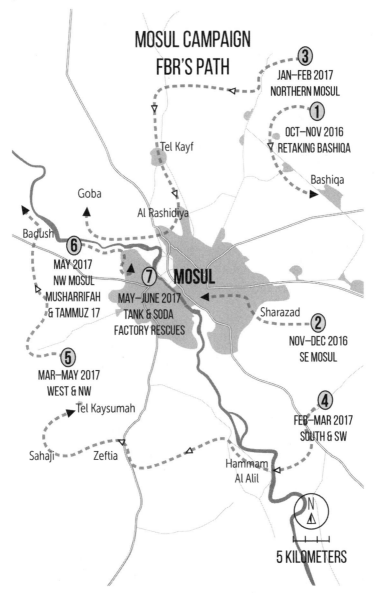

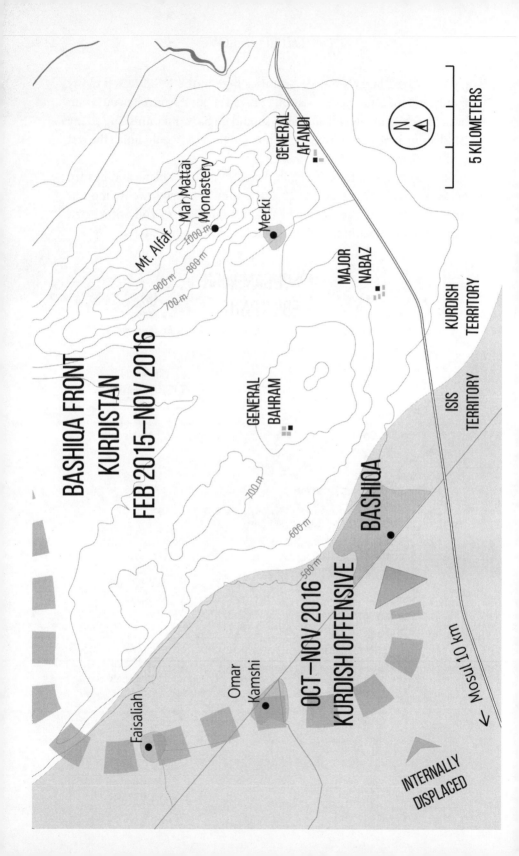

BASHIQA FRONT
KURDISTAN
FEB 2015–NOV 2016

Mt. Alfaf
Mar Mattai Monastery
1000 m
900 m
800 m
700 m
Merki
GENERAL AFANDI
MAJOR NABAZ
GENERAL BAHRAM
700 m
600 m
500 m
KURDISH TERRITORY
ISIS TERRITORY
OCT–NOV 2016
KURDISH OFFENSIVE
BASHIQA
Faisaliah
Omar Kamshi
Mosul 10 km
INTERNALLY DISPLACED

N

5 KILOMETERS

CHAPTER EIGHT

The Battle Begins

"Dave, always be the first to apologize."
—ALLAN EUBANK, DAVE'S FATHER

Zau Seng and I landed in Erbil and met up with Dave Dawson, Dlo, and Shaheen. We organized our gear. Then I went for a run and showered before we loaded our Land Cruiser and drove to the front lines north of Bashiqa near Nouron. We arrived at night, crossing the berm used to hold off ISIS after dark. Peshmerga troops manning a position there stopped us and asked where we were going. "To link up with General Bahram," I replied through Shaheen.

The soldiers said, "Very dangerous," and shrugged. We drove on through in the dark, stirring up a cloud of dust in the still-warm October air.

A few days earlier, the Kurds had pushed through the berm, driving ISIS back across the arid plains. ISIS was able to hold one village and inflict casualties from there, so the Kurds left a unit to keep ISIS fixed there while the main body swung east and then south. The Peshmerga were driving a wedge between ISIS positions along the foot of the Nouron-Bashiqa mountains to the east and the Nineveh plains and Mosul to the west.

The Peshmerga units were strung out in battalion-sized positions along this south-pointing line. There were large gaps between each unit, and ISIS could move between them. We carefully followed the tracks of the advancing Peshmerga columns through abandoned wheat fields and desert. As we drove from one position to the next, we knew ISIS could potentially hit us from any side at any time.

The Peshmerga felt this potential threat too, so as we approached every position, we flashed our headlights, turned on the interior lights, did everything we could to make sure they knew we were not ISIS. We would pull up and ask, "Where is General Bahram?"

They usually said something like, "That's down the next few hills or somewhere. But it's dangerous out here at night. You sure you want to keep going?" We assured them we'd be careful and continued, connecting the dots of these scattered outposts in the new front "line." We were fortunate ISIS didn't hit us in the gaps.

Finally, around midnight, we rolled into Bahram's command post. We pulled our vehicles into their armored circle. There were two APCs, two T62 tanks, some Humvees, and Toyota Land Cruiser pickup trucks with machine guns mounted on them. The PAK, the Iranian Kurds, were there too. There was a big perimeter, about one hundred and fifty meters long by about seventy meters deep. It was a long rectangle, and we set up a casualty collection point (CCP) in the back corner of the rectangle, with our two thin-skinned Toyota Land Cruiser ambulances.

At that point, the primary team was Dave Dawson, Micah, Zau Seng as videographer, Dlo and Shaheen as translators, and me; Joseph, our Karen medic, joined us two days later.

The next day, we woke before dawn as Peshmerga armored bulldozers and backhoes dug a long trench to the west of us, about three meters deep and two meters wide. This was both tactical, as a block against ISIS suicide vehicles and a wedge between ISIS forces in Bashiqa and Mosul; and it was strategic, demarcating the new border the Kurds hoped to secure by driving out ISIS and reclaiming the Nineveh plains territory they lost to Iraq earlier in their history. General Bahram had his men preparing for an attack on the village of Omar Kamshi to our east. ISIS shot mortars and machine guns at us sporadically from both Omar Kamshi and other positions to our west in the Nineveh plains. At this point, we had ISIS on two sides of us.

Early the next morning, the attack started. Zau Seng and I crammed into General Bahram's command vehicle along with the general, fourteen Peshmerga, and Alan Duncan, a Scottish volunteer with the Peshmerga. Alan was an ex-British soldier, an infantryman who was with the Kurds almost from the beginning of the ISIS fight, and the Kurds loved him. There were also a couple of journalists, bringing our total to twenty, all wedged in a vehicle made to carry ten. With elbows in faces and stepping all over each other, it felt like I was in a clown car as we rolled into battle. The tanks took the lead, main guns blazing, as the battle for Omar Kamshi began.

ISIS defended on foot and were hammered by the tanks, Humvees, and APCs with machine guns on top. Our APC was hit by small-arms fire, but we kept moving. Our vehicles drove up and down the streets and killed about fifteen ISIS; the rest fled. At one point, the vehicle stopped, and I got out, along with Alan, to take photographs and document what we saw. There were four dead ISIS fighters lying in the street, one with a suicide vest that was smoking but did not go off. As I shot some photos, our vehicle and the others suddenly took off again, leaving me and Alan standing exposed in the street. ISIS took advantage and started shooting at us.

It was a good thing I liked running because, at that point, we had no choice: we took off, ISIS shooting as we tried to chase down the vehicles that had been giving us cover. At this point I was also grateful for the gift Edo had presented me with earlier as a thank-you for standing with the Yezidis: an AK-47 that I was carrying now. Alan and I ran and shot, aiming at windows and other openings possibly hiding ISIS shooters, praying we wouldn't get hit first. After a couple blocks, the armored convoy stopped again, and we piled back into our vehicle, laughing with excitement and relief.

This kind of fighting went on for a few days, clearing out any last resistance as ISIS fighters withdrew west to Mosul. We'd go back to our position at night, then to the village in the day. It was a one-sided battle with ISIS on the run, and there were only a few casualties on the Peshmerga side. Joseph was able to care for these men and Dave Dawson, Micah, Zau, and I helped move them. In addition to the men who were shot or hit by shrapnel, we also treated several Peshmerga sickened by chemical attacks, which looked to me like the same sulfur mustard gas we faced earlier in Sinjar. About five Peshmerga were affected by this, and we treated and evacuated them, documenting ISIS's use of chemical weapons.

About a week into the fight, I was in our position getting ready to go to sleep. I slept in one of the Land Cruisers at the back of the perimeter. We got a message that the Peshmerga position next to us, about a kilometer away, might get attacked, so we should get ready. That happened almost every night, an attack somewhere, except it hadn't happened to us. I got all my gear ready and planned to go to sleep, and if shooting started, I'd wake up and we could respond. I got in my sleeping bag and maybe fifteen minutes later the attack started—but it wasn't a kilometer away; it was right on top of us.

The first thing that happened was machine gun rounds came in, right over our vehicle and to the side, and then an RPG exploded to the left of us. I jumped up, put on my boots, and grabbed my AK, helmet, and ammunition. It was dark except for flashes of light from explosions and vehicles where guys were frantically trying to get their gear together. I ran up to the middle of the perimeter where the armored vehicles were.

Some of the Peshmerga were there, including Captain Mohammed. He yelled at me: "Daoud, get out! Get down!"

I told him, "No, I gotta go help!" I ran forward in the dark toward where the Peshmerga were shooting back. An RPG streaked by me, impacting ten meters away with a roar that almost knocked me down. The explosion illuminated the ground, and I saw that the RPG had landed in a pit dug earlier that day for one of the armored vehicles. The pit absorbed the shrapnel, but I felt the blast next to me. I thanked God I was still on my feet.

I got to the forward position berm and could see muzzle flashes about fifty meters away. ISIS had already taken the berm forward of us. But the Peshmerga were ready, and within less than a minute, half of our element was up and shooting back. I dropped down and started shooting also, emptying about five magazines in five minutes. Above us, heavy machine guns opened up, and about five minutes later, the tanks got going as well.

ISIS came back at us with RPGs and machine guns, and we kept pounding away from the forward berm. It was loud. Dave Dawson ran back and forth, bringing us more ammo from the trucks. He was like my squire and a brave one, too—every time he popped over the middle berm behind us, he was exposed to direct fire but never stopped and was never hit.

Since the beginning of our time in Kurdistan, we had informal but good relationships with the U.S. Army. Some of the generals, such as General Gary Volesky, with whom I served in the 2nd Ranger Battalion, I knew from before. Others, such as Mark Odom, Steven Gilland, Scott Efflandt, and John Richardson, would soon become friends. I shared all I saw with them. General Efflandt called me a "two-meter drone." As this fight continued, I called General Gilland, in command at that time, and described what was happening. They sent a drone over, ISIS pulled back, and later, we saw air strikes. The whole battle was over in fifty minutes.

We had two casualties. One was a gunner on a tank, shot in the leg. The other was a foot soldier shot in the face. Joseph and Micah treated them, and neither injury was life-threatening.

The next day, we moved on to take another town, Faisaliah. In that area, the villages were all built in the midst of wheat farms and olive groves, with plenty of houses off on their own in the middle of their farms. It turned out there were only a few ISIS in this town and most of them were killed outside in trenches and bunkers they built in the olive groves. They had emplaced improvised explosive devices (IEDs) along all the roads, and we stopped several times to check for them. We discovered several this way, bypassed them slowly, and had no problems.

We got all the way into town and cleared it street by street. The ISIS fighters were either dead or had run away, and, except for some sniper fire and a few RPGs, the battle here was over. We took no casualties. As we drove through, people lined the streets, yelling that they were villagers so they wouldn't be suspected of being ISIS. There were about two thousand of them and it soon turned into a full-blown celebration.

We walked down the street with the Peshmerga. Women ran out holding their babies up for us to kiss, to hold, to take pictures with. They hugged us, grabbed our hands to shake, thanked us, and prayed blessings on us and our children and grandchildren—they were so happy ISIS was gone. I tried to pray with them as well.

Off to the side of the village, the celebration seemed to end. There was a crowd of about two hundred men gathered. They were all very solemn-looking, and I asked Shaheen, "What's that?"

"It's a funeral." I asked him if he could find out what was happening, and he walked over.

He came back, very serious. "David, I say, stay away from this." He told me there was an American air strike just a couple of days ago on a suspected ISIS position. One of the bombs hit ISIS in an olive grove and killed them. But the other missed and hit a house about one hundred meters away. There were eight people in it, including kids. "Now they bury them. They have dug their bodies out of the rubble. They bury them now."

I prayed and thought maybe I should stay away out of respect. I also thought maybe they'd be really angry with me, as an American. I prayed and felt, *No, you should go to them. You are an ambassador of Jesus.* My dad has always said, "Dave, be the first to apologize." I walked to the group; everyone looked at me and I could see the anger in their eyes. Micah was with me and I told him, "Stay back, stay out of this. I'll go alone. If they go crazy, you pray and use your weapon anywhere you need to. I'm just going to do what God tells me."

I had a Glock pistol stuck in my back waistband under my shirt. I didn't really know what was going to happen, but I wanted options. I walked up to the man who seemed to have seniority—it turned out it was his brother and his brother's family who were killed. The circle of men closed around me and I felt surrounded by a wall of rage; one big, young guy standing next to the leader clenched his fists with barely-contained violence. I looked straight at the man whose family had been killed and said, "I'm an American. I am so sorry the Americans did this. It was an accident. I'm sure the pilot would feel terrible. He probably has kids himself and he was trying to hit ISIS and missed. I'm really sorry. We apologize. As an American, I'm sorry. We were wrong. Please forgive us." Shaheen was translating.

I prayed again and felt, *This isn't enough, you should do the next step.* I got on my knees and said, "I'm going to pray for you all and ask for forgiveness." I finished praying and looked up into their perplexed eyes. I said, "I have nothing else to say or give you except my life. I have a wife and three children, and I have no time to ask them if I can offer my life. But I do it out of love. My life is not worth eight of yours, but it is all I have, and I give it to you. I want you to know I've got a pistol in my back waistband. If you want to use it to kill me, if that will make it right for you, you can do that. I will not resist. That is all I can give. I pray for mercy and healing." Shaheen translated all of this.

I started to pray again. And the brother, who'd lost so many people, including a newborn baby who was still buried in the rubble—the brother bent down and, with tears coming down his face, lifted me to my feet and said, "No. No, no, we won't kill you. Only we are very sad. Thank you for caring and thank you for apologizing. It was a mistake. We know it was a mistake, but we're still sad. But we forgive you, we love you."

Asking forgiveness from the man who lost family to a U.S. airstrike, 2016.

He lifted me to my feet and I turned to the young man who stood next to him, who had been glowering at me. "I know you hate me," I said. "I'm sorry."

Now he was crying too, and said, "No, we forgive you." I realized the whole crowd had softened. The anger had dissipated. Jesus had worked a miracle.

We prayed together and it was like I had new friends and family. We went to the site where the bombing happened. On the way, we found the bodies of ISIS in a position the U.S. hit successfully, a hundred meters away. Just to the north was the house, flattened. It smelled of death. The baby was down there somewhere, under tons of rubble, and we had no way to dig. Some action was better than none so we dug with our hands until we got to two huge pieces we couldn't lift.

There was one other thing I could do too: I recorded everything, got the grid coordinates and all the details and took photos of the dead ISIS and their position. I found pieces of U.S. munitions with serial numbers on it. I sent it to our friend Tom Malinowski at the State Department, as well as to the U.S. military and my military friends to see if they could help, maybe pay some kind of restitution to this family. And I gave the family a thousand dollars right there.

Our team—Joseph, Micah, Dave Dawson, Shaheen, Paul Bradley, Zau Seng, and myself with a Kurdish tank near Omar Kamshi, 2016.

We didn't have much more than that at the time, but we prayed with them. Later, we were able to install a playground in that town in honor of those who were lost.

Faisaliah was the last of the outlying villages before the town of Bashiqa. The Peshmerga units we were with paused to start ramping up for what would be their biggest fight yet.

At the same time, ISIS continued to attack us any way they could. They fired more chemical weapons, and we treated three more Peshmerga who were sickened, but no one was killed. The gas they were using was what the U.S. Army calls low-grade or non-weapons-grade sulfur mustard, and it was the same as they had used in Sinjar. We knew of one child who had died from it, but mostly people were just sickened. Occasionally, ISIS would also attack from a distance with sniper fire, but there were no more ground assaults. It was the lull before the big battle.

In this lull, we were able to get a lot of food supplies from other, larger, aid organizations also working in the area but not at the front. No one knew how many people would be displaced by the upcoming fighting, or what condition they'd be in, but the projections went as high as a million, so much preparation was required. One night, around October

31, 2016, we got word: families were running from Mosul. They were crossing the berm at the Kurd positions just south of us.

We drove down, and there were about five hundred people who'd crossed the lines that night. We set up an impromptu medical clinic for the sick and injured and started distributing food packs for every family. It didn't take long for these people to turn into a mob, crushing us to get the supplies. We were too small a group to hold them off. It looked like it was going to get violent pretty quickly. We also had no time to check people, and I started thinking, *What if someone came here to blow themselves up?* That fell into the category of things we couldn't control, so we prayed against it and kept handing out food packs.

The press of the crowd didn't let up. I was starting to get mad. I prayed and told myself, *I serve Jesus, not these people. I can be patient.* I grabbed the biggest guy pushing me—he was about six foot four— and hugged him. I said, "I love you, brother!" I smiled, and he kind of relaxed right there. Through Shaheen, I said, "You're a big leader. I need your help to distribute this food. Don't worry, I'll take care of you and give you extra." And he took charge; he calmed the group down. We were praying in Jesus's name for love and order, and love and order happened.

This location became the main avenue of escape for people fleeing Mosul. These were the people we needed to help and had supplies for, so we left our position with General Bahram and moved to an abandoned house near a break in the berm the people were fleeing through so we could better care for them. We pulled our own security and were on hand to help new groups as they arrived. We gave them food, medical care, and helped drive them to refugee camps.

By the end of October, the Peshmerga had mostly pushed ISIS out of the valley between Nouron and Bashiqa, leaving them only in the town of Bashiqa and the area west, up to and including Mosul. But ISIS was being slowly surrounded: the Kurds had pushed them out of Sinjar to the west and were pushing them from the east, while the oncoming Iraqi Army was pressuring them from the south.

As the fighting drew closer to Mosul, more civilians were starting to run for it. About five thousand people came through our berm position in two weeks at the end of October and beginning of November. They came on foot mostly, or sometimes driving in convoys across the desert. They came in groups of two hundred to five hundred. They walked through the night, four or five miles, carrying their kids and their loads. The Peshmerga stopped them outside the berm and held them until they could be checked for ISIS ties. While they waited, we brought them food and water and prayed with them. If they got clearance, the Peshmerga would bulldoze a ramp through the berm and over the trench and let the people through. That was where the system started to break down.

As IDPs came through, we'd call the U.N. contact to let them know because we'd been told they had prepared buses to bring these people to a reception zone. "Hey, we got hundreds of people here. We're ready for the buses." But the buses never came, and we didn't know why. There were paved roads to the front, controlled by the Peshmerga. Once, I was told they would be brought up later in the evening but they never came. We could fit ten or twelve people at a time in our vehicles, but there were hundreds of people, including babies and old people. The shuttle was twenty to thirty minutes each direction. It would have been more efficient to have dedicated buses for this purpose.

(This isn't meant as a criticism of the entire U.N., and we had many areas we needed to improve too. We were all learning as we went. And people are grateful for all the organizations helping to feed and care for the refugees once they were in camps.)

We did this for a week or so, giving out food and water, which was being supplied to us by the Barzani Foundation and other NGOs. Joseph treated patients as they came through. Every few nights, we'd go back to our old position at General Bahram's perimeter, where there was occasional shelling and sniper fire. The Peshmerga and Iraqis were prepping for the assault on Bashiqa, which was the last big town before Mosul.

Finally, we heard the attack was to be the next day. Bahram was on the ridges above Bashiqa, where the Peshmerga closed the loop to encircle ISIS. We went there and confirmed the plan with him: the main body would stay up on the mountain that night and launch the attack early in the morning.

Our FBR team met to make our own plan. We had added three to our number: Paul Bradley, who had rejoined us a week before; Jeremy Moore, who'd just gotten out of the U.S. military after twenty years in special operations and was visiting us for just a few days; and Jake Hamby, a journalist friend. Our first idea was to follow the main attack in our armored SUV, loaned to us by Victor Marx. It was a five-seater, but we could jam nine people in with their gear and some medical supplies. Trailing the assault would be our unarmored ambulance, which would hold at a casualty collection point we would set up and shuttle medical supplies and people as needed. We'd also leave Dlo or someone with our cache of relief supplies, blankets, food, and water that we were giving out to the IDPs. Otherwise, they'd be stolen by the people around that site.

It was November 4 and cold. We slept in our trucks on the mountain, but not very much, and woke early. In the predawn darkness, all the vehicles were rumbling around, ready to go in a long line down the mountain. As we watched this prep, we started doubting if this was the best place for us. We'd heard the PAK, the Iranian Kurds, were going down on foot, which was better for us anyway because we didn't really have a proper armored fighting vehicle. We decided to drive down to their position and see if we could go with them.

When we got there, they were gone—there was no sign of them. They'd already started to move down to the assault position. We turned around and headed back to Bahram's convoy—they were gone too. We said a prayer, I put the pedal to the metal and we hurtled down the mountain, to the south, trying to catch up. At the bottom of the mountain, we had to turn right, or south, and there was the column, all lined up. We slipped in right at the back and got ourselves in position—a classic Mr. Bean maneuver.

Then the column started moving again, and it was not at lightning speed. There were over one hundred vehicles, a motley lot including tanks, armored vehicles, Land Cruisers, an old Russian BMP, some Humvees, and pickup trucks. Leading the charge were two armored bulldozers that cleared IEDs and broke down walls for the assault element to follow. Behind the bulldozers was a team of men walking with mine detectors. It was a very slow advance.

After twenty minutes of crawling along, I decided I could walk faster. I got out with Micah, Zau, and Jeremy, and we walked up the line. We took fire as we got to the edge of the city. ISIS was shooting back with rifles, machine guns, and RPGs, but so far, the only damage was to a parked bus that had blown up in front of us after a direct hit.

Then an RPG hit one of the bulldozers. The driver was badly injured, and the dozer caught fire. About seven other Peshmerga were injured, but the column kept moving. I was still on foot ahead of our armored vehicle, with Micah, Jeremy, and Zau Seng. Paul, Jake, and Joseph followed us in the armored vehicle. Back in the thin-skinned ambulance were Dave Dawson and Shaheen.

As we entered the city, we started running alongside the MRAPs (mine-resistant ambush-protected vehicles made by the U.S., who supplied the Peshmerga with a few). ISIS was shooting at us, and we wanted to keep the vehicles between the incoming fire and us. Then, as we ran, metal .50-caliber boxes started raining down on us from above; the gunners were throwing them over the sides as they emptied—it was still better than getting shot by ISIS.

We ran into the city, guns out, with ISIS shooting at us. There were about ten journalists running along with us—from ISIS's perspective, it must have looked like a deployed infantry, ten journalists plus four FBR running into the fight. It was wild, and funny too—mostly because none of us got hit.

We went through the whole city like this and pushed ISIS out, running from block to block and shooting any ISIS or potential ISIS positions we saw. We finally stopped near a big mosque. ISIS had mostly fled, it seemed, and we had only about seven casualties. We were stopped there long enough I realized no one had cleared any buildings. I turned to Jeremy and said, "We should get up on top of this building and see what's going on here. No one's cleared any buildings." He and I cleared that house, covering each other as we went room to room, weapons at ready, making sure there were no ISIS. It was probably the first building cleared in Bashiqa.

As we waited, Dave and Shaheen approached in the thin-skinned ambulance, still tagging along at the end of the column. Just then, ISIS fired two RPGs at them, both of which narrowly missed and exploded harmlessly nearby. As they pulled up safely, I thanked God and went running up to them. "Did you see how close those two RPGs came to you?" I asked. Dave looked at me blankly.

"No," he said. Then he laughed. "We were too busy arguing, like usual!" We all laughed. They spent a lot of time together, both on the front and in Erbil, and, both possessed of strong opinions, argued like brothers.

I knew the Kurds had their own way of doing things and they certainly knew the situation better than we did and didn't want to die needlessly. But it was different from the U.S. Army. The Peshmerga stayed buttoned up in their vehicles and blasted everything that moved but didn't clear any buildings.

As everyone got ready to move again, an ISIS sniper opened up and killed the driver of the lead vehicle, a T62 tank. The same sniper shot three more people; then ISIS mortared a support position behind us on the hill where the PAK were and killed three girls who were bringing food to soldiers. The battle definitely was not over.

All back in the car, I was driving as we ran a gauntlet to get out. We were still going really slowly and came to a long straightaway. I could see where ISIS was firing at the convoy from down a cross street. I didn't want to get stuck in that slow convoy in the open. We'd be shot to pieces. I stopped in a place where we weren't exposed, hoping ISIS wouldn't see. I said a prayer out loud—"God, please help us"—and waited. I let the convoy get about one hundred meters ahead as ISIS machine gun, rocket, and mortar fire peppered the vehicles ahead of us from the cross streets.

The Peshmerga fired back as they slowly moved back the way we came. I was letting the convoy get a little further ahead, thinking I could pull out any minute—then ISIS figured out what we were up to. Bang! They were shooting all the time, but this time, the bullet kicked up the dirt right in front of our vehicle. It became apparent: now was the time to move. The guys around the corner shot at us but missed. We rolled slowly forward, and I prayed out loud again: "Lord, if the shooter does something, make it miss." Right when I said the word "miss," a mortar or RPG landed right in front of us but missed. We all laughed, and I stepped on the accelerator. Thank you, Lord!

We raced forward, crossing the open intersection at speed, and caught the column as they reached the edge of town with their guns blazing. There we stopped for a Peshmerga who had been shot in the hand. Joseph and Micah bandaged him, and we followed the main group to a spot about a mile into the desert outside Bashiqa, where they all circled up.

"What's the plan?" I asked.

"Sleep here. Tomorrow morning, go hit it again. We keep hitting this place until every ISIS is gone."

The next morning—same thing: the Peshmerga hit the city, guns blazing, shooting everything that could be hiding ISIS militants. There was a prolonged firefight where ISIS tried to counterattack but without causing us any casualties. ISIS lost a few guys, though, and some fled. We also started seeing tunnels, which meant we didn't really know how many fighters could be there.

I had told our guys from the beginning, "There are two things we're not going to do: we're not going to lead the assault or clear buildings. And second, we're not going to clear tunnels. That's not our job." By the second day, I realized, *No one's going into the tunnels.* It was too dangerous. I prayed, "Lord, is that my job?" And it came to me: *Someone has to do it. You know how to do it.* I prayed, and the next tunnel we came to, I volunteered to clear. I had my 9mm pistol in one hand, a grenade in the other hand, and my light in my teeth. It was totally committing, and I was afraid—but I pushed that aside to concentrate on the job. I crept slowly through the narrow space, and it ended up being empty except for digging tools and wire. I emerged out the other end, where it opened into a gutter on the side of the main road. I was happy to see that gutter.

The Peshmerga thanked me, and from then on, whenever we came across tunnels, they asked me to clear them. Fortunately, we found no ISIS. There were fans and lights and jackhammers and tools, but ISIS was gone.

The assault went on for four straight days. We pushed back ISIS, and some died, while most ran. We cleared more tunnels and buildings. In one building from which ISIS had shot at us, I captured a .50-caliber sniper rifle that had pinned us down for a while. I later gave it to General Bahram. I also found some magazines and other things, ISIS paraphernalia.

Finally, it seemed Bashiqa was pretty well cleared. They figured it might take one more day to finish. On the fourth night, we all went to sleep back in our little compound with our supplies. Everything was quiet, so we figured we wouldn't miss anything that night and planned to rejoin the assault element in the morning. Also, more IDPs were coming and might need help.

That night we pulled security, one hour each on rotation. My turn was at 5 a.m. I was just waking up when bullets started smacking into our building and the steel gate of our little compound. We were under fire—the battle had come to us.

CHAPTER NINE

Do Your Best

"We will never recover from these deep wounds. The world is proud of the Peshmerga—they embody heroism."

—KRG President Massoud Barzani, on the occasion of the defeat of ISIS in Kurdistan

There were stairs going up to the roof along the wall next to the gate. I ran up and opened fire over the wall with my pistol where I thought the ISIS attackers might be. I emptied it around the gate, where I could see muzzle flashes, though no people. At that point, my pistol started to jam, which was disconcerting. But that one magazine seemed to have turned them, and things quieted.

I ran back down and got my boots and gear on. It was now dawn, and we heard a gunfight break out up the line. I yelled to our team, who had been awakened by the shooting, "First four people ready with their gear, get in the vehicle! Everybody else, hold this position."

I jumped into Victor's armored Land Cruiser with Micah, Dlo, Zau Seng, and Dave Dawson. We drove toward the shooting, coming to the trench positions. There were two squad-size Kurdish elements engaged in a gunfight with an enemy I couldn't quite see as we pulled up. Bullets were flying, and I soon found out that thirteen ISIS had broken out of Bashiqa and were trying to go west across the trench line to Mosul. This was likely part of the same group who had bumped into us earlier in the morning and were driven off by our shooting and the fire of the Peshmerga units around us. They had flanked around to the north and run into the Peshmerga there. The sun was coming up as they tried to sneak through and exposed them in the open with no cover. The Peshmerga gunned them down from their bunkered positions.

Ten of the ISIS fighters were quickly killed, but three made it into the trench and were firing effectively at the two Peshmerga squads who had pinned them down from behind berms about thirty meters from the trench. The Peshmerga were having a hard time dislodging them. It was a stalemate and a dangerous one.

We all ran up to the rear berm around one of the bunkers, bullets flying around us. Some would go by, zing!—which meant not too close. And some came by, crack!—which was really close. The Peshmerga yelled at us, "Get down! Big danger."

I was carrying all the firepower I had: the AK-47 Edo gave me earlier, a pistol, and three extra magazines for the AK. I also had two hand grenades Jeremy had handed me the night before as he was leaving. "You might need these," he said before he walked out. We didn't have very many weapons because our main job was not to fight; we hadn't bought guns to give our guys when we came. We just said, "Lord, if we need an AK please give it to us. I mean, maybe even from the enemy." That was a real prayer; it was our prayer. And also, "God bless our enemies to change."

We were happy for every weapon given to us but felt we could use a few more because we were in the middle of so much fighting. If we were going to be useful to injured civilians or Peshmerga, we also had to be able to defend ourselves and the patients we treated. I was glad to get the grenades.

I practiced with them right away, moved through all the motions, refreshing my muscle memory. If you don't use them all the time, it's easy to forget the technique, and in an emergency, every step has to be automatic and fluid. Then I stuck them in my pouches—I had a Vietnam-era flak jacket, which basically could stop shrapnel and maybe a pistol shot but not a rifle. It was better than nothing. So, an AK, a pistol, an ammo belt, and two grenades: that was what I had when I jumped out of the car, and I had a knit cap on my head because it was cold.

With bullets flying by, I was getting ready to sprint out to the forward berm and remembered I had a helmet in the car. "Dave!" I yelled at my nephew. "Go grab my helmet from the car! Please!" Ever the dutiful squire, he ran back and got it. With a protected head, I ran and got behind the forward berm, which was taking fire. I shot back as well as I could, but I couldn't see the ISIS guys. I asked the Peshmerga next to me, "How many?" They said three and pointed out where the ISIS fighters were in the trench. Then I could see the muzzle flashes and knew right away we weren't going to get them out of there just shooting like we were. If we went into the trench after them, we could win, but someone would probably get shot.

I prayed about what to do. I thought, *I don't need to do this one; it's not my job as a relief worker.* Also, if we got involved in this kind of direct fighting, it might confuse things with the Kurds; this was their job. I could lose a lot of supporters and my reputation as a missionary if I got in a fight like this. And, the main thing: I could get killed, especially if I went in there alone.

I prayed about it again and realized everyone was thinking the same thing. Nobody wanted to go in there because they'd get shot. No one was going to move. They didn't have the training or experience to do this kind of thing. If they just rushed in, they'd win eventually, but many would die. And they all had wives and kids. We were all the same. I prayed again: "Lord, what do you want me to do?" I felt I heard God say, *Do your best.*

Do your best, okay. My best is not that great, but I do know how to use grenades. I know how to shoot. I know how to maneuver to take people out of a trench. I told the Kurds, "I'm gonna go!"

They said, "No! Danger, dangerous!" Micah was behind me, also with an AK-47 someone had handed him, and I told him to follow, stay a little back, and support as he could.

I said another prayer, telling God this was my best, and I ran out. I knew what I was going to do, and for that moment, I was in the infantry again. Quite a few things had to go just right for me, and not so good for ISIS, for me to come out alive. I ran to within about fifteen meters of the trench and threw a grenade in. It went off, loud, a big cloud of dust and smoke billowed up, and I rushed the trench with Micah trailing me. As I fired, I saw one ISIS militant was dead.

I was at the edge of the trench when suddenly bullets from my right started going by my face. I jumped and twisted away, my body moving automatically, but at the same time, my head turned to see the source of the fire. I locked eyes with the ISIS fighter trying to kill me, about fifteen meters away. His gun was at his shoulder and he was looking down the barrel, his finger methodically working the trigger, firing, firing, firing; his eyes burned into mine, and in an instant, I read three things in those eyes. One was, "You made a mistake. You

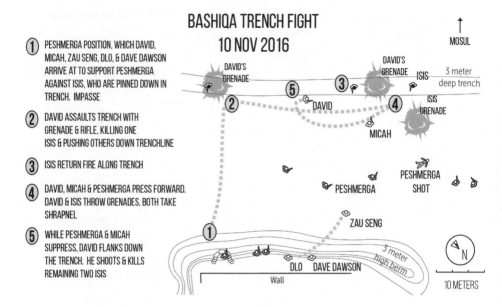

BASHIQA TRENCH FIGHT
10 NOV 2016

↑ MOSUL

(1) PESHMERGA POSITION, WHICH DAVID, MICAH, ZAU SENG, DLO, & DAVE DAWSON ARRIVE AT TO SUPPORT PESHMERGA AGAINST ISIS, WHO ARE PINNED DOWN IN TRENCH. IMPASSE

(2) DAVID ASSAULTS TRENCH WITH GRENADE & RIFLE, KILLING ONE ISIS & PUSHING OTHERS DOWN TRENCHLINE

(3) ISIS RETURN FIRE ALONG TRENCH

(4) DAVID, MICAH & PESHMERGA PRESS FORWARD. DAVID & ISIS THROW GRENADES, BOTH TAKE SHRAPNEL

(5) WHILE PESHMERGA & MICAH SUPPRESS, DAVID FLANKS DOWN THE TRENCH. HE SHOOTS & KILLS REMAINING TWO ISIS

DAVID'S GRENADE
DAVID'S GRENADE
ISIS — 3 meter deep trench
DAVID
MICAH
ISIS GRENADE
PESHMERGA SHOT
PESHMERGA
ZAU SENG
DLO   DAVE DAWSON
3 meter high berm
Wall
N
10 METERS

shot my buddy. You thought we were all dead, but we're not. And now you're dead. You die." The second thing I felt was sheer hate, powerful hate, a hate incomprehensible to me because he didn't even know me. The third thing was not really in his eyes, but I felt this force of evil around him. It was a force bigger than him; maybe he didn't even know about it. But it was like a freight train coming at me.

I spun away, and his shots barely missed my face. I ran parallel to the trench, just out of sight of the remaining ISIS fighters, and prepped the second grenade as I ran. When I was across from where I thought they were in the trench, I cut back towards it and threw in the grenade. It was my last one. As it exploded, I assaulted the trench, shooting directly into it.

As I fired, an ISIS grenade came out of the trench, landing about four meters away from me on the right side and blew up. A blast that close should have killed or seriously wounded me, but it did not. It did rock my head pretty good. I remember seeing the flash and hearing the explosion and thinking, "I'm alive, thank God!" while I kept shooting into the trench. In my mind, from the time the grenade went off next to me to the time I recovered and started firing again was only a couple seconds. Afterward, I looked at Zau's film and saw what really happened: the grenade went off, my legs bent, my head wobbled, and I spent ten seconds looking at my weapon. I looked down at my gun. I looked up. I looked back down and took the magazine out. I put another one in. It was very slow. I was concussed and was lucky one of the two remaining ISIS fighters didn't pop up right then and shoot me point blank in the chest. I was trying to gather my wits just three meters away from where they were in the trench.

I couldn't go forward because the second ISIS guy was also shooting at me, so I circled around to the left to try to engage him. I was met with a burst of automatic fire. By then, the Kurds had come up behind me. They had fallen back when ISIS started shooting, but when I was on the offensive again, they followed me. One of the Kurds tried to circle around to the right and got shot in the chest. He hit the ground, and his fellow soldiers picked him up and carried him back, with Dlo running up to help get him out. The Peshmerga then fell back.

Zau was back behind the berm, filming, and Dave Dawson was with him while Micah was still right behind me. I was shooting from about four meters at the two ISIS fighters but couldn't quite see them through all the dust and smoke, and with them down in the trench, which was pretty deep. Then I ran out of ammo.

I turned and yelled at Micah, "Give me your weapon!" and threw my gun down—Micah immediately handed me his, grabbed mine, and started reloading it. I resumed firing. As he finished reloading, I yelled to him, "I'm going to try to crawl and roll sideways to the trench and shoot the one closest to me. You suppress him if he comes up."

I crawled and then rolled over with my upper body halfway on the trench, hoping to surprise him. I was on my side, two meters from the nearest ISIS fighter, looking him straight in the face. He looked at me, and we both shot. I think I hit him in the shoulder. I'm not sure, but he opened up full auto at me, his bullets just missing my face. Looking in his eyes again, I saw something different: they showed fear. I rolled back out as bullets flew over my face. I was out of ammunition again, and I pulled my pistol out. I yelled at Micah that I needed more ammo. I had my pistol ready to shoot, my head pressed low as I waited for a reload. And then I prayed, "Lord, change this man's heart. This could have a different ending." Instead, more shots came out over my head, barely missing me.

Micah tossed me another magazine. Now I had twenty-five rounds, while Micah had about eight. I told him: "You fire right at the trench. Keep a little bit back and that'll hopefully distract and suppress him. I'm gonna go left and try to flank him." Micah jumped up and started shooting. I ran down the trench, turned, could see both men, and started shooting at them both, shooting one then the other, back and forth.

The far ISIS fighter crumpled to the ground right away, but the nearer ISIS man turned and locked eyes on me one more time. This time, I could see in his eyes he knew it was over. As I shot him again, he collapsed and died.

I jumped into the trench and grabbed the ISIS rifle. The Peshmerga came piling into the trench too and began to strip the far body of weapons and ammo. I heard someone yell, "No, don't! He's got a suicide vest!" I looked up and saw one of them machine-gun the body on full auto. The vest went off in a big explosion; one of the legs flew down the trench and hit me in the leg, almost knocking me over. I thought I'd been hit by shrapnel, there was blood all over my legs—then I realized it was his leg. Three Peshmerga were wounded from the explosion, but nobody died. The situation calmed down as we all realized the fight was over.

I went over to the bodies and prayed for those men. I closed their eyes and tried to arrange them in a more dignified position. I felt bad they devoted themselves to such a hateful and murderous cause. Jesus says we can ask for anything and that He came to save so I prayed that if it was possible, they would have an opportunity to meet Jesus, repent, and that we would see each other in heaven. I am saved by grace, and I wished they had the same opportunity to know grace.

I felt grateful to be alive. I had prayed for another way, but there hadn't been one. I had thought God told me to do my best, and I did, with His help. I knew people were praying for me. Later, I realized the lesson learned was when God tells you to do your best, He doesn't leave you. He goes with you. I had one Psalm in my head when I first ran out there, and later, I thought, "Wow, God was with me."

As I was in the middle of thinking this, all these Peshmerga, including generals, came down, congratulating me and thanking me. "Great job." "You're a hero." "Thanks for showing us how to do it." They were very humble and gracious. They said, "We thought you were just the humanitarian NGO. I'm glad you can fight as well. You were in the Special Forces, weren't you?" One soldier even came up and handed me some more grenades. "You know how to use these," he said.

There was all this handshaking and me saying, "Yes, but God helped me." After about an hour, people started kind of fading away from that position, and it quieted down.

My thoughts drifted back to the ISIS guys I killed. Suddenly, I had a sickening thought: *What will the parents think when they find out their sons were killed?* No parents want their children to be killed, no matter what they've done. I felt sad for the parents, but what else could we do? These men were devoted to destruction and would have kept killing until they were killed. These three dead men, who looked to be in their late twenties or thirties, were hard, tough guys. I didn't know who they'd killed, raped, or tortured. But they were people, and they were someone's kids. My heart went out to their parents.

I prayed again, "Lord Jesus, please comfort these parents, and if I can do anything to help them, please help us meet someday."

The whole trench fight was over by about 9 a.m., and we still had the main assault of the day to do in Bashiqa. We gathered the rest of our team back at our position and joined the Peshmerga column heading into Bashiqa. This ended up being the last assault. There was no return fire as we went through the city, so we dismounted and began clearing houses.

As we went, Micah, Shaheen, and I found a motorcycle barricaded in a room we had seen ISIS coming from in earlier fighting. While Micah worked on getting in the front, I ran around to see if I could get in the back. Just as I got back there, an air strike hit one street behind me, exploding with a tremendous blast. I was able to break the door down into the house, but then had to crawl over rubble and through some rafters to get to the motorbike. As I was crawling through the rafters, one of my new grenades fell out of my jacket, dropped to the concrete floor and rolled away. It didn't go off, but I felt like an idiot as I returned it to my pocket. Feeling sheepish, I finally pushed my way to the front of the building, where Micah, Shaheen, and the bike were.

"You're alive!" Micah greeted me with a shout. I looked at him, startled by the enthusiasm. "We thought that air strike killed you," he explained. They had heard the explosion, wondered if it hit me and started yelling my name. I hadn't heard them at all as I broke the door down and made my way through the rubble. Sure I was dead, they were relieved when I finally made it to them. With the dropped

With General Bahram (behind Suu and Peter) near Bashiqa front line, 2016.

grenade scare, that made several of us who were very grateful for my life at the moment.

We finally liberated the motorcycle and drove it around as the Peshmerga cheered. And that was the last day of the battle for Bashiqa.

That night, I called Karen and told her everything that had happened that day, especially killing those three guys. I said, "I felt it was right, and it seems right, but let's ask God what He thinks of it, regardless what we think." We prayed and she was supportive.

"You had to do what you had to do to protect people," she said. I slept well that night, and the next morning, I woke up feeling completely at peace.

About two nights later, Per Ove from Norway, whom we first met on Sinjar Mountain and who was now a close friend, heard the story of the trench fight. He called and said, "Dave, I have a message for you I really believe is from the Lord. It is that God gave you mercy to kill those ISIS, and He forgives you. And don't operate outside His mercy."

That was a good word for me because the battle was just beginning and ISIS would attack us many more times. The fighting would become more intense and our participation in it more frequent. Our FBR policy was to fight only in self-defense, but for me, I do not have much of a policy beyond my attempt to obey Jesus, act in love, and be His ambassador in every circumstance. That means there is no template, which sometimes makes it more difficult to know what to do. As I understand it, the commandment not to murder or kill is in the context of God still giving commands to kill. So, what do we do?

I do not want to operate outside of God's mercy; I know I am a sinful man, not an avenging angel. That day, that fight, was not a free pass to fight ISIS, it was not an invitation to condemn them. It was mercy—I'm not exactly sure all the ways, but it was at least mercy to the Peshmerga, our team, and to the next people these ISIS would try to kill. It is up to God, not us, what happens after death. Kneeling beside those men, I prayed for each one killed and for them to repent and for Jesus to forgive them and if it was God's will, to bring them to heaven so one day we could meet. Jesus said He desired that none would be lost and it was in that spirit that I prayed.

Maybe I was wrong to ask that, and if so, I believe God won't do it. God knows, and I prayed this out of the love God gave me for them and gratitude for what Jesus has done for me. I also asked Jesus to forgive me of any sin in this and to help me follow His ways.

Most of the time, it seems Jesus has a way not to kill but to make friends. And sometimes we need to give up our lives rather than defend them. But sometimes people choose death, not life, and then we need to listen to what God says. In the trench fight with ISIS, I heard, "Do your best."

I think daily asking Jesus for help and guidance helps us hear more clearly when a crisis arises; but, in any case, if we ask Jesus in all sincerity and give up our rights to what we think is right or just, and to our own lives, He will show each of us in each case what to do.

Jesus said, "By their fruit you will recognize them" (Matthew 7:16). If we kill, what is the fruit of that? I am not sure, but I believe all we do must be motivated by love. For me, in Mosul, the most loving thing I could do was stopping—with, I believe, God's help—evil actions and saving the lives of those who wanted to live. In stopping ISIS, we were also part of ending their acting in hate and killing. It was an act of love to stop them from further destruction of others.

As a weak and sinful man, I put myself at God's mercy. I also need forgiveness. Are some people totally evil? I am not sure but I believe that even at their worst, every human still has some shred of love and goodness. I believe God is sad when any of His children die, no matter what they have done. Yet, life on Earth is fatal but it is not final. Death here is not the end of the story, or of redemption. God is the final judge and I appeal to Him for myself, a sinner, and for others, including ISIS. I hope I see them in heaven one day and we all will laugh and sing in joy to Him who saved us.

CHAPTER TEN

Filling the Humanitarian Gap–
Food under Fire

*"You're like us. You believe in God. You believe in something higher
than yourself. You are welcome here."*

—GENERAL MUSTAFA, COMMANDER OF THE IRAQI
ARMY 36TH MECHANIZED BRIGADE

The Kurdish victory in Bashiqa was a great day for the Kurds and the
world. The Peshmerga had pushed ISIS out of Kurdistan. They were the
first ones to really stop ISIS in their rampage across Syria and Iraq, and
they were also the first to declare victory. The Kurds continued to be
key in the forthcoming conflict, during which the KRG eventually took
in 1.5 million refugees, housing them in camps and within local communities. Many of these were refugees from Mosul, families who lived
under ISIS for three years—and many were people who had sympa-
thized with ISIS but were now desperate and afraid.

From our little compound, we continued to give food, water, medical care, and prayer to those fleeing. Night and day, they came through,
and we helped them and then shuttled them back to the refugee processing centers where they were checked before being sent on to camps.

It was during this time Oliver North, Chuck Holton, and Dennis
Azato with Fox News, and Chris Mitchell with CBN visited us. We
had met Holton, North, and Mitchell a year earlier when they were
doing stories in Kurdistan. Ollie is like an uncle to me. He is a direct
and forthright man, a man of God. I admire his courage. In Vietnam,
he was wounded multiple times and was a brave combat leader. He is
a real warrior, and at the same time, his humility and love draw people to him. I have learned a lot from him. Chuck and Dennis are two

old Ranger friends, and I love Chuck's books. Chris Mitchell is also a friend and one of the best reporters I know. He has a gentle, loving demeanor and the gift of putting people at ease when he interviews them. Victor Marx came back and provided more supplies and generous support for our team.

These men visited us on the new front line between the Kurdish positions and ISIS, and Ollie also stayed the night in our position. Ollie's security team, led by a cheerful South African named Eric, joined us in pulling nighttime security. They made our position stronger and the bond of love between Ollie, his team, and us grew stronger. Ollie led us in devotions in the morning, and after he went back to the U.S., his stories helped others better understand the situation in Kurdistan and Iraq. North, Mitchell, Marx, and their teams made us stronger and were an example of people who cared and came to help.

The relief work we were doing was needed, but with the end of the fighting here, there were lots of people and organizations who could do it. We were useful if it was a dangerous situation because we had a skilled team with years of experience in areas of combat and didn't have too many security rules. But once things settled down, other groups could better handle the job of caring for large numbers of refugees. As mid-November 2016 passed, we started asking ourselves if we were done here. The battle for Mosul was raging in front of us: we could see helicopters and artillery fire flashing in the distance all through the night and could hear small-arms fire not too far away—but that was an Iraqi Army and coalition fight. We had no ties with the Iraqis and didn't want to go chasing action. We prayed, "Lord, if you want us to go help in Mosul, we will. If not, should we pack up and go back to Burma to continue our work there?"

The work in Burma hadn't stopped. We had excellent ethnic leadership, more than fifty ethnic relief teams, and a solid headquarters staff there keeping it going and enabling us to be here. But we had been gone a long time and now our primary mission to help the Kurds was about over. I wondered if maybe it was time for us to go back. Then, on November 19, we got a call from a big NGO (who does not want to be named) from which we were already getting food for distribution. They said, "We've got a shipment of food for IDPs from Mosul. But we can't take it to them because they're too close to the fighting. Can you do it?"

We prayed about it and felt, "Yes." This seemed a direct answer to our prayer about whether we had a job to do in Mosul. We were staying.

We linked up with the truck full of food and found out there were no permits for us to pass checkpoints. In addition, no one knew exactly where the Iraqi Army unit we were to meet was located—just that the unit was the 36th Mechanized Brigade of the 9th Armored Division and they were somewhere near the villages of Ali Rash and Sharazad in southeast Mosul.

In the meantime, Victor Marx had come back, and I asked him if he wanted to come along. We were still using the armored Land Cruiser SUV he had bought and lent us. He only had about a day but said he'd come and see what happened.

We left for Mosul: the FBR team and I in Victor's vehicle and one of our Land Cruiser ambulances full of our supplies and meds, with Victor and his team following us. Last was the big cargo truck full of food. We navigated to the front line, making our way through checkpoints, some more easily than others. We came to one where they weren't letting anyone through. We were stuck in a line of cars, so I walked with Shaheen up to the soldiers manning the checkpoint. I said, "I'm an American, and we're on our way to help the Iraqi Army."

The soldier responded with more enthusiasm than I anticipated. "You American! Michael Jackson! I love Michael Jackson! You go." We got through and continued, asking for Ali Rash, Sharazad, and the 36th Brigade. We were slowly working our way past the main defensive positions, which were all in smaller villages on the outskirts of the main city. We passed Ali Rash, where we saw some damaged Iraqi vehicles being fixed in what looked like the brigade's supply depot. We continued, rounded a big bend in the road, and suddenly were in the open. We were between the last little village and the main city. It felt very exposed, driving out in the open.

My vehicle was in the lead, on the lookout for ISIS and trying to figure out how to locate the Iraqi Army position. As we rolled down a small hill past the abandoned and destroyed village of Al Lak, we came to three big rocks seemingly arranged across the road. We stopped and got out. Rubble on the road wasn't that unusual, but this looked like it could be intentional. Maybe it was a message that we should not go farther on this road. In Burma, we placed branches across trails we weren't supposed to go down. This was a land of rocks and not branches, so maybe this was the same kind of signal.

Somewhere ahead of us was Sharazad, but we were not sure where. In the distance, we could see the city's skyline and hear shooting. Off to the right, about a kilometer away across some empty land, we could see the buildings of a little village. I got out my binoculars and glassed around, then handed them to Micah. "That's an Iraqi flag," he said, pointing toward the village. We noticed a set of tracks taking off from this paved road to the right, and going through the dirt toward the Iraqi position we could see through the binoculars. You could tell the tracks were made recently. We prayed and decided: "We can see the Iraqi flag there. We should try to get there and figure it out rather than just blindly going ahead."

We turned off the paved road and started making our way through the fields, following the dirt track. Right away, a machine gun opened fire, bullets flying close to us. Two mortars landed in front of us, and I cracked a joke to Micah and Shaheen about the Iraqis dropping errant rounds on us. Then I looked left and realized it was ISIS shooting at us. We had just missed them when we turned off the main road. Had we driven straight instead of turning off, we would have driven directly into their position. But now they saw us and opened up. Bullets whizzed by, and mortars exploded around us. The big truck accelerated, moving as fast as it could, bouncing over the rutted track, the driver's terror intensifying along with the ISIS fire.

We made it untouched to the little walled village with the Iraqi flag flying above it and pulled in. I got out and asked for the commander. It wasn't every day a convoy of food trucks and American civilians came screeching into his position in a hail of gunfire, so he came walking out pretty quickly to see what was going on. His name was General Mustafa. He looked like a kindly grandfather in uniform, a lined and weathered face with a mustache, balding, and with a star, swords, and eagle on his shoulder to indicate he was the brigade commander. This was Sharazad, and these guys were the 36th. We were in the right place. He didn't know it yet, though. "Who are you and how did you get here?"

I said, "I'm David Eubank, or 'Daoud Shingali.' I'm with the Free Burma Rangers. God sent us here to help you in any way we can. We have medics, we have an ambulance, and we have food for civilians. We'll try to get you even more, as much as we can." He looked at us like, what in the world? We talked for a few more minutes, and then I asked if I could pray.

"Of course," he said. I closed my eyes and then felt what was, by now, a familiar voice: *Get on your knees.* What? Get on my knees? Not again. This was an Iraqi general. But there it was again: Get on your knees and pray. So I did. There, on the muddy brick patio where we were talking, I knelt, held my hands out, open, in front of me, and prayed. I thanked God for General Mustafa and the Iraqi Army and all their sacrifice. I thanked Him for the chance to meet General Mustafa and for new friends. Then, I prayed He would bless General Mustafa and his men. Shaheen translated. I finished in Jesus's name and stood up. General Mustafa was smiling out from under his mustache, and he said, "You're like us. You believe in God. You believe in something higher than yourself. You are welcome here." It was exactly what General Afandi said.

We unloaded the food truck and sent it back, and Victor went back too. The Iraqis first put our team in the CCP, their field hospital, where they stabilized patients before sending them on to Erbil or somewhere else for better care. Soon, though, we moved into one of the headquarters buildings next to General Mustafa's place. Most of the houses were abandoned, as many of the people had fled the village. It was close to the front.

At night, ISIS opened up with rifles, machine guns, and mortars—our walls were bullet-pocked—but we didn't have any casualties here. There was a trickle of wounded guys coming into the CCP from the front, and Joseph and Micah started helping out there. We had Dave Dawson helping with coordination, Jake Hamby and Zau Seng on camera, and Dlo and Shaheen as coordinators and translators. Paul had gone back a few days before.

We started coordinating food and hygiene supplies for the families liberated by the Iraqi Army. The NGO supplying us was happy to be able to provide supplies to these people in need and when they had a new shipment ready, we'd go pick it up. Sometimes it would be multiple seven-ton trucks of food. General Mustafa helped us coordinate getting in and out of his position.

Two nights after our dramatic arrival, we were feeling more settled. We were used to the pattern of ISIS shooting, occasional sniper bullets whizzing over our heads, or mortars dropping nearby. On this night, we heard a big explosion and could hear gunfire in the distance, about a mile away, back toward the way we had come our first day. We could see about a mile across the open area around Sharazad, and looking directly south, we saw the flashes of a battle.

Then the Iraqis got a phone call. An Iraqi Army food truck with three unit cooks bringing a resupply of food for the unit was coming down the same road we used just a couple days previously, but, in a pitch-black night and driving without lights to avoid drawing fire, they missed the turnoff into the field, drove right over the rocks and straight into ISIS. Right away, they were hit with an RPG, which ISIS followed by peppering the vehicle with small-arms fire. They were all wounded in the initial RPG blast and had bailed out of the truck, firing back for their lives. They were hiding in a ditch near the burning truck, fighting, and calling for help.

The RPG had come from a position about two hundred meters away from them. There was a machine gun position about three hundred meters away and another heavy machine gun seven hundred meters away. These three worked together to pin the three soldiers down. In the dark, another group of ISIS fighters began maneuvering on foot to get around the pinned-down soldiers to finish them off.

I was outside our house with Jake and Joseph when the call came. The rest of the team gathered as the soldiers around us hustled into action. I told the commander, "We're with you. We'll help you whatever you decide to do."

As they prepped the three rescue Humvees, the officer said, "This is dangerous."

I told him, "We've got a medic, we can help, and we want to go." They pointed out one of the three Humvees, and I got in, with Jake, Joseph, and Zau Seng jumping in behind me. The driver was Khalid, a soldier who looked like the genie in the Aladdin cartoon, a big swarthy man with a scar on his face, powerfully built, but with a wide smile. He joined the Iraqi Army when ISIS captured his sister and vowed to fight until she was set free. He was a dangerous man. Up in the turret on the machine gun was Benz. He had a big Fu Manchu mustache, and when he laughed, his head wobbled from side to side.

That night, neither man was laughing as we loaded up. I was in the front seat next to Khalid, with the others in the back. With no night vision devices, the Iraqis drove straight toward the fighting with lights full on, which was terrifying because ISIS saw us right away and started shooting. Heavy machine guns, light machine guns, and RPGs were all coming at us as we drove with lights blazing through the night. I realized: these guys are brave. They were risking soldiers and three Humvees for those three cooks. That was the first example I saw of the Iraqis' bravery and care. It really impressed me and continued to through the whole battle of Mosul.

We were barreling into action with Khalid at the wheel, bullets pinging off our vehicle. I suddenly became very afraid. I knew we could get hit with an RPG or run over an IED in the dark. This was crazy. *What am I doing here?* I thought. *What kind of value can I really add?* I asked God. I said, "I'm sorry, God, if I came for the wrong reason, for adventure or pride, but if you want me here, please protect me."

Something came to me then. It was a Bible verse, one I had quoted many times, "Greater love has no one than this: to lay down one's life for one's friends" (John 15:13). I realized, *Oh, that's what we're doing. I love these guys; they're my friends.* And I thought, *Okay then, if I die, I die for the right reason.* Peace came over me, and I prayed again for protection.

We pulled up to the burning truck as the fire from ISIS intensified, but I couldn't see where the three wounded cooks were fighting from. There was an element of ISIS maneuvering out to our right and a machine gun to our front left, shooting and hitting our vehicle. The heavy machine gun was farther away to our left. Rounds were hitting our vehicle, and the ISIS maneuver element to the right had closed to within fifty meters of us, trying to overwhelm us and kill the cooks. Our Humvee was in the front with Benz on the machine gun hammering away at the ISIS positions on our left. The machine gunners in the other Humvees followed, sending tracers streaking into the ISIS positions.

I didn't know what to do but wanted to do something. I could help shoot, but I didn't know where the cooks were and wasn't sure I could tell the difference, at night, between the cooks and ISIS running at me. In this Humvee, my window wouldn't open, and the door also sometimes jammed so that, once it was closed, it had to be opened from the outside. I had held it partially open as we drove so that I would have options.

I opened the door just a bit more and got a hand grenade ready. I figured I could tell the difference between the cooks and ISIS if they got close enough to me and could use a grenade then, if needed.

We were about fifteen meters away from the ditch, and in the lights of the vehicles, I saw the cooks jump out of the ditch and run to the vehicle behind us. On the radio came the order to pull out; the cooks were in, and we needed to get out now before more people were hit or our vehicles disabled. I'd done nothing but pray and prepare. I wanted in on the action. As we rolled forward and began the turn to exit the ambush area, I pushed the door open further, nosed my AK out with one arm, bracing it under my armpit, and started shooting back at the muzzle flashes. Right then, the Humvee sped up in the turn; also, right then, my gun jammed.

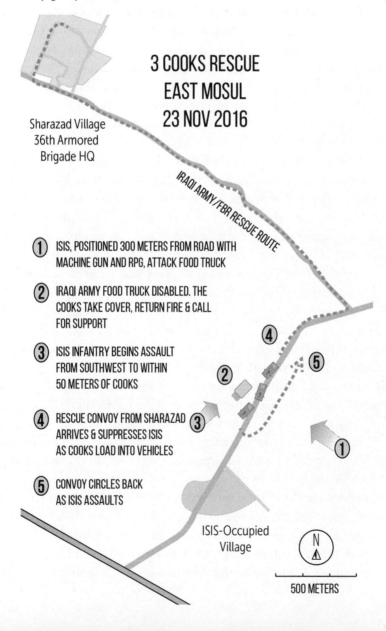

3 COOKS RESCUE
EAST MOSUL
23 NOV 2016

Sharazad Village
36th Armored
Brigade HQ

IRAQI ARMY/FBR RESCUE ROUTE

(1) ISIS, POSITIONED 300 METERS FROM ROAD WITH
MACHINE GUN AND RPG, ATTACK FOOD TRUCK

(2) IRAQI ARMY FOOD TRUCK DISABLED. THE
COOKS TAKE COVER, RETURN FIRE & CALL
FOR SUPPORT

(3) ISIS INFANTRY BEGINS ASSAULT
FROM SOUTHWEST TO WITHIN
50 METERS OF COOKS

(4) RESCUE CONVOY FROM SHARAZAD
ARRIVES & SUPPRESSES ISIS
AS COOKS LOAD INTO VEHICLES

(5) CONVOY CIRCLES BACK
AS ISIS ASSAULTS

ISIS-Occupied
Village

N

500 METERS

Distracted by my jammed weapon, I wasn't ready when the Humvee suddenly lurched violently left, and the door, two hundred pounds of steel, swung completely open, dragging me with it. Now I had a jammed weapon in one hand and was being dragged out of the vehicle by the heavy, swinging door; the open door was exposing the driver and all the other people in the vehicle to enemy fire. *What an idiot*, I thought. I prayed a frantic prayer: "Help me!" With all my might, I managed to slam the door shut and threw my jammed weapon in the back seat, where it hit Zau Seng in the head. "Pass me your weapon!" I shouted.

"Yes sir," he said, thinking it was all part of the action, and handed his gun up to me.

We barreled out of the kill zone, up over a hill and stopped. Some of the Iraqis got out of their vehicles and started shooting back at ISIS, and I did too. Then in came the American jets, and pummeled the ISIS positions with air strikes.

Back at the CCP, Joseph began to work on the three wounded cooks as well as one of the Iraqi soldiers, who was hit seven times in the rescue. I helped treat the minor wounds, and we thanked God everyone made it.

I was feeling a little chastened though. I had learned a couple things. One of them was: when God calls you into battle, He goes with you. Always remember why you're going, because if your love is enough that you're willing to lay your life down, you'll have peace. And call on Jesus's name.

The other thing I learned was more humbling: don't take matters into your own hands, either for pride or because you think you're more efficient. I tried to get some action out of pride and selfishness; then my gun jammed, the door swung open, and I was almost pulled out. I could have got myself killed along with those in my vehicle. It was a big mistake, but no one saw me. Benz was busy shooting; Khalid was driving and shooting out his window. I felt ashamed, and that night when we reassembled, I told my team what a foolish thing I did and how wrong I was. I hoped we could all learn from my mistakes.

I was grateful when, after the rescue of the cooks, General Mustafa began to look at us like part of his team. He hadn't seen my mistakes, only that we'd risked our lives to go out there, and he was grateful. "Thank you. Thank you. You belong with us," he said.

We gave out FBR Stars of Valor to those who helped rescue the cooks near Sharazad in November, 2016. Benz is in the middle; the man on the left was shot seven times

I became close to the Iraqi medical team: the Chief Medical Officer of 36th Brigade, Major Naseem, and also Dr. Osama—the medical officer of the 9th Division. Major Naseem was a quiet, thoughtful professional; he talked about faith and family with our team as we worked together more and more. Dr. Osama was a mustachioed, jolly guy with a perfect American accent and some American humor to match it. Joseph was working under them, and later, as we had more team members show up, Dr. Osama pulled them all into helping out.

Every day, the building we were in was hit with small-arms fire, and mortars dropped close by. ISIS was about a kilometer away, but sometimes, at night, they would close in and attack. Up ahead of this headquarters position, in the Intisar District of southeast Mosul, the three battalions of the 36th were fighting block by block, but they were stalled by dug-in ISIS forces.

Each newly liberated city block was full of hungry people who hadn't left their homes when the fighting started. They stayed because most of them were Sunni, and they were afraid if they left and went to a refugee camp, the men would be arrested as suspected ISIS. Also, they were afraid their homes would be looted by the Iraqi Army, their neighbors, or other militias who were also fighting. Food, cooking gas, and other supplies were running out, so a lot of these people were pretty desperate.

Each day, we positioned behind the forward battalions, providing food and other supplies to the civilians, using our trucks and the Iraqi Army trucks. Every day, we ran a gauntlet of ISIS fire as we approached the front line, and our supply truck was sometimes hit by machine-gun fire. In the neighborhoods, we announced the food distribution; sometimes, there'd be four thousand people crammed into just a few blocks.

The Iraqi Army secured buildings surrounding the selected distribution site, and then we would go in. The people would line up, and the head of every household would come and show his I.D. and ration card. We'd have a table set up, checking everyone and recording all who came through. Shaheen did a great job organizing this with the neighborhood headmen and the local Iraqi Army battalion commanders. They would get the signatures, check people off, log the names, and mark their hands with indelible ink. Then they'd come to the truck and we'd start handing out food.

Sometimes ISIS was only one or two streets over, and they would attack the distributions. The first seven out of ten distributions were attacked by ISIS, usually within thirty minutes of starting. They would figure out what was going on and start mortaring, machine gunning, and then trying to break through the security perimeter, which they did a couple times, trying to kill the people in the streets and us too. ISIS drones flew over us to guide attacking fighters and suicide vehicles.

When we were attacked, the Iraqis would counterattack and push the assault back. Often, they shielded civilians and exposed themselves to direct fire, and I again saw the quality and courage of the Iraqi soldiers. ISIS launched their assaults on foot from a network of tunnels, or rat holes they'd knocked into walls connecting houses; they also used suicide vehicles and IEDs. They did not spare those distributing food, and they did not distinguish between civilians receiving it and soldiers protecting it.

The Iraqi soldiers did a courageous job of holding back attacking forces and taking care of civilians. This was wonderful to watch, especially as many of the Iraqi Army soldiers were Shiite while most of the population was Sunni.

The civilians we met were grateful for our food and help. However, we knew some of them still supported ISIS, and many were wary to trust us. On some occasions, after receiving their rations, the small group of civilians who supported ISIS would call in our position and we'd be attacked. Once, two men placed a land mine on the road we used to approach the distribution site, intending to kill us on our way out. The Iraqi Army caught them in the act and stopped the attack.

Toward the end of one distribution, while we were under fire, I gave a "Jesus" film in Arabic to one of the men. I said, "This is a film about my leader, but if you don't like it you can throw it away."

He looked at the cover and said, "Jesus. We need Jesus because Jesus brings love, forgiveness and truth; we need Him. Thank you for loving us and sharing about Jesus." I prayed with this man that he would survive the war and that freedom and peace would come to his land. He told us his name was Haman and he would help us any way he could. His face was radiant and warm as he said thank you and goodbye.

When we were attacked, while the Iraqis fended off ISIS, we helped civilians get to cover, and we sometimes helped the Iraqis fighting. This was risky in a lot of ways as I found out. We were on a roof, and bullets were flying everywhere. I asked the soldiers who were with me, "Where's ISIS?" They pointed at a green building right in front of us and said everything from there and left was ISIS. Right then, I saw two men pop up, one wearing a turban, in the green building I'd just been told was ISIS.

They crossed in front of me on the open roof with their weapons. I started to shoot, but something about them made me hesitate. At the same time, I yelled, "Daesh! Daesh!"—which is an Arabic acronym for ISIS. I fired a couple shots, mostly as a warning, as I wasn't sure it was ISIS. That was fortunate: it turned out they were Iraqi soldiers, one of whom didn't have a helmet on, who had gotten into the wrong building. I had come close to shooting them and thanked God I hadn't.

Toward the end of November, our team grew. We were joined by two more FBR volunteers: Riley Ewen, a former U.S. Army infantry officer, and Sky Barkley, a former Marine. Riley left the army to start medical school and was volunteering with us until school started. He and his wife, Jessica, had been working with our team in Thailand, but decided he could maybe be more useful here. He was a quiet, thoughtful, good-humored man, and I was happy to have him. Sky was medically discharged from the Marines after a car wreck and came with his wife to help us in Burma. He was a handsome, muscled gym rat who was once paid to advertise Harley-Davidsons. He was impulsive, funny, made friends easily, and had some basic medical training; he'd been deployed in Iraq and wanted to come back and help in a different way. We had also been joined by a French woman named Aude who became a part-time volunteer.

Karen and the kids arrived the day before Sky and Riley; it had been about six weeks since I'd seen them. Hosie had arrived about a week earlier. The family landed in Erbil, was picked up at the airport by Hosie and Dlo, and came straight to the front line. We met them just outside the checkpoint because we had food trucks coming in at the same time. We all worked together for two hours to move the food from one truck to another, then headed to Sharazad right in time for a sunset ISIS attack. Mortar rounds were landing nearby, and bullets smacked into our sandbagged building as we pulled in.

Karen looked around, taking it all in. "What is this place? Is this where we're all staying?" I knew this wasn't exactly her favorite environment, but she said, "I'm glad we're all together." We were happy to see each other. The whole team settled into the house. At night, sleeping bags were spread out all over the floor. The winter rains had started, so sometimes there was quite a lot of mud, but the house we were in, right next to General Mustafa's headquarters, was in pretty good shape. We had our own cooking supplies, a couple of burners and propane tanks, with pots and pans we'd brought from Erbil.

Karen and I decided to set up on the roof so we could have some privacy. The roof had about a five-foot wall all around it, so we had cover from direct fire; it was starting to freeze at night, so we set up our tent and had some time to talk. I showed her the video of the trench fight outside Bashiqa from a couple of weeks before. We'd already talked about it, but seeing the video upset her. "Now you're killing people?" she asked.

"Honey, I told you about this right after it happened. We prayed, and you said you felt peace. No, I'm not here to fight, but in that situation, there was no choice unless I wanted to let ISIS keep killing people. Remember, they were killing people, they were trying to kill everyone, and us. There was no other way to get them out so they wouldn't get past us to villages. I didn't want to do it. I wanted the soldiers to do it. But they wouldn't or couldn't, I don't know. It was too dangerous to not do anything. I knew I could get myself killed, but I prayed about what my place was and just felt God say, 'Do your best.' I knew all my years of training could make a real difference. I knew the guys beside me hadn't trained for this. I did pray that ISIS in the trench would give up, that it could be talked out or something. But they didn't, so I went."

She told me she got that, but it would still take a bit to grasp it all. She said, "I guess it's just new."

"What's new?" I asked. I had, after all, been a soldier when I met her, and then been in the middle of the Burma conflicts for years.

"I guess I've just never really seen 'soldier Dave' before, the Dave before we got married. I mean, I've seen all the photos and heard the stories, even ones your mom told about how much you loved the Ranger Battalion, but I've only known 'jungle Dave.' Our Burma missions, even the intense parts, have looked very different from all this. Backpacks and pack-mule trains, and Rangers who travel light—they're different than this, not nearly as much heavy, loud, and big weapons. I mean, considering the enemy, I'm really glad for all this stuff—mortars and tanks and air strikes to match what ISIS has. It's good, just different." She paused. "It's just going to take me a little bit to get used to it."

Karen is the toughest woman I know. She had already said, "I'm glad we're together, even if this place is scary" and "It's good to be here." If she was on board spiritually and in theory, I knew her emotions would catch up soon. And I was grateful. What a gift from God to have Karen and the kids here with me—and not just for me, for all these people who would be able to feel their love and, through them, God's love. Sahale, Suu, and Peter were unfazed by the shooting and our place here. "No problem, Dad."

The next day, the commander of the 9th Division, General Kasem, came to visit General Mustafa. He told Mustafa, "I want to see the American family." We walked next door to Mustafa's headquarters, and General Kasem shook my hand. He met my whole family. On my order to "attack," the kids all gave him hugs. He said, "Thank you for standing with us. It is so inspiring for us that you Americans count us worthy to bring your families and stand with our families. You make us feel that Iraqis count as much as Americans. Welcome, welcome, welcome." We thanked him and prayed for him.

That same day, we met with General Mustafa to explain the GLC children's program of singing, dramas, and health lessons, to him and see if we could organize one. He was excited and thought it was a great idea. He thought we could conduct one in a school near where we'd been doing food distributions. The school was abandoned but defendable, a solid structure with a big wall around it. ISIS had been pushed out of this neighborhood just a few days before.

We decided we would divide our group: some of us would do a food distribution while others would conduct the GLC program. Dave Dawson, Riley, Micah, and I all went to the distribution site, taking Shaheen with us as our translator, while Karen, the kids, Hosie, Sky, Joseph, Dlo, and Ezadine, our friend and translator from Sinjar, went to the GLC program. We each had our own Iraqi Army security contingent as well, and General Mustafa went with the GLC group.

Our distribution almost immediately came under attack. Before we knew it, we were in the middle of a big firefight. Bullets pinged down the side streets, and civilians hunkered down in what cover they could find as we tried to figure out where ISIS had infiltrated. As I ran down a little alley, I realized I only had my pistol. I yelled at Dave Dawson, "Dave, I'm going up to the roof where I can see! Bring me up my weapon and armor." I ran up there and could see ISIS flitting around on the roofs of nearby buildings, shooting at us. Our guys were shooting back, and it was chaotic. Dave, my faithful squire, ran through the gunfire and brought my gear.

The fighting went on for about thirty minutes, until the Iraqis brought up armor and blasted ISIS. The surviving ISIS fighters fell back. We went back to feeding people and then headed over to the GLC program, hoping things would be calmer there.

CHAPTER ELEVEN

The Enemy Has a Vote-Southeast Mosul

"I asked God for help and he sent me the two worst possible things: a Christian and an American!"

—GENERAL MUSTAFA, COMMANDER, 36TH
MECHANIZED BRIGADE

There was a mob of kids and adults around the walls of the school compound; as the convoy had driven slowly through the streets, it had picked up curious followers along the way. By the time the convoy reached the school, it was a large crowd. The Iraqi Army brought the team inside and closed the gates. Karen, Hosie, and General Mustafa, with Ezadine, were making a plan. The soldiers ended up letting the kids and their moms in one by one through the gate and into the main floor of the school. The kids all sat on a big staircase that went up from the main entrance hall, and the team was below.

They started running through the program, singing songs and giving health lessons, with the soldiers jumping in and contributing their own comic relief. These guys hadn't had any opportunities for fun in a while. They all had their own kids at home and seemed to love the program and the chance to laugh with these kids. Sahale, Suu, and Peter sang "Iraqis Lead the Way," an adaptation of an FBR song a Karen villager wrote years ago that originally said "Rangers lead the way." The kids loved all of it.

The last part of the program was the Good Samaritan play about a Jew who was robbed and left for dead, ignored by his own people but rescued by a Samaritan, a then-outcast of the Jewish people. The story is about love, risk, and forgiveness that crosses religious and ethnic lines. We modified the play to be about the local people, Sunni and Shiite and ISIS. Peter pretended to be a beat-up Arab who'd been attacked by ISIS,

161

and Suu pretended to be the donkey carrying him, hee-hawing with enthusiasm. As the kids shouted with laughter, however, the real ISIS started launching mortars and RPGs at the school and began an assault on the building with rifles and machine guns.

The Iraqi Army asked us to finish the program quickly as the sound of explosions and machine-gun fire echoed through the building. We ended with a prayer and quickly handed out all the GLC shirts and bracelets we brought for the kids, who were more interested in getting the shirts and bracelets than they were in getting away. As one man was leaving with his children, he thanked me profusely, saying, "That was the most wonderful play because it describes our people. We should be like that Samaritan."

Under the cover of Iraqi Army fire, we escorted the kids out of the school to a side street, making sure they were out of the direct line of fire so they could get home. ISIS was getting closer, and the soldiers were afraid they were going to lose the school. As we loaded up to leave, we thanked the soldiers for their help. One of them turned to me and said, "Thank you. We love helping the children." All the children and their families made it back home, and we drove out under fire, back to Sharazad.

The next day, we did a more peaceful GLC program back in Kurdistan. We'd promised to put in a playground at Faisaliah, where the family was killed by the air strike. Our Reload Love friends , Lenya Heitzig and Jen Santiago, and a man named Rick Whittlesey funded the playground, which Dlo and Dave Dawson coordinated to get delivered from Erbil. I introduced Karen and the kids to the family who had lost their loved ones, and we had a wonderful and warm visit. We did a GLC program in the school, and some Barzani Foundation team members joined us. We also reunited with Major Nabaz and other Peshmerga we had served with earlier.

Afterward, we returned to Sharazad to continue the food distributions and GLC programs. It was December 2 and we had until about December 10 before we had planned to return to Burma for our relief team graduation and a quick mission with the new teams. The Iraqi Army was making slow, block-by-block progress in the neighborhoods of southeast Mosul. We were feeding thousands of people and giving some medical support. Around December 3, General Mustafa came by. He said, "There's a plan for us to launch an attack deep in ISIS territory, to take the Salam Hospital. It's near one of the bridges."

Sahale with kids at a food distribution in Intisar, E. Mosul, 2016.

Sahale rides a horse we found in a newly liberated area of East Mosul, 2016.

The idea was the 36th would push a salient into ISIS territory, grab a wedge, and separate part of east Mosul. "Intelligence says we can surprise them and do it."

This was going to be a mission for the 36th Bde of the 9th Division with a few divisional assets from the 15th Division and a few other units. All the Iraqi commanders met to plan it. I attended the planning meetings, which were two nights in a smoky room with lots of tea and Arabic discussion over maps and tablets as they hammered out the details. The morning after the second night of planning, I went for a run with Karen—the running here wasn't great because we had to stay in a tiny area between the buildings controlled by the Iraq Army. By then it was freezing, so we'd be all bundled up in mittens and balaclavas in the semidarkness at 6:30 a.m. because, if it was fully light, we'd get shot at by ISIS snipers in the open spots. We were running little circles around the group of buildings where our guys were, and I said, "I think they're going to do this attack. Should I go?"

I was still pretty new to this unit and didn't want to be chasing fights. Our job was to help people, not fight. This was different than when we had rescued the cooks because it was an attack, not a rescue. If I went, it would just be me because there wasn't enough room in the assault vehicles for everyone; I didn't want to abandon the team. I didn't know what God wanted. We prayed as we ran, and as we finished, I could see the Iraqis were loading their vehicles. I asked General Mustafa, "Do you need me?"

He said, "If you can go further up the front and set up a more forward casualty collection point and help us there, that's the biggest thing. If we need you forward, we'll call you up later. This should be a pretty simple mission."

They all took off, and our team divided: Karen, the kids, and Riley stayed at the division CCP with Dr. Osama (Hosie had just left to meet other commitments), while I took Joseph, Zau Seng, Sky, Ezadine, Shaheen, Jake, and an Iraqi medic named Faiz to set up the forward brigade CCP, which was to be located in an abandoned school.

At the school, we met a private named Mohammed, who was part of the 36th. He was a smiling, soft-spoken man and, as we introduced ourselves, he said, "Welcome. Are you from America? I want to go to America." He was a Humvee driver who would eventually become my driver and a key part of our team.

For the first thirty minutes, we waited, just listening to the booms and machine-gun fire from the hospital complex the 36th was attacking. Then the first casualties came in. At first, there weren't many, just three or four wounded, but soon more, and more seriously wounded, started coming in—and then came the first of those killed in action.

By about 2 p.m., it was becoming a pretty big fight. Joseph and Sky were busy with patients, and I jumped in to help. I knew basic stop-the-bleeding first aid and helped where I could. Soon, everyone had a job trying to keep these guys alive and shuttling them back to the Sharazad CCP.

Things got worse and worse for the guys at the front. I wanted to go up, but no one was moving up there. Taking heavy casualties, Mustafa's men took the hospital, but then ISIS reinforcements arrived, and they counterattacked. By nightfall, ISIS had completely surrounded the hospital and cut off all possible movement to and from it—the 36th couldn't even evacuate their casualties. General Mustafa was in trouble.

That night, I went back to Sharazad and listened to the radio with General Mustafa's executive officer (XO), Colonel Ali. It was bad. The Iraqi Army tried to get reinforcements in, but they were ambushed. They fought through the night. By morning, they had thirty casualties, and it was getting worse.

In the morning, the 9th Division brought up more reinforcements, including some units from the Golden Division. They formed a big convoy and were going to try to power through the ISIS lines. I said, "I'm going." But the division commander, General Kasem, said, "No, it's too dangerous."

"Look," I said. "I'm part of this brigade. Those are my friends, and they're in trouble. And I came to help. I've got a good medic, and we're going to go."

He said, "Okay, follow me." I got in the convoy line in Victor's armored Land Cruiser. I was driving and had Faiz, Jake, Joseph as our chief medic with Sky to help, Zau as our FBR cameraman, and Shaheen as my translator.

We got in the relief convoy with the 9th Division, a line of tanks, APCs, and Humvees, just as they started to move. Suddenly, two other Humvees with different markings pulled in front of me and blocked my way. I got out and so did they. An Iraqi general walked up to me and asked, "Where are you going? Who are you?"

I said, "I'm with the 9th Division. I'm going to go help the 36th, trapped in the hospital."

The general said, "No, you're not. I'm not going to let you go there."

"I'm part of the unit."

"You're an American. You could get killed."

"Well, we care about these people and we can help. And General Kasem said I could go. I'm going."

"Well," came the response. "I'm General Kasem's boss."

That changed my tone a little bit. "Sorry, sir, I apologize. But, sir, can I go, please? I'm an old U.S. Army Ranger and Special Forces officer. I have a very good medic, and they are like my family in there. Please let me go?"

And he said, "You're serious, right?"

"Yes."

"Okay, follow me." He pulled in behind the division convoy, and I followed him. We went into the city and got to a big intersection, taking fire. Suddenly, a shell from a 175 mm Howitzer came crashing by and hit about a hundred meters to our left. Another round blew up a wall in a building next to us. We kept moving.

A few minutes later, the corps commander stopped, and we stopped right behind him. He motioned us to stay there, and he pulled over a bit and the 9th Division vehicles behind us pulled ahead and disappeared down the street. A couple of vehicles went back behind us, to the big intersection and posted up there. I realized: they're setting up their command post here. We weren't going to get any closer.

I prayed, "Lord, we can't help anybody here. What should I do?" I felt, "Go." So I said, "Guys, I'm going."

"No," Shaheen and Faiz said in unison. "No, no, no, stop. Oh my God! It's crazy. Don't go."

I said, "No, we've got to go. We can't help them here. They're dying there. We can't leave them." So I prayed, we prayed together, and we took off. We headed in the general direction I'd seen the 9th Division vehicles disappear, and I followed faint tracks left by the vehicles as they passed through puddles left from rain a few days before.

We came to a vacant lot of dirt, mud, trash, and grass. I looked around and saw where the tracks of vehicles had left a little mud. We followed those and drove through another part of town to another big, open, empty lot. Following more tread marks across the dirt and rocks eventually dumped me into a three-way intersection. Now I really had no idea where the Iraqi Army vehicles had gone. I thought, *Man, I could get myself really lost right now.* I was okay with the general risk of going, but now it felt more like a gamble than a risk. I didn't want to gamble. I slowed down and prayed, "Lord, where do I go?" Right at that moment, we started taking fire: bullets smacked into our vehicle from three sides, left, front, and right.

That solved my dilemma for the moment: "We'll take cover wherever we can." The closest building was fifty meters to the left and we were taking fire from somewhere beyond it. As I turned that direction, an Iraqi soldier popped out of the building and came running toward us, waving his arms. Bullets hit the side of the building where he'd just been, and as I opened my car door to talk to him, two bullets hit the doorframe. He ducked, flinched, looked at me wide-eyed and said, "Get out of here! Come with me, you'll be killed here."

I nodded and started driving slowly towards his building while he ran beside us using our vehicle for cover until he was close. Then he pointed to an empty building across the street where we could park and took off back to his building. There, they had set up a strongpoint, making a defensive position with two Humvees, a .50-cal that I could see, and about ten men. Our vehicle was still in the open and taking fire, so I started backing it inside the empty building's compound, while the team jumped out and ran inside. The parking area was too small to fit the Land Cruiser, leaving the front exposed and the gate unable to be closed. ISIS took notice and started shooting at the car again. AK rounds smacked off the windshield; I could see them hit. I'd had no idea if the glass worked, until it did. A machine gun opened fire on us, then a sniper rifle, and pretty soon, the windshield showed a couple of cracks in it. Then, they started hitting the hood of the truck.

I had backed the Land Cruiser in as far as I could and I decided to bail out. I rolled out into the driveway behind a wall and, with all my gear on, joined the team in the empty building. We then all dashed across the road to the house which the Iraqi Army had strongpointed and, in addition to the .50-cal, was bristling with machine guns and RPGs. We were probably going to sleep there that night, so I had to go back and forth a few times to get equipment from the car. I eventually took off all my body armor because it was so heavy I decided it was safer to go light and run faster.

In the next building, we got up to the rooftop and tried to look over but instantly came under fire; ISIS was shooting at this building constantly. Every now and then, the Iraqi Army would shoot back. Here, we were about seven hundred meters from the Salam Hospital where Mustafa was under siege. I could see it in the distance in the last light of day. The main advance went past us and pushed to the hospital; now this position was cut off by itself. ISIS could easily have surrounded us. I went to the next building and prayed help would come for our friends in the hospital.

Paul Bradley called me while I was there, and we prayed together. Then I called Victor and asked him to pray as well. We prayed that help would come and that our friends in the hospital would be rescued. I hadn't given up on getting there, though we were cut off from them. As it got darker, we could hear huge explosions at the hospital. An armored convoy raced by us and another series of explosions soon after showed where they were attacked by ISIS with vehicle-borne explosive devices (VBEDs) and IEDs. Now we were taking more fire. An RPG round exploded not far from us, and mortars were landing nearby. From the roof, we tried to get a bead on where the RPG fire was coming from. We opened fire on that spot, and the RPG seemed to stop. Then a machine gun opened up on our left, and we returned fire there also, suppressing it.

There was a lull, and I realized I was thirsty. It had been a long, tense day. I grabbed a titanium canteen and went to twist the lid off, but it had warped somehow and was stuck closed; I worked it and worked it, but as hard as I tried, I could not twist that cap off. Another frustration. I handed it to Sky, and in one motion, he opened it. "Eight hours in the gym, baby," he said with a laugh. I laughed too and was again thankful for our team, both for their physical abilities and their humor.

Night came fully, and we continued to take intermittent fire from mortars, RPGs and machine guns. Then the mosques came alive and the cadence of pronouncements in Arabic echoed throughout the city; the call to prayer was normal, but I could tell this was different. I asked Shaheen what they were saying, and he translated: "We know where you are. All you infidels, we are going to kill you. This will be the second Mogadishu, the second *Black Hawk Down*. We will kill you. You will die tonight. Brothers in the city, join us and let us wipe out the infidels."

That was chilling. As it echoed through the city, I was pretty afraid and thought our house could easily get overwhelmed. We were just one building with fifteen people in it, surrounded by ISIS. I prayed a lot. And I think ISIS lost track of where we were, with the focus on the hospital. Everyone was just going by us to attack the hospital.

By then, there were about seventy casualties and the generals were starting to realize they were in big trouble. They called for more help and later in the night, the U.S. was able to respond, with General Efflandt sending an AC-130 Specter gunship. There had been a misunderstanding between the Iraqis and Americans on when and how much air support they would get, but the Specter was just the beginning and they would now get all they needed. I could hear the booms of the cannons and air strike explosions as they started to hammer ISIS. This opened a route for reinforcements to the hospital and again, a rescue convoy from the 9th and Golden divisions attempted get through with bulldozers and tanks to push through and over all the rubble.

Even with the help from the Americans, it wasn't easy. ISIS was still holed up in all the buildings and fired on the convoy the whole way with everything they had.

The Iraqis finally broke through the ISIS cordon, drove straight through the wall of the hospital, and started evacuating everyone. It was around 10 p.m. when we started seeing the evacuation vehicles flying by us back to Sharazad. One vehicle with some badly wounded soldiers stopped, and Joseph treated them. One of the wounded was Major Ali, shot in the stomach. Joseph saved his life that night. At first, they wanted us to go with them as they returned to the Sharazad CCP, but I said, "No, we'll come back when we're sure everyone has been evacuated." When every living person was out of there, we returned to the 36th base in Sharazad. The 36th had lost eleven people and had seventy-one wounded.

Back at the CCP in Sharazad, it was a fast-paced but organized scene, with so many casualties. Riley, my family, and the team were there, helping Dr. Osama and the other Iraqi medics. General Mustafa and Major Naseem were also there, and Naseem had a wound in his foot. They were both pretty shaken up.

They'd almost been massacred. ISIS had said they would take the head of General Mustafa and parade it around the city. And they almost did. It was really only the intervention of the U.S. that saved the 36th, along with the 9th and Golden divisions pushing through. General

Mustafa did a great job of keeping his men together and getting out. There were a lot of heroics in this operation, even though it was technically a failure.

It's a reality of war that the enemy has a vote. They're committed too. I talked to Major Naseem later, and he was distraught. "We lost so many people," he said. "We were betrayed. The Americans said they'd have support for this, and they didn't." I didn't know what the misunderstanding between the Iraqis and Americans was, but was grateful the help did come and at the same time I grieved with him the loss of his men.

I hugged him and said, "I'm sorry. I'm so sorry." The next day, we gave medals to everyone who was in the fight. (In FBR, we have our own medal system similar to the U.S. Army's. We have five medals, for meritorious service, achievement, being wounded, valor, and a medal of honor for superlative bravery and accomplishment.) Then the 36th was pulled back to refit. They'd been seriously damaged. This coincided with our schedule, as we wanted to head back to Burma in time to graduate our new relief teams there. So we prepared to return to Thailand.

Before we left, many of the soldiers of the 36th thanked us: "Thank you. Thank you for trying to come to the hospital. We know you didn't make it because of ISIS, but thank you for trying. Thank you for being with us and helping treat the wounded and feed the people and be part of us." This battle was another step in our friendships with the Iraqis and especially the guys of the 36th. They all became closer to us. "Please come back soon," they said.

"We will," I promised. We prayed together, and it was with sad hearts we left.

Later, I heard that maybe the reason for the delay of U.S. support was part of the fallout of an earlier U.S. bombing of a hospital in Afghanistan. They had bombed a hospital the Taliban was using, but civilians were killed as well. When it broke in the news, there was a big uproar. So, with another hospital in the picture, the military proceeded with extreme caution. General Scott Efflandt of the U.S. Army made sure the help arrived, but it took him a while to get permission. Still, because of his actions, General Mustafa and his surviving men got out. I was sorry we couldn't do more to help but was very thankful for the U.S. help we received. As I headed back to Thailand to be with our teams, I was already planning when I could come back to be with these guys. They were my brothers.

CHAPTER TWELVE

Enemy Without a Face– Suicide Cars and Drones

"If no commo with me—pray and take charge and serve."

—DAVE, HIS MESSAGE TO THE TEAM

JANUARY 2017

The silence was almost complete as dawn crept over the Salween River and jungle-shrouded mountains rising steeply up from its banks. A soft breeze stirred the air on the porch of the little bamboo house where I sat alone, replaying in my head the images of the previous couple of weeks. Behind me, in the house, Monkey was still sleeping. Miles away, across the mountains, over the Yunzalin River, and across a Burma Army-controlled car road, were Karen, Sahale, Suu, Peter, and the rest of the team.

My ears still seemed to buzz with the roar of the dirt bike I'd raced for hours, away from them, to get here, to this border crossing—my heart getting heavier the further I traveled away. Roads in this area were a new development, and it felt strange to move so quickly and even stranger to be moving without my family. Now I sat here questioning myself and God: *What am I doing? Isn't that my place, with them in Burma, with the new teams? Am I doing the right thing?*

What I was doing was getting on the fast track back to Mosul and leaving my family, teams, and this beautiful land. I had just sent out this report:

> Thank you for all of your love and support. 17 new relief teams have graduated from ranger training in Burma and they are now on missions. Karen, the children and I came back from Mosul, Iraq, for the graduation of the new teams, and we joined them

on their first mission. We walked all day from our camp to the first village of our mission, a village that had been attacked by the Burma Army and burned three times before. There, the new teams gathered the people from three villages for Good Life Club (GLC) and medical programs. The day started with a Run for Relief, and we ran with the kids across rice fields and over muddy streams and around clumps of towering bamboo. After the run, the teams performed skits and songs and they gave basic hygiene and anatomy lessons for the children and played games. The FBR medics ran a clinic under a tarp, and our friend Dr. Bob Arnold did eye exams and dispensed glasses.

One of the skits was about carrying burdens such as hate, jealousy, fear, and greed and how Jesus saves us from these. As I stood under the shade of giant bamboos swaying in the light breeze, with rice fields stretching out to the steep mountains in front of us in this narrow valley, I was in awe of the beauty of this place. In the midst of this beauty were the new teams from different ethnic groups, singing and laughing together with the villagers. I thanked God to be here and to be part of this program in this beautiful place. It was so good for my soul. I was so grateful to be able to come back to Burma, our main work, and, as our kids call it, "our home."

Our leaders, the new teams, and my family would do well without me, but I missed them. I prayed again but felt no peace. When Monkey woke up, I told him what I was feeling. He was our team chaplain, and I knew he'd tell me what he really thought and also if he didn't know. We prayed together, and he said, "They need you there in Mosul. I think God wants you there—they need God. We're okay here. They need you to play a greater role. Keep going. I think it's right."

We prayed again, and I said, "I'm going to ask God to tell you, as my chaplain, what I should do, to give you that authority. I really don't know. I don't trust my decision on this issue."

I prayed: "Lord Jesus, please give us the truth of what to do, especially to Monkey right now." Then we got on the boat and headed downriver. It was a long ride, and I spent it looking at the beauty all around me—and praying that God would speak to Monkey and to me, too, that I would get the right answer. The boat ride ended, and as we climbed out and stopped on the sandy riverbank, I asked, "Monkey, what did God tell you?" This was my last chance to turn around.

He said, "I'm a little scared to tell you, but I think to keep the same plan. I think you should keep going. Don't go back."

"All right. I promised to go with that." I felt sad but kept on track to Iraq. I repacked in Thailand, was joined by Eliya and Zau Seng, and we all got on the plane to Erbil. Dave Dawson, Sky, Riley and his wife Jessica, Hosie, Aude, and Justin were there already and were helping the CCP of the Iraqi Emergency Response Division (ERD), mostly in Intisar, where we'd been when we left back in December. We'd gained a new volunteer, Bradley Brincka, who was formerly U.S. Army and had done some work with a different organization in Kurdistan before coming to see if he could help us. And we had a new friend, Darrell, who was a Mennonite we met through mutual friends from Thailand; he helped us provide relief and later joined us for some of our supply distributions.

The team had done a few food distribution projects with General Mustafa and the 36th, but the brigade was still recovering from their losses at Salam Hospital and wasn't back in the fight yet. Other elements of the Iraqi forces were pressing ISIS hard, and by the time I got there, most of eastern Mosul was liberated and ISIS was being pushed back across the Tigris River to the western part of the city. As we walked the streets where we had been under fire before, we met families returning to their homes. Children came up to thank us.

One little boy told us, "ISIS was very bad, they beat people, and in their school we had very strange math problems like, 'How many land mines do you need to plant to kill a certain number of infidels?' And 'Ten bullets plus fifty bullets equals how many bullets?' This was a terrible school. Now we are free, and we are so thankful." A fruit vendor talked about how freeing it was to be able to do business without fear of getting beaten for not having a proper beard, or receiving blows measured out for each cigarette ISIS might catch him with.

Even though the east side of Mosul was mostly under the control of the Iraqi Army, ISIS was still launching mortars, using drones and car bombs, and had mined most of the places from where they retreated— so casualties continued to come even if a lot of the active fighting here was done.

Right away, I met up with General Mustafa. He was still sad and discouraged after the Salam Hospital fight. "I think they're going to fire me. They already don't like me because I'm Sunni."

I knew he was an effective general and thought it unlikely he'd be fired. But he was like a brother, and I wanted to comfort him. I prayed and then told him, "Don't give up. God will redeem you because you are brave, humble, and care about your people."

And he wasn't fired. Instead, he and his men were deployed north of Mosul and assigned to take the town of Tel Kayf and then work their way south toward the Tigris River. They would meet it right where it bent south and began to bisect the city proper. This area was called Al Rashidiya and would tie in all areas north of the river bend with the coalition-controlled east side, isolating ISIS on one side of the river only. General Mustafa told me, "Come on!" So the team and I geared up, said goodbye to the Emergency Response Division, and headed out to join our old friends.

We had to go back through Kurdish lines, circling east then north through Kurdistan, then recrossing the Kurdish lines, to get in place. The attack would launch from a small farming settlement north of Tel Kayf. Our team set up in the compound the 36th decided to use as their CCP once the attack started—an abandoned gas station, walled all around, with a big awning and a single building inside the wall. Once we arrived, I joined Mustafa at his field headquarters as they completed the plan. I stayed there that night and rejoined the team the next morning as the attack started.

On January 19, 2017, I sent the following message to our team:

Dear team, great job and I thank God for you all.

Finished all prep back at HQ with General—we will come to you tomorrow early—Be up at 6am ready to go.

The CCP is where you are now as planned and as we last discussed. The plan is same but tell Zau Seng and Eliya to be ready to roll with me and General—need aid bag with Eliya—we will move with General and support by prayer, medical and film.

Rest of team at CCP support Maj Naseem, need ambulance empty to use for medivac to rear (I am bringing this back to you early am) and then armored Landcruiser empty to use as medivac forward. Main mission is at CCP—prayer, treat, support, evac and resupply as needed. Hosie in charge of all, chain of command: Hosie - Justin - Sky. Take advice of D'lo and Ezadine and obey Maj. Naseem. Pray about all things and stay united—God will lead us all in love. Be ready to split into 3 groups when needed- 1) with ambulance to take back to Osama CCP- Div CCP =Hosie, Dlo or Aude 2) to come forward in armored Land Cruiser on call-

Sky and Justin, Ezadine and optional Bradley.

3) whoever is left stay and support Maj. Naseem at CCP—that is main priority—so when 1 and 2 are not in effect then all of you stay at CCP and respond to Maj Naseem—and if he needs more supplies check with me first—if no contact with me and it is urgent then pray and do as you feel best and support Naseem with what he needs ASAP.

Note: Eliya initially with me and Zau Seng—to medically cover front group with General but if too busy at CCP we will send him back. Thanks and Coms= phone and radios, check in at 6am.

If no commo with me—pray and take charge and serve.

Thank you and God bless you, Dave
Ps 23

This message went to our team all over the world, including in Burma, our board and supporters in the U.S., and the team on the ground. We were all in it together—but not just here. We all knew we were united behind each of our missions, wherever they were. Hosie, on the ground at the CCP, responded right away:

Roger that. Team CCP will be all hands on deck at 0600. Should Eliya go to the front and I am in charge, given my unextensive military experience, I will be assembling a team of advisers. (However I will continue to take all literary situations in hand.)

Team Chiang Mai, operate as usual. I expect coffee in the pot by 0930 and Larry to have drunk it all by 1000.

Team Burma, keep your socks dry and the tee klaw (tee klaw is Karen for hot water) hot and plentiful. Don't make us run up the mountain with you when we get back because you're getting all the exercise.

Team America…please remember us in your bedtime prayers.

What a blessing to be caught in this wide-thrown net that is the family of God! I thank Him for each of you and tonight especially for this team camping out here under these Iraqi stars together (actually, if you want to get literal I'm stretched out in the front seat between the driver's and the passenger's door because being a midget has to pay off sometime). But the stars are bright.

God bless you all from here,
Hosie

From Burma satellite coms, Jesse wrote in:

> Tee Klaw is hot and flowing here up at Hah Toh Per! Sitting on the front porch of their new wooden church. 1 group doing recon of Thay Ah Hta camp today. Tomorrow GLC program here in the morning then heading to Saw Wa Der. Plan to go to Bawgli Gee. Motorbikes everywhere but we are not smart enough to use them so we get to walk over all these K2 mountains. Pretty good PT though, especially after SWD we will walk straight to TDD in 3 or 4 days.

> Thanks
> Red Panda and Betel Nut (Jesse and Benita were part of the tradition of getting "animal" nicknames)

Riley wrote from Erbil, where he and Jessica were preparing to fly home: "Jess and I are praying for a peaceful operation from Erbil. God bless."

Dr. John Shaw, who helped start and helps run our Jungle School of Medicine, wrote from the U.S.:

> We are holding up our end of the bargain with daily lattes and pancakes every Saturday.... And yet, our hearts are bent often your way, following and thinking and loving. There are storms stateside as well, of the hot air variety, with a great deal of angst, and very little compassion or generosity. In this we are trying not to be stingy or flummoxed by sophistic wizards, but rather, as we are enjoined, to speak the truth in love.

> Praying for you and the team.
> John and Christa.

We were not in this alone and, as was often the case, I felt gratitude well up in me at the blessing of the team God brought to this work of His.

The morning of the attack dawned, beautiful, clear, sunny, and freezing cold as the troops assembled. The desert was just starting to green up with the winter rains, and the world was a bright place that morning. The column of armored vehicles was lined up as far as you could see. We did not actually start rolling on schedule, so I had extra time to enjoy it.

In the lead element, I rolled out with Mustafa to the rally point from which the whole unit would arrange into battle order. We dismounted our vehicle behind a berm to wait for everyone to organize. A few mortars dropped about fifty meters away on the right, then one exploded right in front of our Humvee. That was a jolt. Obviously, this wasn't a surprise attack and I wondered what kind of resistance we'd meet. Tel Kayf was not just a village, it was a town. Before ISIS, three thousand families lived there, including around five hundred Christian families. There was potential for serious resistance if ISIS really dug in.

Finally, the armor element came rolling in, T-72 and Abrams tanks and BMPs—Soviet-made APCs—churning through the grass, arrayed for battle. It was time. Mustafa poked his head up over the berm and scanned the field ahead. Bam! A sniper's bullet zipped by and almost took his head off. The shot smacked into the dirt behind us as he ducked quickly away from the berm. We all laughed, but it was a near miss.

The signal to move came. The tanks and BMPs led out, pivoting over the berm and spreading out in a line. They started firing their main guns right at the town and the dismounted infantry followed, assaulting the houses one by one. Initially, there was some resistance, and many mortar rounds landed near us. ISIS machine guns and rifles opened up on us as we advanced, but before long, the few ISIS defenders who stood their ground were killed and the others retreated. We swept through the neighborhoods, checking houses and shops. While ISIS was mostly gone, we found plenty of tripwires and IEDs.

And the town was taken, just like that. We had four casualties. The Iraqis raised their flag over it, turned on the loudspeakers, and started playing Shia music out of the back of a couple of Humvees, singing and dancing in the street, hoisting their guns in the air and shouting. An entourage of Iraqi generals came, led by the Iraqi ground force commander, General Raad. I shook hands with them and told them we were there to help. They thanked our team. Then we went over the battle together and made plans for the next day.

I called the rest of the team and had them drive forward to us. We all slept in the ruins of Tel Kayf that night. The house we stayed in was nice, with carpet and gilded mirrors. It was on the edge of town across from a small park. Sky found a puppy he decided to adopt. He named it "Howan," which means "mortar" in Arabic. We set up our kitchen in the courtyard, Eliya and Zau Seng cooked, and we thanked God for the victory.

The next day was similar: a bright, beautiful day with the might of the Iraqi Army ranged out for battle and our forward FBR team at the front with Mustafa while the rest supported the CCP. We had about five miles of open fields to cross to get to the next village, and the brigade drove in echeloned wedges, through gold and green countryside that looked like a bumpy Kansas. We were rolling and firing at ISIS, who shot back with mortars and machine guns. As the Iraqi Army located the source of the return fire, they pounded it with cannon and machine-gun fire.

As we neared the village, General Mustafa dismounted and walked, not behind any armor, but in the lead with his entourage of about twenty men, including bodyguards, operations officers, and radio operators. They had their tablets out, plotting, and calling in air strikes. The U.S. bombers dropped a few air strikes, and there were two Iraqi helicopters buzzing around, doing more than almost anybody else. One was a smaller, armed scout helicopter and the other was a Hind attack helicopter, and they were shooting with rockets and machine guns from dawn to dusk every day of the battle.

On that day, three Iraqi soldiers were killed and four wounded. Eliya treated the ones near us, and we kept advancing. We were in an industrial free-trade zone directly west of Tel Kayf that normally received huge shipments of goods. Along with the other warehouse-type buildings, there was also a chemical factory there. ISIS attacked with small-arms fire and sent two armored suicide cars at us. Both of those were blasted apart by the tanks before they reached us. Many of the Iraqis had dismounted and were walking through that zone along with General Mustafa. They opened up against anything they thought was ISIS but weren't being too careful about being behind cover. Suddenly, there was a thunderous explosion.

It came from a building toward the end of the warehouse zone, and we all ran over. A soldier lay on his back, hurt badly. He had hit a trip wire, setting off an IED. A few of his buddies were gathered around, and he was moaning on the ground. His right foot was nearly severed, held on only by a flap of skin. His head was bleeding, and, as I lifted him to look at his back, I saw a hole the size of a football. I told Eliya to take the back wound, and I moved to work on his foot. We stopped the bleeding, bandaged him up, and carefully lifted him into a vehicle. They took off, and we continued.

Sporadic fire was coming from the west edge of the complex, and the Iraqis answered with a hail of their own fire. The firing stopped, and we continued to the end of the industrial area. The Iraqi armor was lined up in the road waiting for orders. There was a bit of a lull. I saw a huge ISIS flag, about one by two meters, six meters up on a scaffolding. That was a prize. I wanted it. I said a quick prayer and looked around, calculating the danger.

I could see no enemy and started running for it. The Humvee driver, Ali, and machine gunner, Najim, hollered at me, "It's dangerous, Daoud, come back!" I kept going, climbed the scaffolding, and cut down the flag. Back on the ground, I rolled the flag up and sprinted back. The soldiers were all excited now. "Daoud, give us the flag!"

"No way!" I said, laughing. They laughed too, and we all looked for a minute at this flag, the symbol of such evil, now defeated. I tucked it away in our Humvee.

We cleared that whole zone and lost four men I knew about, the ones close to me; there may have been more. We started pushing to the next area, getting closer to Al Rashidiya, the last district of Mosul still held by ISIS on this side of the Tigris. The Iraqi Golden Division, Federal Police, and ERD already held most of the other main areas of eastern Mosul, including the University of Mosul. People were returning to their homes, and small shops were opening.

We moved past the economic zone, meeting little resistance as we progressed. We reached a large compound with a huge mansion and the resident sheik, who'd stayed on throughout all of ISIS's time. We pulled in, and he instantly came out, welcoming us, ranting about how much he hated ISIS, gushing about how glad he was to see us, thank you so much for saving us, and so on. I didn't really believe him; I felt sure he'd said the same things to ISIS. But we went into the compound since it provided some protection—and right away, ISIS started attacking, first with mortars and machine guns and then two suicide vehicles came our way. The Iraqi tanks and the machine guns on the Humvees opened up and they took out the vehicles, but it was close. Shooting continued for about half an hour before quieting down.

By now, it was night and starting to freeze. Inside the house was cold, but the sheik invited us into his inner sanctum, which turned out to be warmed by a space heater. General Mustafa and his staff went in, inviting Eliya, Zau Seng, and me to join them. In addition to a heater and furniture, they had a TV. They turned it on for us and there, on the screen, was a different world: President Donald Trump's inauguration. Wow. I had lost track of days, but it was January 20, Inauguration Day. There was our friend, Franklin Graham, praying and reading Scripture, and Trump giving his speech—and I was in Mosul, Iraq, watching it in real time. Everyone in the room was cheering. The sheik loved Trump. Shaheen was also in favor: "He's got a beautiful daughter. Of course, he should be president."

The next day, we were standing outside the compound preparing to continue the advance. The armor and Humvees were spread out outside the compound. Suddenly, everyone started yelling and diving for cover. A suicide vehicle was barreling right toward our line of vehicles. It had made it through the perimeter and by the line of tanks before anyone saw it. By then, it was almost on top of us at one hundred meters and closing.

We all scrambled for weapons and cover. I was standing next to the second vehicle from the front of a line of about five vehicles. I dove with the Iraqi soldiers near me through the open gate of the compound, and crouched behind the concrete wall, hoping it might shield us from the coming blast.

At that moment, Hyder, who had always seemed to me a rude, friendless soldier, stepped out in front of the oncoming vehicle. He pulled his machine gun up to his hip and started firing at point-blank range, bellowing his defiance at the onrushing death machine. His bullets pinged off the armor, but it would be over his dead body, literally, that the suicide vehicle came in to kill Mustafa, his commander, and the rest of us.

It was the bravest thing I'd ever seen, a lone figure standing in the face of that onrushing two thousand pounds of TNT. I was thinking, "He's gonna die, and we're gonna die." At the last second, the vehicle swerved suddenly to the left, hit a parked tank, and blew up. Hyder dove behind a Humvee as jagged chunks of metal flew by him, lodging in the vehicles we were all sheltering behind.

One tank was blown up, another one damaged a bit, and men were wounded, but no one died. I went out with our crew, along with Khalid, who was carrying an RPG, and we took a position on the roof of a house to our front, where we could see any other suicide vehicles that might be headed our way. We wanted a bit more advance notice next time.

No more came as the men finished preparations. We loaded up again and pushed forward about three more kilometers, taking just a little bit of fire as we went. We started meeting more civilians. Unlike at other places, these people did not seem happy to see us. Khalid said he was sure they were all ISIS. "They'd all like to kill us, so be careful."

By then, it was noon, and we stopped to secure a cluster of houses on a small hill. The rear Iraqi element sent up rice, chicken, and tomato soup for lunch, and I took a big plateful. I was getting ready to eat when I saw two men hurrying away from us, down over the edge of the hill. One was limping on crutches, and the other was trying to help him and run at the same time. "Look!" I shouted.

"Daesh, Daesh, let's go!" yelled Khalid, starting his Humvee. Benz was already up in the turret on the machine gun, and I jumped in the vehicle with them. We took off, and my plate of food went everywhere as Khalid raced down the hill. The two men disappeared by a huge house that had an even bigger warehouse of some sort beside it. We piled out, and the house owner hurried to meet us; he had some kids with him and a smile on his face—but it didn't go to his eyes. Something else was going on.

That's weird, I thought. *Why the kids? Why the fake friendly?* It didn't feel right. I wanted to get a better handle on what was happening. When Benz and Khalid went in the house with the man and kids, I started walking over to the warehouse, my boots crunching on the gravel outside a big sliding steel door. I went to the far side where I could see behind the house. As I did, I noticed a side door to the big building. I thought about testing it but wondered where the two men we'd seen running were. Suddenly I heard Khalid yelling, "Come back! Come back!"

I went back around the house and saw Khalid already at the Humvee, and Benz running out of the house. "We gotta get out of here—we just got a radio call that there's a suicide vehicle near our position and it's coming to hit Mustafa." We jumped in and headed back up the hill. We only made it about one hundred meters when people started running by. I looked back and saw a suicide vehicle close to the warehouse I'd almost walked into and moving toward us. Had that VBED been there all along? Were the two wounded ISIS running to that? If so, had I opened that door I'd probably have gotten my head blown off.

The armored suicide car was approaching fast. As I watched it, I felt a palpable sense of immense evil around it, almost propelling it toward us. The road we were on formed a Y, and Khalid stopped our Humvee on the left arm of it, putting us in front of all the 36th armored vehicles and General Mustafa. The vehicle was coming straight at us, with Mustafa behind us as the main target. *Oh man,* I thought. *Here we go again. My gun's not going to stop this.*

Bullets from Benz's machine gun were bouncing off it, and I dropped to a knee and started firing my AK—I hit it every time, but every bullet bounced off. Khalid was next to me, prepping an RPG. "Khalid, steady!" I yelled. "I'm not gonna leave you, take your time." He was down on one knee, with the ISIS vehicle barreling down on us, now at about one hundred meters. He settled, sighted, and fired. It was our best chance. The shot clipped the back end of the vehicle and blew up, making it swerve but barely slowing it at all. Uh-oh. I kept firing and thought, *This is it, we die here. But we will not back off: we will shoot till it stops or we are dead.*

Then, right as the vehicle got to the Y, it veered off to the other side and went up another road, passing us at one hundred meters. We kept firing until it disappeared behind some buildings. What we did not know was Mustafa was not directly behind us in his command Humvee but had gone down to a house to talk to a local leader. An ISIS sympathizer alerted them and guided that suicide vehicle to his new location.

But Mustafa knew how to stay alive. He had parked an armored BMP right beside the building he was meeting in. As the suicide vehicle turned, it ran right into the cannon fire of the BMP, which blew it apart with a tremendous explosion. A huge fireball rose into the sky and metal flew everywhere. The engine from the vehicle flew about one hundred meters and embedded in a wall. Pieces of the driver flew everywhere. The men in the BMP who'd fired on it were concussed but otherwise okay. Our Humvee was hit by metal fragments, and a small piece of shrapnel even made its way into my shin.

Benz, Khalid, and I burst out laughing. We'd thought we were dead. I kidded Khalid about how he hadn't led the vehicle enough with his RPG. But there was no time for relaxing: suddenly, soldiers started pointing up, aiming their guns and shooting.

An ISIS drone was overhead. Everyone was taking shots at it when a larger drone came over. This was ISIS drone strategy: one drone was

Major Ali, Khalid, Benz, and their buddies have some fun and share a laugh on the front line near Al Rashidiya, 2017.

a command control drone used to guide in suicide vehicles while the other would drop grenades.

I started firing with everyone else and prayed, "Lord, this is a deadly thing. Let me help. Help me get it down." I took careful aim at the larger drone, pulled the trigger, and down it came. We all ran over and checked it out. It had about a two-meter wingspan. We looked for the bullet hole that brought it down: there was an AK round in it, and I felt a little rush of elation. I was the only one shooting an AK there; the Iraqis had M-16s. The soldiers congratulated me, and I told them I had prayed and thanked God for helping me shoot it down. The smaller drone dropped its payload without effect and disappeared.

We moved to another position that night, and it started raining; now it was cold and muddy. It had been about three days since I had been able to work out because we'd been moving and fighting. I wanted to get a little run in, so I went out into the small courtyard where our armored vehicles were and ran some tight little circles about half the size of a basketball court; it was many laps to a mile. After that, I joined those who weren't pulling security in the building and looked for food. We hadn't eaten anything all day because the suicide car had interrupted our lunch. We found a sack of potatoes in the house, ate some raw, and went to sleep.

CHAPTER THIRTEEN

Al Rashidiya-The Last Battle of the East Side

"Don't worry, they're bad shots."

—LIEUTENANT COLONEL AHMED

The next day was January 23. Karen and the kids had arrived on the 21st, and some of the team went back to help them get their one-year visa paperwork started. We could get thirty days on arrival, but this battle was looking like it was going to go longer than that. My visa also needed renewing—I wondered if I should go to Erbil for a couple days. I knew I didn't have to. So I asked General Mustafa what he thought. He said, "Go back, this is a good time. No problem. We're going to pause here for a bit before we head into Al Rashidiya." We all went back to Erbil and had a good reunion.

Karen, the kids, and David Tun Aung Kyaw (DTAK), one our Karen cameramen, had come from Thailand, along with Noelle Barkley, Sky's wife. Riley Ewen and his wife, Jessica, who had been there since January 1, left on the 23, and I was able to say goodbye to them. Riley had been a good hand; he was an ex-infantry officer, a skilled medic, a good thinker, brave, and caring. He quietly called me out once when I got angry and too rough with an IDP man who was clearly in the wrong and trying to get more than his share, and, after a few hours, I saw Riley was right. I appreciated having solid guys like him around.

Jessica had stayed in Erbil and did a great job of setting up our new office and getting support out to us. She set up our office in a house Dave Dawson found in December and Victor had helped us rent. Before that, we crashed in other people's places, but our operation grew to be too big for that. We were grateful to Victor for getting us our own space, and Jessica did a lot to make it a home as well as an office.

Dave Dawson, my nephew, left a few days before the Ewens, and I was sorry to see him go. He had plans to go to seminary and become a pastor. He was brave and had followed me into many dangerous situations, carrying equipment, ferrying ammo—my faithful squire. He also did the grinding administrative work in Erbil, getting our organization officially registered with the KRG, opening bank accounts, renting vehicles, and sorting supplies before and after missions.

Eliya and Zau took over the kitchen, and soon the spicy smells of curry filled the house, along with their laughter. We reupped our medical supply with help from Bring Hope Foundation and Dr. Mariwan Baker, the director. Bring Hope is a Swedish-based NGO set up to receive large donations of medicine from all over the world and pass them on to those who needed it, including field practitioners like us. That saved us a lot of money because we were running through trauma supplies quickly, supplying ourselves and filling the lists we got from both Major Naseem and Dr. Osama.

Karen updated me on the rest of their mission in Karen State, which had been good. It wasn't the first Burma mission they'd done without me, but usually I was just a few mountains over on my own mission. It was great to have them there, and Karen was happy to have the house in a neighborhood where we could spread out and have our own space. And there was good running. One lap around the neighborhood was about a mile, and there was a back road that took off from the side we could run down without much traffic and only a few dogs. I was happy with that after the tight little circles I'd been eking out at the front.

We had a good couple of days doing admin and resupply, then headed back to the front. The 36th had moved itself into Al Rashidiya. General Mustafa was headquartered in one wing of an abandoned school. They set up the CCP in the other wing and his staff and bodyguards were scattered throughout the building.

We took a couple of empty classrooms for sleeping and cooking; some of the team slept in the trucks as well. The backyard of the school was walled and had a concrete basketball court, which became our new workout space. Every morning, my family and I and some of the team ran laps around that for about four miles.

Al Rashidiya was a densely packed neighborhood and was the last little enclave of ISIS on the east side of the river. Most of the ISIS fighters had already fled across to the west side, so the fighting was intermittent. Still, there were thousands of desperate civilians here, and General Mustafa asked us to focus on helping them as much as possible. Just because most of ISIS fled across the river didn't mean they were done here. We were still within striking distance of mortars and drone attacks launched from across the river.

While there weren't many ISIS left in this part of Mosul, there were enough to make forays into the city dangerous. Though we were focusing on helping the civilians, who came in crowds from the homes where they'd been living in quiet desperation for the previous couple of years, we still went out on a few recons with the Iraqi Army.

On January 28, we heard word that a captured Yezidi boy was somewhere in the neighborhood. According to the local residents who contacted us, he was captured by ISIS two years earlier in the village of Hardan, in the Sinjar area. His family was separated by ISIS and sent to locations in Syria and Tal Afar, Iraq. Some escaped to a refugee camp in Dohuk, Kurdistan. The little boy, Ayman Amin, four years old, was taken to Tal Afar and sold to an Arab family in Mosul.

Right away, General Mustafa started organizing a rescue. Major Wathaq, one of his extremely competent operations officers, would lead it, and some of us went along as well. The section of Al Rashidiya we were directed to hadn't been completely cleared of ISIS, and as we approached the area, we could hear shooting between ISIS and Iraqi soldiers. There was a firefight going on nearby. Despite the chaos, the Iraqi soldiers never lost their cool and kept searching the area until they finally found Ayman. They put the rescued boy in one of their Humvees and brought along the man who had purchased him from ISIS.

The man said he knew the boy should go back to his family, but he always wanted children of his own. Because he and his wife couldn't have children, he purchased Ayman to be his son. Now struck by grief, he said he loved him as his child, but knew he had to give him up. General Mustafa, the Iraqi soldiers, Shaheen, and my family tried to comfort the boy while Mustafa and Shaheen coordinated Ayman's reunification with his family.

We took Ayman Amin to the Kurdistan border, where we were met by his grandmother and uncle. His grandmother cried with joy, saying,

Shaheen, General Mustafa, Peter, Major Wathaq, and I with Yezidi Ayman Amin and the man who bought him, before he is restored to his family, 2017.

"Oh God, God, thank God, thank you all, thank God. Thank you, Iraqi Army for bringing him back." She cried, laughed, and held Ayman tightly.

An Iraqi soldier asked the boy, "Where do you want to be?"

"With my grandmother, with her," he said as he clung to her.

The grandmother told us no one knew where his parents were, and she had also been captured by ISIS. But since she was so old, they later released her, and she had fled to a refugee camp in Dohuk, Kurdistan. His parents and more than ten members of his extended family were still missing. This rescue and restoration was another example of how much the Iraqi Army cared for all the people they were helping.

And it wasn't just humans: some of the soldiers also found and rescued three Saluki dogs in a compound they liberated. Someone said they may have been held by an ISIS emir who took them from a villager—but everyone in the area was gone or dead. General Mustafa took possession of the dogs and asked my kids if they wanted one of them, a female. "Oh yes, yes, we love her," Suuzanne said as she hugged the dog's neck and stroked her gently. The dog was so weak she could barely stand and so traumatized by violence she trembled constantly.

The general asked Karen and me if it was okay, and I agreed immediately. I felt very sorry for her, our kids loved her, and she needed love. I have always admired Salukis, which are one of the fastest breeds of dog in the world. They were prized by ancient Egyptian kings as hunting

My family with our new Saluki dog, Nineveh, rescued in Mosul, 2017.

dogs. Now we had one—a beautiful, elegant, calm, athletic, sweet, and swift (or at least she would be after some care) dog.

The kids showered her with affection, and she grew livelier and happier. We named her Nineveh after the region of Iraq she came from. The IDPs and villagers loved her as did the soldiers, and every day, someone offered to buy her. DTAK says she understands Karen language but just can't speak it. Her eyes are deep, full of love, the desire to be loved, and a kind of innocent wisdom. But she can also bite, as other dogs who try to push her around soon find out. Nineveh became a part of our family in Iraq and then in Thailand and Burma when we took her back with us.

On January 30, we conducted a GLC program in Al Rashidiya, inviting the kids into our base of operations—their old school. The team sang songs, performed the Good Samaritan skit again, and played games with around one hundred bright-eyed, curious children. The kids were curious about us. What place did smiling, singing foreigners teaching about the deep and wide love of God ("deeper and wider than the Tigris!" as Karen said) have here, where fear stalked the people, where violence was in the air they breathed?

The children here who went to school under ISIS learned math by figuring out how to divide a limited number of bullets between various kinds of infidels. Violence wasn't only a cloud they lived under, scurrying along, head down, hugging walls and staying low to stay safe; it was a poison ISIS used to try to corrupt them from the inside out. Now, they looked on as we reenacted the story of a traveler beaten by robbers who is helped not by an NGO or a rich man or a priest, but by a villager, just like them. "This we can all do for each other—this is part of the secret of abundant life," we told them.

Then we played games. No lessons here, just running in the sun for fun. Still they watched us carefully, but they also ran freely; they also laughed. The Iraqi soldiers—most of them dads who were regularly showing us pictures of their kids or having us say hello to their families during a phone call home—some of these laughing, goofy guys joined in as well, hamming it up with their M-16s slung over their shoulders. What did those curious kids think of laughing soldiers and playful adults, an afternoon event devoted to them, even as mortars and gunfire could be heard in the background?

We gave each child a bracelet with five colors through which we shared about God's good plan for us, which the enemy wants to destroy, and God's love, which can overcome that evil and give us a destiny and hope no man can destroy. We gave them shirts that summed it up with the words drawn from John 10:10: "Good life comes from God." This day of fun and joy, overflowing and untainted by the surrounding conflict, felt like life irrepressible, like the table prepared in the presence of the enemies from Psalm 23, like victory. General Mustafa even joined us, handing out shirts and taking photos with the kids.

The next morning, ISIS fired a mortar that landed less than a kilometer away from us in the midst of a group of kids playing. People came running to our CCP, some pushing awkward hand carts with bodies on them. Four children and one adult were dead, or nearly so, before they got to us.

The first boy the team saw in the improvised clinic was about eight and wasn't moving. He let out a single gasp and shuddered. Pulling back his shirt, we saw a piece of intestine protruding. Seconds later, one of the Iraqi medics pronounced him dead. Seven kids came in wounded; for these, we controlled bleeding, cleaned wounds, patched as well as we could, and mostly tried to get them to the hospital as quickly as possible. Two more died in the hospital that day, young sisters, and we drove their bodies back home with their grieving father.

And so our five-colored GLC bracelet had come to life. We talked about the gold bead, God's good creation, His good plan, His value for each of us. We were given a golden day, full of laughter and joy. We talked about the black bead, sin, hatred—our enemy. We were given a black day, with stilled, broken bodies, and frenzied grief. We talked about the red bead, and love—God's great love that embraces and shares our suffering and, we believe, has the power to redeem and transform suffering and our lives together. We clung to that red one as we tried to patch together broken bodies, and prayed over broken hearts. We talked about the white bead, a clean heart, untainted by hate or anger, loving God and the world with clear eyes. We prayed for that heart clarity. Finally, we talked about the green bead, the hope of new life.

We hoped the message of the bracelet had dropped like a seed into the heart of each child we met, to sprout like a shoot growing toward the sun, rooted in the Spirit, and ready for whatever the next day would bring. We talked about all these things and gave each child a bracelet to take with them into their next day.

This was a message we would need over and over. As families here slowly started moving around more freely, little shops opened, and we had thousands of people come for food and cooking fuel distributions, as well as medical care. But ISIS continued to attack the people of Al Rashidiya for many days after the fighters were physically pushed out of the area. During our time there, we had a lot of help from Partners Relief and Development and others in buying and distributing supplies. The Iraqi Army provided security and organization and we were able to help thousands of people.

Around February 3, even though there were still occasional attacks in Al Rashidiya, the 36th pulled back to refit and get set for the next big phase of the operation: the west side. The Iraqi Army officially declared the east side liberated on January 24, but as anyone on the ground could see, ISIS was certainly still there. The army maintained a presence in the newly liberated areas.

While the 36th refitted, we moved over to Goba to the northeast and linked up with a brigade from the 15th Division. This unit was set up out in the country in a big house in a compound up on a hill. Fields surrounded the hill and small settlements were scattered across the countryside. Bernard Genier, who had been on many missions with us in Burma decided to join us here around this time, doing a story on the battle for a French YouTube channel. Our friend Brian Moore also came and helped us with this mission.

The families in Goba and the country villages were desperate. We did several food distributions and GLC programs and the Iraqi Army was key for organizing and providing security. The 1st battalion commander, Lieutenant Colonel Ahmed, accompanied us on the GLC and food distribution missions, and we became close friends. He taught us much about Iraqi history and we shared about our respective faiths, him a Muslim and me a Christian.

Once we went on a patrol with him and his men. We were walking down a street in Goba, near the Tigris on the outskirts of Al Rashidiya, checking on his troops. We began taking fire from some buildings to our west. "Don't worry, they're bad shots," he said, laughing. We completed our patrol and were walking back, on the same street. There were several sharp cracks in quick succession and a sniper's bullets winged by, just missing me. We were out in the open, between buildings, with little cover, so we were all soon running, ducking, and zigzagging around, looking for whatever cover we could find from which to return fire. We suppressed the sniper until one of Ahmed's Humvees came up, and we jogged out of the area using the Humvee as a shield.

Around the middle of February, we headed back toward Kurdish lines and rejoined General Mustafa and the 36th, ready to cross the Tigris and start the campaign for the west side. Before ISIS, Mosul was served by five bridges; ISIS destroyed two, and coalition air strikes took out the other three in an effort to disrupt ISIS logistics. To cross the Tigris, a pontoon bridge south of Mosul was set up near the town of Hammam Al Alil. It was here the entire Iraqi column, moving from the east to the west side, planned to cross the river and take up their positions to launch the next and, hopefully, final phase of the campaign to defeat ISIS in Iraq.

CHAPTER FOURTEEN

Let High Adventure Begin: Crossing the Tigris

"We're not going back. If we die, we die together."

—MOHAMMED AHMED

On February 17, the day before the troop movement was to begin, U.S. General Richardson of the coalition (who temporarily replaced General Efflandt after he went home to care for his wife, recently diagnosed with cancer) made an announcement: "D-Day is at dawn. Let high adventure begin!" What a great leader—he motivated me! He shared the feeling of the happy warrior who is fighting not for hate or vengeance, but for love; who believes life on Earth is fatal but not final and so it can be risked for what is eternal. I felt good for the Americans under him, and I would have followed him anywhere.

On the 18th, we crossed the Tigris in a slow-moving column and went through the town of Hammam Al Alil on the west side of the pontoon bridge. ISIS had moved through this area as they were pushed out of their southern holdings back in the fall. According to reports, they had swept up groups of civilians from their homes and taken them into the city to use as human shields. Reportedly, sixteen hundred people were forcibly removed from this town to Mosul or Tal Afar. It was also the site of a massacre of at least one hundred people whose beheaded bodies were found by the Iraqi troops who retook the town back in November 2016. Now, Hammam Al Alil was bustling as the people tried to resume their normal lives.

Our column stopped about an hour away in Zeftia, a little farming village that was one of several in the area, most close enough together you could see them across the fields from each other. This would be the headquarters of the 36th for the first part of the west Mosul battle. Here, we were reunited with Dr. Osama, the 9th Division's medical officer, and they began to set up the division CCP here.

Victor and his team showed up along with our Mennonite friends Darrell, Brent, and Darrell's parents, who were in their eighties. Brian Moore, Tim Hayes, and his eye doctor friend Todd Pierson had been with us in Goba and were just leaving. Todd was able to do eye exams and hand out glasses, which was really appreciated by the Iraqi Army.

We set ourselves up in a couple of low, adobe farming huts, making a kitchen, unclogging a pit toilet, and sweeping out rooms to sleep in. It was a little rustic, but the team and visitors didn't mind. Short of rooms for all the people, we found the stable, which was dusty and full of hay—Darrell's mother, in a headscarf and homespun dress, was unfazed: "This was the stable? It's just like where Jesus was born! Of course, we can sleep here." After we cleaned it, she and her husband gamely set up their beds there.

The 36th Brigade and 9th Division spent three days preparing to launch the assault, setting up communications and mapping out lines of attack. While they prepped, we did GLC programs and food distributions in a couple of the neighboring villages. These quickly turned into mob scenes as people fought each other for the supplies we were handing out.

Our team and the soldiers helping us did a good job of keeping calm, smiling, and handing stuff out so everyone got something. We were even able to share about Jesus—Shaheen was wonderful as a translator and organizer. In the evenings, we went back and had dinner with General Mustafa, and in the mornings, we ran laps around the little village, looking across the winter-brown fields and enjoying the wide views after running inside the walls of the Al Rashidiya school.

On February 21, there was an operation order, and we were told the attack on west Mosul would start the next day. There was one Humvee allocated for us, so we divided our team: Karen, the kids, Hosie, and Paul Bradley, our chaplain, along with all our guests, would be with the rear group in Zeftia, with our armored ambulance and the other four vehicles. The kids would do homeschool, and the team would support Dr. Osama at the division CCP, if needed.

In the Humvee going with me to the front would be Eliya, Monkey as videographer, Shaheen, and a rotating fifth man—Bradley Brincka,

Sky, or Justin. Zau would ride with General Mustafa to film specifically for him. Also, I wanted to give Victor a chance to come, so he climbed into the last remaining spot.

Our old Humvee driver and gunner, Ali and Najim, had been sent on another mission that day, and we had a new crew: Mohammed, whom we'd met earlier back near the Salam Hospital fight, and a very large, portly, and smiling Iraqi soldier named Mohan. It was a good thing Monkey was small because he was going to ride into battle filming while squeezed into the turret with Mohan.

The plan for the battle for the west side was roughly as follows: the Federal Police, the ERD, and the Golden Division would attack from the south, taking the airport, military base, and other installations, The 35th and 37th brigades of the 9th Armored Division would attack from the southwest. The 36th Brigade was to swing further out west, reinforced by the Hashid Shabi, also known as the Popular Mobilization Units (PMUs). Their position on the extreme western flank of the attack meant their mission was to sweep the western desert and hills clear of ISIS and cut off Mosul from Tal Afar and, further to the west, Syria.

The PMUs were Iraqi militias that sprang up to help fight ISIS. At that time, the most revered Shiite cleric, Ali Al Sistani, issued a fatwa inaugurating the PMUs. Iran got involved and supported some of these units, which made the coalition nervous, as some of them threatened to attack Americans after ISIS was finished. Because of this Iranian influence, U.S. and coalition units were prohibited from working with the PMUs. There would be no U.S. advise-and-assist teams or coalition units with us helping to coordinate air and artillery strikes.

The PMU Abbas brigade was attached to us, and the morning of the assault, they pulled in and lined up, looking like a Mad Max army with a hodgepodge of armored vehicles, many with do-it-yourself armor welded on and bristling with an assortment of light cannons and machine guns. General Mustafa had warned me, "Don't get too close to the Hashid. They don't like Americans. Be careful."

I thought, *Well, I've got to meet them sometime*, so I went forward to the Hashid commander, bringing Shaheen with me. I walked up to the leader and said, "My name is Daoud Shingali. I believe God sent me here to help you. All I have is yours. Armored vehicles, my ambulances, my family, everything is at your service to help you." I had his attention and continued: "I'm very sorry for what America's done wrong to the

Iraqi people in the past. We are only human and trying to help. We want to try to be friends again. We're here to serve you." I stopped, looked him in the eye, then asked, "Can I pray?"

He was still processing everything I'd said and agreed. Why not? We prayed, and then General Mustafa walked up and told him, "Don't worry. They're just like us. They believe in God," and we felt a real friendship. Later, as we talked, I asked them not to consider us Americans as either Satan or God—we were neither. We were just people, like our government, and we wanted to help.

The morning of the assault dawned clear and cool, the sky slowly turning from the pearl gray of dawn to blue as the sun rose over the brown, fallow fields of Zeftia. The long convoy of armored vehicles—tanks and BMPs all lined up in front of the Humvees—roared to life, shattering the silence, and began its slow, inexorable lumber across the fields. All that power moving through the beauty of the morning was a stirring sight.

It stirred ISIS too—to action. They started firing mortars at us, but nothing came close. We headed north, then swung west, getting into low foothills. We started seeing destroyed vehicles, knocked out earlier by air strikes. We took fire from a small village, and a truck driver was killed there by a sniper, who, in turn, was taken out by the Iraqis. We stopped in the small village, now empty of ISIS. While we waited, I took the chance to drive an armored bulldozer that was also stopped there—it was good to know how to work these just in case, and my Iraqi teacher had a good laugh as he taught me.

We resumed the attack, and by afternoon, reached the town of Tel Kaysuma. There were probably only ten or twenty ISIS fighters in the village, but there were many more in the hills behind it. The BMPs and tanks led, all firing their guns as ISIS mortars landed around us. To my right, I noticed a stream of people coming over the hills to the south. It turned out to be the Hashid and they came running down the hill, yelling and shooting, sweeping across the open ground. It looked like a scene from World War II as they ran behind the advancing BMPs.

We advanced to about four hundred meters from the village, and I noticed a little hill to the left that looked like it could hold fighting positions. I kept an eye on it as we kept moving. Soon a mortar landed forty meters or so to our right. Nobody flinched, and we kept walking as Mustafa yelled orders into his radio, impervious to the firing. ISIS had pulled back but were still in the northern part of Tel Kaysuma. Soon we were able to make out their location in a part of town across an open field—firing on us. Unexpectedly, the BMP right next to me fired at them and nearly blew my eardrums out. I changed my position and the BMP kept firing, trying to suppress the ISIS fire.

By sunset, the Iraqi Army and the Hashid Shabi had taken and secured the entire town. They set up security between the town and the hills, which were about 500 meters from the town and rose one hundred meters higher than the surrounding plains. These are the same hills that guard the western approaches to Mosul and go around to the south almost to the Tigris River. We took over an abandoned compound, secured it, and set up camp.

Our little FBR team had our own food, but the general's staff had already set up a cook station, so we got to eat a great dinner with them. Then we settled down for the night. I was up early for a quick workout and bucket bath. Then our mortars started firing, so we went to check it out. The Iraqis had their 120mm set up and offered to let us fire it. We each took a turn sliding the mortar round down the tube and yanking the lanyard like they showed us, which released a firing pin and launched the round out of the tube.

This was a good opportunity to talk with some of the soldiers, a quiet moment between movements. Victor and I shared our faith and why we were there with the fire support officer; he told us he was there for his family's sake and his country's. He was a soft-spoken, kind man with glasses, who was always cool under pressure.

Suddenly, we heard a shout and a bustle of movement behind us. Guys were pointing at the sky, and I looked up: four little Phantom drones, with 40mm grenades attached, were flying above us. ISIS did this all the time, releasing the grenades at anywhere from thirty to three hundred meters up, trying to land them in the hatch of a Humvee or a tank.

I saw one right over me, probably one hundred and fifty meters up; there was a tank to my right with the hatch open, and I guessed the drone was trying to drop the grenade into that tank. We were shooting at it but realized it was going to drop. Out of the corner of my eye, I saw a big vehicle. I ran behind it and started shooting from there; this way, I would have one side covered and could see where it dropped.

I'd then have a couple seconds to jump to the other side of the vehicle if necessary.

The grenade was released. Zau actually got a photo of it as it fell. It came down on my left, and I jumped the other way. It landed in a piece of low ground. Rain the night before had made the ground soft, and the grenade buried itself about a foot deep before it blew up, which saved me. I was hit with a little shrapnel, which put holes through my three layers of clothes but only scratched me; the vehicle shielded me from the rest of it. Zau laughed and said, "Sir, you almost die." Eventually, someone shot the drone down, and we loaded up for the attack.

We left soon after that, leaving an element there in Tel Kaysuma.

The next village was called Sahaji. About a kilometer from the village, we popped over a rise and immediately started taking fire. To our right were the tanks of the 36th and to our left were armored bulldozers. I dismounted, moving behind a BMP with other BMPs to the left and right. The tanks fired with their main guns, then the dismounted infantry began shooting. We advanced slowly, men on foot moving behind the armor, letting the tanks shoot first as the whole group moved forward. We could see ISIS fighters running from position to position, trying to shoot at us.

I was following an armored bulldozer; to my right Major Wathaq was leading the infantry assault. The Hashid Shabi fell in behind us with their mix of armored vehicles, Humvees, and pickups. Once their vehicles linked up with the rest of the brigade, the foot soldiers dismounted and began an infantry assault, running ahead. I joined them as they pushed into the village, and the way became narrower streets instead of roads. There was a slight bend in the street ahead and a wall to my left. The Hashid were running and shooting, and I was all set to go with them. I thought I would be in the very front, so I could help take care of casualties.

As the rush of bodies, yelling and firing, went by me in a cloud of dust, I suddenly felt a strong check, like a voice saying, "No—that's not your place right now. Don't rush headlong into something you don't need to be doing." *That's God's voice,* I thought. I slowed and moved to the side, near the wall.

Then, up ahead and around the bend, there was a huge explosion. A suicide vehicle had come around the corner about ninety meters ahead of us and plowed into the first group of guys. It blew up and killed four or five men instantly and wounded more. One piece of metal went through the man in front of me and hit me in the hand with an impact like a baseball bat. It spun me around, and I thought for a minute I'd lost my hand. I didn't have time to check because ahead of me the ground was littered with wounded and dead.

I yelled: "Medic! Medic!" and ran forward to help the closest wounded man. The metal had torn through him, ripping through his arm. As I picked him up, I looked down at my hand. That same piece of metal had probably slowed down enough by the time it hit my hand that it only bruised it badly. Eliya came running up, and we started working on the downed soldier. The air filter from the truck also hit his arm, breaking it in about ten places; it looked like spaghetti.

Our Humvee moved up with Monkey, Victor, and Shaheen. They all jumped out and started helping. While we cleaned and bandaged those in front of us, there was a steady stream of other casualties passing by to the rear. I realized the Hashid commander I had prayed with the day before had died right in front of me. His second-in-command was wounded, and we helped care for him.

We became friends with the Hashid that day. We were the only medical providers there taking care of their people.

After that first mass casualty event, we occupied the town. I thought back to the small voice that had called me back from the point of that attack, and I was grateful. It was like someone slapped my hand to make me pay attention and not chase a fight I didn't need to. I thought of the quote I told Eliya long ago, which had become his favorite warning back to me: "Thara, remember, don't wrestle with the pig. You both get dirty, and only the pig likes it."

In the town, we found suicide vests, hand grenades, and grenades with no fuses. ISIS was making their own explosives and modifying others. They had hand grenades with time fuses and .50-caliber casings packed with explosives and a time fuse. They had jars with metal balls packed inside and a time fuse. Some of the suicide vests had detonators that looked Russian.

We stayed the night there uneventfully; the next day, there were suicide cars sighted, but none made it close. Once, I saw an ambulance tearing out of the town across our right front. Then, a second later, it turned around and came tearing back—with a VBED right behind it. The Iraqis were in position and engaged the suicide car immediately with tank fire, BMPs, and machine guns. It blew up before it could hurt anyone, though some metal pieces did land on our roof. Armed ISIS drones came that day as well, so I wouldn't say Sahaji was a relaxing place.

That evening, Paul drove to our position with Karen, the kids, and Nineveh, the dog, in the armored ambulance. They were going back to Thailand, for homeschool and other commitments they had, and I wanted to say goodbye. It was good to see them and say goodbye, but I was sad they were leaving. We prayed together, and they loaded up and drove away, taking Victor with them. A few mortars dropped as they drove off, but none close to them.

That night, we strongpointed a school and slept there. ISIS tried to attack but was repulsed. The next day, we got word from the outer security perimeter that ISIS had twenty suicide vehicles coming at us. We decided to call up the Americans. We were talking to General Richardson or his aide, Lieutenant Shawn Sororian, every day, with situation updates and battlefield descriptions. This, I hoped, was useful, given the absence of the advise-and-assist teams. This time, we gave them coordinates for these vehicles, telling them their likely target was us. The next thing we knew, there were aircraft overhead, and they took out at least six of the vehicles. The rest dispersed.

This happened more than once: the enemy would come, and we would describe the targets with a SALUTE report (size, activity, location, unit, time, equipment) giving GPS coordinates. The Americans then evaluated the report, verified it, and decided whether or not to attack the ISIS targets. They were already in the air with recon aircraft, and majors Ali and Wathaq were in regular radio contact. The Iraqi Army and the U.S. had a very good partnership, and I was just adding what I could.

Generals Efflandt and Richardson and their staffs were people of God, and we prayed on the phone every chance we could. Their care for the Iraqis was impressive and their assistance, especially in the western desert, won the love of the Iraqi Army and the Hashid Shabi.

We were pushing into the hills on the west side of Mosul, where Jonah, famous in the Old Testament for his experience in the belly of a whale, would have come on his journey long ago (after being spit up by the whale). The first day in the hills, we were walking up the middle of a paved road following a bulldozer that was clearing IEDs. The men shot out any positions that looked like they could contain ISIS snipers.

We took a whole day to get up to the pass of the first line of mountains. From the top, we looked down the other side. The valley was full of homemade oil refineries, fifty-five-gallon drums, little huts, or two semis pulled together. People were processing their own oil all over the place.

There was a small village and the 37th Brigade, on our right flank, was approaching the east side of the town. We watched a suicide bomber chase a BMP through the town, then get stuck and explode to no effect. (VBEDs were distinctive even from a distance because of the heavy armor they were encased in to protect the driver from getting shot before arriving to his target.) We swept the hills above the town until it got dark. I assumed we'd stay out at the forward limit of our advance, but we fell back to Mustafa, who had set up a position in Tel Kaysuma.

The 36th moved their headquarters and casualty collection point up to Tel Kaysuma, and the rest of our team moved up as well. This became our pattern: we moved out in the morning, pushed further into the hills, and then returned to Tel Kaysuma at night. It was a different kind of battle strategy. We'd have a good dinner with General Mustafa and make plans for the next day.

In the morning, I ran around the compound, took a water-bottle bath, drank coffee, ate cereal and yogurt, had prayer with our team—sometimes this would just be all of us reciting the Lord's Prayer together—and then headed back to the front.

We still had limited room in the Humvee, so our team rotated on a daily basis, while Hosie and Aude stayed back at the CCP with Major Naseem and the rotating Iraqi soldiers. Along with Eliya, Monkey, Zau, and DTAK, we had Justin, Bradley, Sky, Paul, and Shaheen, with Dlo going back and forth between the front and Erbil for admin work.

After several days, we were cautiously approaching the highest line of hills. Suddenly, shots rang out and the Hashid Shabi, who were in the lead, got nailed. Just like that, one of them was shot in the head. There wasn't anything we could do about it. The fire came from a nearby hilltop ISIS controlled. It turned out that hilltop position guarded a long, deep trench dug not just to fight from, but also to stop the Iraqi armor. It was over twenty kilometers long, running north-south from the highway near Badush, and it was from four to six meters deep and up to seven meters wide.

We ran up to evacuate the dead man and treat other wounded. Everyone started firing back at ISIS on the hill, and it became a shooting match at about four hundred meters. We crept to the crest of the hill, looked over and saw a big tunnel on the slope across from us. The advance stopped. The Iraqi Army and Hashid Shabi would not go forward unless something was done about that tunnel. Night fell with ISIS holding the hilltop and the tunnel, menacing like a poisonous snake in the trail, silently controlling the space in front of us.

The next day, the Iraqis asked me to call General Richardson and ask for more help. We gave him a situation report, and the Iraqis put in a request for the air support. Major Ali provided the coordinates, the FLOT (forward line of troops), location of friendlies, the limits of our advance, and where ISIS was, describing them as a target, their size, activity, location, the grid coordinates for that, the azimuth from us to them.

There were no civilians or structures in the area, only ISIS trenches, fighters, and tunnels. We reported the equipment they had: light weapons plus unknown weapons in the tunnel. Very quickly, the U.S. had a fighter up, we confirmed the target again, and they put a bomb right into the tunnel.

A huge cheer went up from the Hashid, who'd lost men the day before to these ISIS fighters. They shouted in unison, "Long live America!" Then, "Long live Trump!"—and me, and the pilots. They came up, patted me on the back and asked for more. Right about then, ISIS started attacking again, with machine guns and mortars on our right flank so the Iraqis asked for more support.

No more air support was available at the moment, but General Richardson and his aide, now Captain Sororian, put the French 155mm artillery on it, and with the grid coordinates we gave them, the French soon destroyed the ISIS counterattack. It was very impressive. Later, we went forward and gathered some ISIS memorabilia, scraps of weapons and such that I put in a bag and sent back to General Richardson to give to the French to thank them for their help.

After that, we still had to take the hilltop. This wasn't easy, either. With the tunnels wrecked, the Hashid advanced to a little toehold in a cliffy band of rocks partway up but were pinned down by heavy ISIS fire and without much support. I told the team, "I think we should go up there. Nobody has to, but I think we should." When we prayed together about it, everyone agreed to go. We ran down the hill, hit a trail that paralleled the ridge but was below the crest, and turned north. Running along this trail at the bottom of the hill, we were sometimes masked from ISIS but sometimes exposed. When we came to an open area between two hills that looked pretty risky, we paused and reassessed.

Below us, I saw an Iraqi bulldozer coming up, clearing mines. I decided to wait for it, and when it reached us, we followed it, using it as a shield from ISIS fire. ISIS mortars hit to our left, spraying us with rock pieces, but the bulldozer blocked all the metal fragments. That brought us to the base of the hill ISIS occupied, with the pinned-down Hashid right above us. We were planning our movement up the hill to them when, out of nowhere, a Humvee flew up behind us. It was ours, with Mohammed driving and Mohan on top with the machine gun. "What are you doing?" I yelled. "You're not supposed to be here."

Mohammed said, "We came to help you." Mohan looked down at us with a wide grin and nodded.

The Humvee couldn't go up the hill, but it could pull security below us as we ran up, so I said, "Okay, you stay here and provide security. We're going to run up there to try to help those guys out. But if you get attacked, you gotta go back." The hill in front of us had a ridge running down into the valley to where ISIS was. They could easily come up the ridge out of our sight, around that hill, and catch our guys alone.

Mohammed pulled an RPG out of the vehicle and put it on the hood. "We're not going back. If we die, we die together." He meant it. I came around the vehicle, took his hand, and we prayed.

We made our dash up the hill to the Hashid, a few bullets skipping harmlessly over our heads. Pinned down by heavy fire on top, they definitely weren't advancing any further at the moment, so we stayed with them until it started to get dark. Then we all pulled back together and returned to Tel Kaysuma for the night.

The next day, the hilltop was pounded again, and ISIS pulled back a bit. This enabled the Hashid to take the top of the hill, which gave us control of the high ground west of Mosul. We stood on top, looking out; we could see the plains of Mosul to the east, the city, and the Tigris River to the north. We were on the verge of snapping the trap on ISIS in the city.

The people of the city knew it and started to flee. First, it was a trickle, five or ten or twenty. Pretty soon, however, it became hundreds a day. One day, it was about three thousand people, escaping Mosul and the surrounding areas. Those who fled through the mountains met us, and we were back to giving out food and evacuating people, just like we did in Kurdistan. The team back at the CCP was able to help with medical care and did a small GLC program in a mosque with some of the IDPs. But the Iraqis didn't want them hanging around, never knowing who might be ISIS fighters, and the people also were in a hurry, never knowing when they might be mistaken for ISIS. They wanted to get to the refugee camps and under the protection of the international community.

We had just one more line of hills to take before dropping down to the plains. ISIS was dug in pretty heavily and shooting back at us. We were lying below the same small rocky outcropping we'd run to before, but this time on the other side. Our three ambulances were behind and below us, in the cover of the hill. The Hashid ran by, dashing across the open ground with bullets flying overhead.

An Iraqi vehicle drove up and ran over a land mine, injuring three of the occupants. I sent Paul back with them in one of our ambulances. Then we started slowly moving down a finger ridge below the crest of the hill, trailing the Hashid. I realized no one was looking to our right flank, so I crawled up to look over the ridge. There, four hundred meters in front of me, I saw six ISIS fighters running across the hilltop, from my right to left. I realized the 37th Brigade, which was on our right flank but hadn't been visible, was pushing them back toward us. I started yelling, "ISIS! Daesh!" and we started shooting at them as they ran. We saw four go down but two disappeared.

We kept moving forward until we were stopped by ISIS fire coming from the trench their hilltop position had previously overwatched. An Iraqi helicopter gunship made a firing run up the long axis of the trench, pouring in machine gun and rocket fire. Another helicopter joined and they strafed it repeatedly. We moved forward cautiously and found seven dead ISIS in the trench and no further threats from there.

Next, we came to the bodies of the four ISIS we shot earlier. We were moving toward the ridge of the last line of hills. When we reached the top, we saw a farmhouse below—and also a blood trail on the ridge. I figured it was from one of the two ISIS who got away.

I called Bradley and Paul over and we started following the blood trail. We tracked it to a small cave. I had them watch the sides while I got out a grenade and crept around to approach from the top. We cautiously looked inside, but no one was there. Suddenly, from behind us, there was a huge explosion. We looked back in time to see pieces of sheet metal flying over our team. It turned out one of the ISIS men was hiding in an outbuilding of the farm and blew himself up. I stopped and said a prayer of thanks: none of our guys were injured.

Paul and Brad headed back toward the main group, but I continued following the trail of blood alone. After a few minutes, the whap-whap-whap of rotors caught my attention and I looked up to see an Iraqi helicopter circling overhead. Suddenly, I realized I was in a nonstandard uniform with an AK-47, which was what ISIS used. I could easily be mistaken for ISIS. I waved my hands at the chopper, put on a big grin and tried to look as friendly and unradical as possible as I turned around and headed straight back to the team.

I found an Iraqi squad to follow the blood trail with me, but they were recalled by radio before we found the wounded ISIS fighter. By the amount of blood, I was following, I reckoned that ISIS guy would probably not survive long anyway, so I rejoined the team, and we went down to the farm together.

We approached the main house carefully. We didn't want to be surprised by any other exploding ISIS members. As we got close, the family emerged from the door of the main house, women and children peeking fearfully out from behind the father, who greeted us in English. We told them they had nothing to fear and that we came to help. "I am an American," I said. "We love your people and want to help. Can I pray?" The father agreed. I prayed in Jesus's name for good things and a new life for them.

The children began to smile shyly. We talked some more and gave them some food. We were becoming friends. I bent down and smiled into the eyes of the little kids, shaking their hands and saying, "God bless you."

They smiled shyly back and one little girl, about three, tugged on my pants. "Ameriki, Ameriki!" she said with excitement. This joy and friendship shared lit up our day. To me, this felt like God's will, done on earth as it is in heaven, and He had given us the gift of being part of it.

We said goodbye, and the family all piled onto their tractor, which pulled a trailer, and began to drive off. We started walking back up the hill, lighter in spirit than we had been. Then, from behind us, there was another big explosion. This time it was accompanied by screams. We turned to run back and saw what happened: the family had made it only a couple hundred meters on their tractor before hitting an ISIS land mine.

On the open trailer, they had no protection and were all thrown off. Blood-covered children screamed in terror and pain. Their mother, seriously injured, sat on the ground wailing. The father, with a bloody gash in his head, looked on in dazed horror. Our moment of peace and joy dissolved in the tears and blood of this family. We ran up and all started working, frantically trying to stanch their wounds, clean and bandage them, and calm down the stunned and terrified family until we could get our ambulance over to evacuate them.

There was one pocket of silence in the chaos, and when I looked up and saw it, my heart sank: there was Faiz, the Iraqi medic who always came to the front with us, bending over the youngest girl where she lay, still and silent and bloody in the dirt. He was doing CPR on her as tears ran down his face. I went over to help, but she was dead. I prayed and asked God to heal her. I thought, *My prayers must not be very effective, and my faith is weak, but what else can I do?* She was dead. We all started crying, our team and the Iraqi soldiers. We had seen many children killed, but this broke our hearts. We had gotten to know her just a little bit, and it was too much.

Our ambulance drove down the hill to evacuate the wounded and we put the lifeless little girl in with her badly wounded mother and the rest of the family. They were all crying. We shut the doors on them, and the ambulance sped away. There was a sudden silence, but it was not a peaceful one. My heart was a clenched fist inside me. I turned to Monkey, our team pastor, and said, "That is why ISIS must be stopped. That is why people need to fight them. We pray their hearts will change, but if not, they should die. I will kill them."

That night as I went to sleep, I was sad and angry. I vowed to kill ISIS but felt no joy in the prospect, only a grim determination. It felt like my world went from full color to a dull, heavy gray. I asked God to show me His truth on all this. The next day, I was up before dawn and prayed and asked again, "Lord Jesus, please show me the truth of what happened yesterday." I opened my Kindle to the Bible and chose a verse at random: "Vengeance is mine says the Lord, I will repay."

What did that mean? I tried again, choosing another random verse. I got the same message. After it happened a third time, I stopped. I confessed to God my desire for vengeance and gave it up to Him. I

The little girl who died after her family ran over an ISIS landmine in their tractor.

Bradley Brincka, David Tun Aung Kyaw, myself, Eliya, Monkey, and Paul Bradley in the hills beyond Tel Kaysuma, West Mosul, 2017.

didn't want to, but I felt I had to. And as I did, as I let go of my plans to avenge that little girl, I felt suddenly free and light. It was like a two-thousand-pound weight fell from my shoulders—a weight I did not know was there until it was gone. What would have happened had I not been freed from it?

I was still sad, but I was free—free to love, free to pray, free to fight if and when God directed, free to heal, free to keep going, and free from the false duty of vengeance. I did not have to do anything but be an ambassador of Jesus. He freed me from revenge masquerading as justice, from a hate that might one day have come back to my team, family, and me. I learned that to get justice, we have to love and care about those who hurt us. Punishment should be what is best for the person who hurts us, to help them know their wrong and give them an opportunity to change. Love keeps our hearts free, regardless of what others do.

Later, this made me think about the Punisher, the fictional comic book character motivated by the loss of his family to take revenge on all evil. He is popular with some soldiers, but there are two problems with the Punisher. One, he is not real—he doesn't have to live with all the variables and nuances of life. Humans aren't comic book characters, and none are either all evil or all good. Two, no human can function well with themselves or others, nor are there good lasting results, with revenge as a motive.

That day, as we walked up the hills and past the now empty farm below, I asked God, "Please be with and heal that family and let them see a vision of their little girl in heaven. Give them comfort and hope. Thank you, Lord, for your patience with me and thank you that I do not have to carry the weight of vengeance. You will do it. We only have to be your servants and do as you direct each day."

I remembered praying earlier for this family. It seems many times my prayers are not very effective. But what else can we do? Jesus said to keep asking and keep trusting God. We have a choice: give up or keep hoping, praying and trying. The things of this world are fatal, but they are not final. We can be sad and live well. I believe we will see that little girl in heaven. Until then, in spite of those who will do evil, we can walk with God so His will is done on earth as it is in heaven.

CHAPTER FIFTEEN

Closing the Trap— The End of the Desert Fight

"And God, in our Easter basket can we please have a boat?"

—DAVE

The day the little girl died was the last day of our push through the hills. We reached the western edge of Mosul, and there was a pause in the offensive to plan for the next stage of the battle in the dense urban terrain of the old city. My team and I went back to Thailand for our 2017 March meetings. We reported to all the ethnic leaders from Burma on the situation, told our stories, and what we were learning. They were supportive, and more of our teammates stepped up, requesting to come. Two of them were medics named Slowly and Silver Horn. Toh also offered to come back.

Two potential volunteers visited us during the March meetings: a Navy SEAL just leaving the service, Ephraim Mattos, and a former Special Forces operator-turned-missionary living with his family in Okinawa, Kevin Johnson. Ephraim had emailed us about coming to help once he discharged from the Navy, and I invited him to our meeting. He came and first thing, I sent him on a night horse ride with the kids—a gallop through trees, hills, and around the lake. When they galloped back in, the kids said, "Dad, he's okay. He's up for anything." First unofficial test passed. The next morning, we ran up the hill behind the house and he passed the second unofficial test. Once I heard some of Kevin's stories of being shot in Iraq, and we prayed together, I invited him also.

Once the meetings were over, we started reassembling the team for the next mission. Sky, Noelle, and Justin went back first to start resupplying, doing vehicle maintenance, and getting things organized. Together with Dlo, they reupped our medicine, started coordinating food and relief supplies, and worked on visas for the new batch of Burma Rangers coming. I went back with Zau Seng, Eliya, and DTAK on March 28. Kevin and Ephraim also joined us in Erbil.

In Erbil, Steve Gumaer and Brad Hazlett of Partners Relief and Development joined us, along with our friend Darrell again, and Larry Hansen from Calvary Chapel in Murrieta, California. These were people who'd been supporting us in different ways, and it was good to have them see the fruits of their support in the field. Reload Love was another big partner that enabled us to help more people. We handed out thousands of shoes, warm jackets, and long-sleeve T-shirts, thanks to them.

When we left for Thailand in early March, Badush was the next objective of the 36th Brigade. By the end of March, ISIS had retreated and the Iraqis took it without a fight. Badush is the site of a huge cement factory and is situated right on a bend in the Tigris River northwest of Mosul. It is surrounded by farmland with little walled villages scattered among the fields, which, in early April, were brilliantly green. It was really beautiful.

We moved in with the 36th, where they were set up in a village near the cement factory. We stayed in a little house at the top of a hill overlooking the Tigris, and we could see the outskirts of Al Rashidiya across the river. It was a scenic spot. In this same house, two kids had died in a rocket attack. They were buried in the front yard, two small piles of fresh soil reminding us daily of the reason we were here. During this time, we were able to give all the villagers who hadn't fled enough food for a month, plus shoes and shirts for everyone.

We found a tunnel system that ran from our house down to the Tigris, with all kinds of ISIS propaganda and paraphernalia, including explosives. One day, the Iraqi soldiers took some of the explosives down to the river, blew them up in the water, and caught a lot of fish to eat. We all laughed, especially the Karen—because they do the same thing in Burma with Burma Army land mines. A different way to fish, and a different use for land mines.

At the beginning of April, we heard the 36th was going to attack Tal Afar. This was far to the west. We would be moving away from Mosul, and there were a lot of smaller villages to take on the way. We were told April 12 would be the launch day. Besides me and the Animals (this is what we still called all the ethnic guys from Burma, harking back to the beginning of FBR when we all had animal nicknames), we had Shaheen, Sky, Bradley, Justin, Kevin, and Ephraim. We organized for the initial roll-out: I would be in front in the Humvee with the Animals and Ephraim. Mohammed was our driver and Mohan was the gunner. The rest of the team would follow in our armored ambulance, driven by Kevin.

The morning of April 12 saw us again moving out with the convoy of the 36th's armor. It was a little smaller and more banged up than when we first rolled across the desert with them toward Tel Kayf. But I was enjoying the familiarity of covering ground with this force, defeating an evil enemy. The familiarity didn't make it any less deadly, however.

As we got to within 1.5 km of the objective, a small village called Garbollah, some of the vehicles stopped, and General Mustafa and his team dismounted. Shaheen and I dismounted as well and started walking behind the BMPs and tanks. There was a large group of civilians fleeing in the opposite direction, some on foot, but most in vehicles. The lucky ones had big trucks that could carry all of their stuff.

As we arrived to within five hundred meters of the village, ISIS engaged the lead vehicles and, at the same time, IEDs ISIS planted started exploding to our left. The civilian convoy panicked, and there was no small amount of chaos just behind our advancing front as swaying, overloaded lorries careened around tiny, overloaded pickups swerving to avoid those on foot, who were probably as likely to get run over as blown up.

While this was happening behind us, mortar rounds started dropping around us. Machine gun rounds zipping over our heads provided the final touch for our standard village welcome from ISIS. The Abrams tanks in our column started shooting back, cutting down ISIS fighters who were trying to make a break for it. I was following the BMPs and Abrams, with the rate of fire increasing the nearer we got to the village. Suddenly, in quick succession, I heard two explosions right behind us: an Iraqi Humvee hit an IED, and almost simultaneously, a T-72 tank hit another land mine. These went off right next to our armored ambulance, but all of our team seemed okay as I looked back. Ephraim and Kevin later told me they were surprised to still be alive.

Meanwhile, Shaheen and I were picking up the pace, making a point of sticking close to a BMP as rounds skipped off its armor. The fire was coming from different parts of the village, from windows, doors, loopholes, and what seemed to be camouflaged tunnel entrances. Suddenly, to our right, a suicide vehicle came flying out of the village. The BMP stopped, I jumped to the left side of it, made myself as small as possible, and curled into the wheel well, ready to jump out if it started moving again.

Shaheen fired off some choice words and crouched behind the BMP's rear hatches. The Abrams behind and to the right of us fired its main gun, scoring a direct hit on the vehicle less than forty meters away. There was a huge explosion and a fireball rolled over, bathing us in heat. The engine block of the car flew all the way over the BMP and metal car parts slammed into its side. As I uncurled myself from the wheel well, I gave it a pat of thanks: it had surely saved our lives.

Ephraim ran up to make sure we were okay. Just as he reached us, the BMP and Abrams wheeled right and left respectively, assaulting into the town. Other vehicles to our left took off to secure the flank. Suddenly, we were completely exposed. Ephraim and I looked at each other and took off running, shooting at the same time into the buildings in front of us. We headed to the right and the cover of the other BMPs, about one hundred meters away. Shaheen followed, but without our urgency, sauntering like he was out for a walk in the park. After a hard hundred-meter sprint, firing the whole way, Ephraim and I pulled up, breathless, in the cover of the other group of BMPs, by now on the south side of the village. Shaheen strolled in behind us and we both scolded him for being so nonchalant.

He laughed. "I do as I like," he said. "Listen, baby, I know what I'm doing. I'm Shaheen. This is my country, boys." He was still alive, so we laughed with him.

Our team pulled up in the vehicles, and we started clearing buildings, working together with the Iraqi Army. We came to one house, and even before we approached it, I saw a machine gun poking out the door and a muzzle flash. I ran around the side of the building and, covered by Ephraim, prepped a hand grenade and threw it in. I stepped back for the explosion then followed it in, shooting. My weapon jammed, but Ephraim was right behind me and backed me up. I cleared my gun, stepped over the abandoned machine gun on the floor, and we finished clearing the building.

We found no one inside, but a tunnel entrance was just inside the door. The ISIS fighters had clearly fled underground. Ephraim and I and the Iraqi soldiers who followed us fired down into it for a minute, but then we all gradually stopped and looked at each other. We knew what needed to be done. No one wanted to do it.

ISIS was down there, waiting to kill anyone who came after them. If we didn't get them now, they'd get us later. I prayed and felt: *someone has to do this and I have the training and have done it in Kurdistan already.* I set my AK down. I would go, with only my pistol and hand grenades in case it got too small to maneuver with an AK. Ephraim volunteered to go with me. Kevin, who came up just then, pulled security above.

I threw a hand grenade down, waited for the boom, and followed it in, with Ephraim right behind. The tunnel was less than a meter wide and about two meters tall. I couldn't see much with all the dust. I moved forward slowly, with my headlamp on, pistol in one hand and a prepped hand grenade in the other.

The tunnel dropped straight down, then twisted to the left. After about ten meters, it turned and there was a five-meter stretch, then another turn and a ten-meter straightaway. At this corner, I threw another grenade down a long hall of the tunnel, trying to bounce it around the next corner.

We jumped back around the previous corner. The grenade went off, and the air became thick with dirt and dust. We couldn't see anything, and it was hard to breathe. As we waited for the dust to settle, I suddenly remembered my pistol was jamming earlier. I looked at it, thinking, "This is stupid. I left my AK up on top, and now I'm down here with a malfunctioning pistol."

Ephraim saw me hesitate and said, "Dave, let me go first." The one who went first was assuming the more dangerous position if we met ISIS. Usually, I would have refused such a suggestion, but I realized that with a faulty pistol, pride would be pushing me not just into normal danger but into bad tactics.

I said "Okay. My pistol isn't working well, go ahead." This was very humbling, and as he stepped ahead of me, I felt love and admiration well up for him. He was a brave, selfless man, a real fighter and warrior. I was grateful to have him with me.

We continued forward and came to a vertical shaft ascending about seven meters. Looking up we could see, about halfway up, another tunnel branching out horizontally. There were scuff marks in the dirt at the base of the shaft and it looked like ISIS could have used a ladder and pulled it up after them. Someone might be up there waiting for us.

Just then, light came through from above. Kevin had found the opening to the vertical shaft and was looking down at us. We kept our weapons pointed up at the opening until we passed, deciding to follow this lower tunnel system first and then come back to check out the higher one.

We passed a small branch to our right that held a small kitchen with pots, pans, and a stove. The main tunnel eventually opened into a big room, about five by six meters. It had four mattress pads, beds, a Koran, tools, cameras, and lots of ammo, including RPG rounds. The tunnel continued out of this room but before moving on, I grabbed a hammer from the floor and tucked it in my belt. Without a working pistol, I would use it if we came into close quarters with an ISIS fighter.

We continued on and found another small room with some mattresses, obviously recently used. The tunnel ended at a dirt wall. Where were the ISIS fighters—or the exit tunnel? We rechecked everywhere we'd been and decided they must be in the upper tunnel we passed earlier. We went back to the vertical shaft, and I told Ephraim my plan: "I'll climb up on your shoulders, pull myself up with one hand, and toss a grenade in with the other; then I'll assault into the shaft." It was a pretty high-risk scenario, but we couldn't see another way.

I started to climb onto Ephraim's shoulders, prepped grenade in hand. Then we heard Lieutenant Colonel Feras yell down from the tunnel entrance. "Hey, you guys, come out! I've got a better plan! A bulldozer!"

Kevin chimed in: "Yeah, come on out! This is a better way." It seemed obvious, but I said a prayer to be sure. The prayer would serve as a motivation check and make sure I wasn't being led by fear. After I prayed, I still agreed. Ephraim and I headed back to the tunnel entrance.

As we reached it, Kevin, who was just outside, stopped us and pointed to the ground. Just an inch away from our boot prints was a land mine. How we missed it coming in, we did not know. It was a close call.

We got out to fresh air, hearts pounding, and happy to see Feras smiling from ear to ear. "Thank you, brave men, for risking your lives for us all! Thank you, Americans, for caring about Iraqis and even doing the most dangerous work." He grinned. "I think we can solve the

ISIS TUNNEL AT GARBOLLA
APRIL 2017

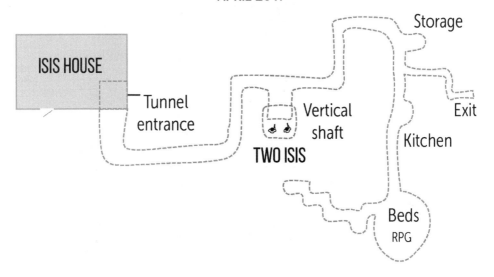

problem of this tunnel." He motioned, and, with a roar, up came an armored bulldozer, which began to bury the tunnel entrance and collapsed the building over it.

"Thanks! Your idea was better than ours," I said. I was grateful for the teamwork we had with the Iraqis.

Later that day, I heard from Feras that two hours after his bulldozer covered the tunnel, there were two muffled explosions from underground. The ISIS fighters trapped up in that high horizontal shaft blew themselves up. *What a way to die,* I thought, picturing them in that dark shaft for hours as the air gradually thinned and their hope with it. And what a way to live—what a waste and tragedy for all.

The next village was near enough we could see ISIS there, setting up defenses against our attack. I was sure we would keep moving and try to get them before they were completely dug in. But no. It was the lunch hour, and we stopped to eat. Our team ate quickly and readied ourselves to move again. Still, we just sat. We waited. Finally, I took a nap.

We couldn't go anywhere until we got the command, no matter how impatient or prepared we were. What we didn't know was right then, the Iraqi high command canceled the attack on Tal Afar and turned the 36th around: the attack in Mosul was bogged down, and they were needed back there. Eventually, the word got around and the command came: turn around. We were headed back toward Mosul.

We returned to Badush to await the new plan. More and more people were fleeing, first hundreds, then thousands. As we waited for the next phase of the battle to start, we were able to help give food and water to all those people.

A few days after we returned to Badush, Karen, the kids, and Hosie came over from Thailand for a few days. The kids were enrolled for two months of international school in Chiang Mai and Karen was teaching a spring term English class for Thai children. At this point, they only had a short spring holiday, four days, but they were able to help with distributions and do a couple of GLC programs.

Easter coincided with their visit, and we were happy we would get to spend it together. Our friends at Samaritan's Purse (SP) invited us to visit them to celebrate at their field hospital in east Mosul, and we agreed. We left most of the team on site with the 36th but took Mohammed, our Humvee driver, and Shaheen with us, along with Eliya and DTAK. It would be a quick trip. The night before we left, Good Friday, Mohammed came to me to say he decided to be a follower of Jesus. "I asked Jesus into my heart and I am so happy," he said, beaming. This trip would be a good opportunity for him to meet other Christians. Early Saturday morning saw us retracing the steps of the last two months of fighting, to cross the same pontoon bridge near Hammam Al Alil.

When we arrived at the bridge we normally used, we found floodwaters had just swept it away. A three-and-a-half-hour drive suddenly got longer. We would be late to the meeting. There was another bridge, an hour's drive south; then, once we crossed, the route was even longer, going back through Kurdish lines, which meant more checkpoints and permissions. We had no choice, so we called our friends to say we would be late and please pray for us to make it.

We crossed at the second bridge, which was another pontoon setup constructed as a temporary replacement for the bridge a hundred meters upstream that had been blown up during the fighting. On the other side, we wound through back roads as fast as we could, trying to make up time. When we reached the Kurd lines, our progress came to an abrupt stop. We were told that without special permission, we could not cross. Frustration rose in me, but I decided to praise God. I had to force myself, but I did it. I said, "Praise you, God, for your plan."

Then I appealed to the local commander, who said, again, "There is no way without a permit."

I didn't know what else to do so I said, "I'll pray to God for a way."

We all prayed in front of the commander, and when we were finished, he said, "I am a Christian, too."

I asked him, "Why did you become a Christian?" He told us he had been interested in Christianity for some time, but it was a friend from SP named Caleb who led him to follow Jesus. My jaw dropped. "He is our friend too!" I said. "And he's the one we're going to meet today!"

The commander's face lit up with a smile and he said, "Since you're Caleb's friend too, I'll ask my leaders to make an exception so that you can go now."

We thanked him, and God, and took off again for the meeting. We were on our seventh hour of driving when we finally arrived. Mohammed spent time with this Christian team and afterward told us, "People are so nice here because of Jesus. I love Jesus."

We had brought many patients to this field hospital when the fighting was on the east side and it was inspiring to be back at this place of world-class medical treatment, love, and prayer. Lives were saved daily by the staff there, and all in Jesus's name.

Franklin Graham, the leader of Samaritan's Purse, was there, along with Caleb, Matt Nowery, and many local SP staff. Franklin wrapped up our meeting with a retelling of the Easter story, starting with, "...the soldiers went to the tomb and saw it was empty and reported...the soldiers saw the empty tomb first..."! They were among the first witnesses that there was no body because Jesus was alive. This was a powerful message for me as a soldier and for Mohammed.

We drove back as fast as we could. We planned to have an Easter sunrise service and GLC program the next day with our team. Sahale, Suu, and Peter were looking forward to riding a newly borrowed horse, a beautiful stallion that belonged to a local villager whose home was liberated from ISIS by the 36th.

We reached the bridge after dark only to find that it, too, had been swept away by the same flood that took out the first bridge. Now we were stuck. We prayed and scouted for a way to cross and made plans to make a raft to cross the next morning. We called our team on the other side and asked them to bring another vehicle, as we would have to leave ours on this side after we crossed. We all curled up on the cold floor of a little hut by the river and tried to sleep. Shaheen was the only one with a blanket, which he gave to the kids to share, and we passed a long night with little sleep and the roar of the flooding river nearby.

The next morning was Easter Sunday. Even though we wanted to get right on to finding a way across the river, we first went down to its edge to thank God for Jesus and celebrate His resurrection. We sang, "He Lives" in English and Karen and shared what Easter meant to each of us.

For me, it all came down to Jesus being alive in my heart and filling it with such overflowing love that it made me want to cry sometimes. The forgiveness, acceptance, fellowship, and pure love of Jesus fills our hearts in a way nothing else can. I am humbled that while I am a sinner and often small-minded and mean to God and people, God still loves me and sent His son to live and die for us, and to live on with us. Jesus rising again gives us assurance, hope, joy, and power to live for Him.

My heart was full as the sun came up over the river. In our closing prayer, we thanked God for His gift of Jesus and I also asked, "…and God, in our Easter basket can we also have a boat?"

As we finished praying, we looked up and there was a boat, crossing the river toward us. "Thank you, Lord, and let's go, Rangers!" I shouted. The river was swift, and the boat landed about a kilometer downstream, so we gathered our things and hurried down after it.

We made friends with the boat driver, who was named Sultan. We weren't the only ones wanting to cross, and there was a bit of a line, with people pushing and shoving to get on. Mohammed was in his Iraqi Army uniform and said we were on official business and we moved to the front of the line. Then we offered to pay Sultan, and we were on the first ride of the day without a problem from anyone. As we pulled away from the riverbank, we heard gunshots behind us. Apparently, it wasn't going to be so easy for everyone else.

We did our best to keep the boat balanced in the fast and muddy current. The engine quit once but started again, and we made it across. We thanked and paid Sultan and linked up with Justin, who had drove from Badush with materials to build a raft and extract us.

We raced across the desert and got back to our base three hours later, with time to do a program. The kids attending the program had been liberated from ISIS a few weeks before, and we had been in this area for those weeks, handing out food, water, clothes, and shoes, slowly making our way from one settlement to another to make sure everyone got something. We worked with the local headman to organize our efforts. For this program, soldiers helped set up an organized distribution chain by laying out shoes and shirts by size, funneling the kids down the line, and keeping the parents in check. The soldiers also provided security.

Toward the end, the Iraqi Army got a tip that two ISIS leaders were hiding out in the village. As we packed up our supplies, they dragged those two men out with the help of the villagers. General Mustafa was furious and went over to the headman, screaming at him: "We've been here for weeks! Just giving you stuff! And now you tell us about these guys! Why did it take you so long? Makes me want to be sick!" That was the reality of the situation; ISIS was successful in taking over Mosul partly because of sympathy in the population, along with distrust of the Iraqi Army. We had put time in here and finally overcome ISIS influence. I thanked God it happened before those guys lashed out at us in any effective way.

After the two ISIS leaders were taken away, someone brought over the borrowed horse, and the kids and I took turns riding it back to our base. Running through the green fields as the Easter sun set, with the Tigris in the background, laughing with the kids as they galloped around on this beautiful horse was a great gift. I couldn't believe it was happening here, outside Mosul, alongside all the death and destruction. As night came, my heart was full of light and joy.

It was a blessed day, and that night we got news topping it all off. Eliya came back from visiting a woman who was brought to us in a wheelchair a few days earlier. She had had a stroke when ISIS was in her village, and her left side was paralyzed. She could not talk or walk. Eliya examined her and told her there was hope she could possibly recover some of her mobility if she did physical therapy every day. He taught her and her husband some exercises to do, and we prayed with her. I gave her an MP3 player loaded with the Bible in Arabic. As soon as she heard the words of Scripture, she smiled widely. I also gave her a print version of the Gospel of John in Arabic and right away, she and her husband began to read it together.

Suuzanne rides a horse we found near the Badush front. Major Naseem is standing in the background, 2017.

After the Easter GLC program, Eliya went to check on her again and gave her vitamin B1. Her husband told him she was doing the prescribed exercises each day and was a little better. With Eliya's encouragement, she raised her hand and then, to everyone's amazement, stood up. She could not stay up very long, but this was the first time she had moved her left hand or stood since the stroke. I said to Eliya, "Thank God! Thank you, too. I love you! And on Easter too! Look at all the things happening today, I am so glad and thank God."

Karen and the kids had to leave after just four days to finish school. They planned to come back in May. Eliya had to go also and complete some responsibilities at home but planned to return later with my family. Hosie and Dlo went out to Erbil with them and were able to pick up Slowly and Silver Horn, who finally got visas and arrived with Jesse Lee, a friend from Alaska, the day after Karen and the kids left.

This was a perfect rotation, Eliya going out and these guys coming in. They were also very experienced medics: Silver Horn had started out years ago as a communications man for us, but within a couple years had requested medic training. Now he helped run the Jungle School of Medicine-Kawthoolei (JSMK), our medical school at the training camp. Slowly started a clinic in his area of Toungoo District, one of the more remote and mountainous parts of Karen State in Burma. He also helped run our large-scale training in the fall. I was glad to have them and Jesse Lee here.

For the rest of April, we were mostly taking care of people fleeing Tal Afar and Mosul as the high command positioned the troops for the final assault on Mosul. We started each day with devotions, finishing with the Lord's Prayer and a song in the Karen language that meant, "Hear our prayer, oh Lord." All day, we handed out food to people leaving the city and treated the wounded. We fed over twenty thousand people during this time. At night, we worked out, ate, and talked in our house.

Devotions were not mandatory, and not everyone attended all the time. Justin, for example, was agnostic and was skeptical though respectful of all my God-talk and praying. As in Burma, no one was required to be a Christian—but because, for me, prayer was such a part of all decisions I had to make involving the whole team, I needed to be sure we were all on the same page. One night, I had a talk with Justin. "I believe in an invisible God I talk to on an 'invisible' radio," I told him. "You don't have to believe, but you need to be able to trust me in action because I do believe God leads us when we ask Him to. Do you trust me?"

Justin shook his head and smiled. "I don't believe like you do, but I do trust you. You can count on me."

"I trust you too," I said. Though Justin trusted me, there were times when he questioned my decisions. I didn't always have time or a ready explanation for him, so I would put my thumb and little finger to my ear imitating a phone call and say, "Invisible radio, man." He would laugh and get to work.

I know that many of you, dear readers, may be like Justin—you do not pray or believe in God. All my praying might be a bit incomprehensible. If nothing else, you can look at it as my way to stop and clear my mind of comfort, fear, or pride as motives for action—all of which can lead you the wrong way. However, for me, I do believe in a living God who answers prayer and has the best way for us, so I pray. And I believe He has helped me be brave where I would have been afraid, be loving where I would have been hateful, act in peace where I might have acted in violence, and stay alive when I should have been killed.

We went back to work each day, giving love and help to families fleeing ISIS. Many of these people had been ISIS and, now that they were losing, were leaving. General Mustafa's care and feeding of them, and using us to help, was a beautiful and, I believe, effective example of loving your enemies and showing them a way different and better than theirs.

By then, the Golden Division and 37th Brigade had ISIS pushed into just a few sections of Mosul, mostly in the old city. The east, south, and north sides of the city had been liberated, the airport had been taken to the south, the desert to the west was secured—which cut off both resupply and escape—and ISIS was jammed into a bend in the river with the Tigris to their north and east. None of this had been easy. While the coalition had been preparing this offensive, ISIS had also been preparing. They had kidnapped thousands of civilians and were preventing tens of thousands more from leaving, to use as human shields. They had tunnels, mines, trenches, and rubble fields set up throughout the city to slow down the progress of the attacking forces. Every step of the advance was fraught with danger, either to the soldiers on the attack or to civilians who were everywhere in the city. The U.S. Army Mosul Report described the challenges of the attacking force in this final field of battle: "The city's narrow streets and corridors, rubble, power lines, and unforeseen environmental hazards negatively impacted mobility and the ability to maneuver. Dense urban terrain aids in the conduct of the defense against a superior force."[6]

CHAPTER SIXTEEN

Into the City-The Beginning
of the End

"Dense urban terrain aids in the conduct of the defense against a superior force."

—U.S. Army Mosul Report

On May 1, 2017, we moved from Badush to Hulayla, which was about four kilometers outside northwest Mosul. This would be our staging area. As we rolled toward this new position, I climbed up into the empty turret of our Humvee. Civilian vehicles coming toward us seemed small from up there, and the scattered people on foot who paused, stepped aside, and looked up at us as we passed seemed smaller.

Standing there, higher than the people and vehicles around and with a machine gun under my hands, I suddenly felt myself inflate with an almost embodied pride. I felt literally puffed up, like my chest expanded and I was torn out of my mortal trappings and became some sort of superhero.

With this came another feeling—of separation from the people we were passing on the road. We were not the same: I had power, and they did not matter. Simply standing in the turret of the armored vehicle behind a machine gun, riding along with more than twenty other armored vehicles, had changed me and my attitude toward everyone around me. *Wow*, I thought. *I'm infected. Power and pride have me. This is bad. Lord Jesus, I am sorry. I give up this power and pride. Help me be loving and be your ambassador of love.*

The prayer burst the bubble. I instantly felt shrunk back to my real size. This was a humbler size, but it was also more real. I saw a choice: give in to power and pride and the illusion that I was greater than I was, or be who I really was, a mere mortal who might need to fight to help others but always wanted to act in love.

The late psychiatrist Dr. M. Scott Peck said, "Mental health is…reality at all costs." I thank God I was shown reality. As I mentally settled back into my real size, I smiled at the Iraqi men, women, and children on the side of the road. They smiled and waved back. We were there to help them, and because of ISIS, we needed the armor and weapons to be of help. But I was only a man, no more or less important than them. We were in this together. This was real and I was humbled, happy, and free.

That experience was one of many demonstrating the supernatural power of Jesus to change my heart and show me another way. I do not want to live life without this gift and I certainly do not want to go to war without it. Without God's help, I would care less about the people I am here to serve and become more like the enemies I am trying to stand against. That was a good lesson to learn as we moved into the next stage of this battle.

On May 4, we joined the attack. The 36th's objective was to liberate the Musharrifah district of Mosul, an area that stretched from the Mosul-Syria highway up to the Tigris River before it bent south. General Mustafa gave us our own Humvee after he reassigned Mohammed and Mohan to support his explosive ordnance disposal (EOD) unit. Paul and Kevin had prepped the vehicle, Justin was the driver, and Kevin was up in the hatch on the light machine gun. With our Humvee and armored ambulance, driven by Bradley, we followed the column. Paul was gone by this time, but the rest of our team included Ephraim, Slowly, Silver Horn, Sky, Zau Seng, Shaheen, and Dlo. We also had been joined by Ephraim's brother, Zeb, who normally worked for an NGO in India but had come to Iraq trying to help out in the refugee camps. The team split up between our vehicles and I joined General Mustafa, walking at the front until we got about one kilometer from the city's edge.

The buildings in this part of Mosul were mostly two- and three-story houses with flat roofs, the minarets of mosques rising up above the rooflines here and there along with a few bigger structures like hotels, hospitals, and office buildings. The approach to the city's edge was over unpaved roads, open fields, and mostly empty plots of land cleared in preparation for new buildings, with a few scattered houses. The terrain was rolling but with few trees; there was very little cover. In the city ahead, near-constant smoke columns rose from one place or another, from air strikes or artillery. Coalition air was pounding ISIS targets.

As we got closer to the edge of town, the Iraqi BMPs and tanks moved to the front and started engaging ISIS ahead of us. Several suicide cars emerged from the alleys of the city's edge, aiming to disrupt the attack. I moved into the Humvee with Shaheen, which, besides Justin and Kevin, carried Slowly and Sky as medics. We were about two hundred meters back from the front and the lead company and platoon BMPs and tanks.

Colonel Haider was the officer leading the assault and we ended up with him and his battalion. Trying to be in the best place to control the attack, General Mustafa dropped back, which was a change from how he operated in the more wide-open theaters we'd been in previously. He was about seven hundred meters from the edge of the city.

As we rolled behind the Iraqis, Shaheen turned to me and said, "You know, I don't hate all these Arabs anymore. I'm actually starting to love them. They are suffering like us and need help." Wow. That was a real change of heart, a softening. He hated them before and stuck with us out of loyalty rather than any great desire to help the Iraqis. This was a transformation. Love was at work in battle-torn Iraq.

We were moving across the open, rolling ground, still outside the city, having just passed a small, blown-up house, when we started to meet fleeing civilians. They were running as fast as they could. Some were injured, some were carrying kids, or old people, or bags. There was

As the fighting entered west Mosul, thousands fled. Musharrifah, May 2017

panic in their faces. I realized: they were getting shot at. Then I heard what they were yelling as they ran: "Sniper! Sniper!"

We stopped, our group and the Iraqi Army, and hastily set up a position using our vehicles to help provide cover so we could get them out of danger and treat the wounded. This terrain was very open and ISIS snipers with long-range rifles were trying to pick them off from elevated positions on the edge of town, about five hundred meters away.

One old man was being carried by his son, going pretty slow as they approached. One soldier jumped out of his vehicle, ran to them and grabbed the old man, sliding him over onto his own back and running with him back to the vehicles. The old man was unconscious when he got to our ambulances; the soldier gently laid him down and Sky started doing CPR while the man's family hovered anxiously around. Within a minute, he coughed and then sat up.

Meanwhile, more people kept coming, women struggling in long burkas with bulky bags and babies, small children struggling to stay on their feet as they were dragged along by an older sibling, one old lady being pushed in a wheelbarrow. Our team and the soldiers went into full evacuation mode, running back and forth, carrying people and their stuff as they frantically ran for cover.

Up at the front, two hundred meters away, a suicide vehicle burst from one of the clusters of buildings making up the city's blocks, detonated, and a huge ball of fire went up. I ducked behind the berm we were parked behind but thought Colonel Haider, who'd been leading the assault, must be dead. (I later found out he had survived). As the number of fleeing civilians fluctuated, our group moved forward haltingly: helping people, advancing, stopping, helping, advancing.

One family came running toward us, two men, an older woman, and a younger woman with a newborn baby in her arms. Just as they got to us, the young mother went down, hit by a sniper's bullet. Sky and I ran over to her, ducking behind the berm the family just reached and tried CPR, but it was no use. She was dead. Her husband collapsed in sobs, and I held him, crying too, rocking him in his grief. We put her on a stretcher and carried her body back to our vehicles, her mourning family following us.

The lead line of armor was pushing ISIS back, and as they did, more people escaped. This was good until ISIS launched a counterattack.

Now it was not only all-out war, it was all-out war on a battlefield full of men, women, and children just trying to get away.

The Iraqi Army started to take casualties. As they began sending back wounded men, we stopped and set up a temporary CCP. We were at the top of a little rise next to a blown-up building just before the dirt road we were on dropped into a dip and started getting into the structures on the edge of the city. There was a little cover with the building and the hill, and the Iraqi command post was nearby. Slowly, Silver Horn and Sky worked on patients there, stabilizing them before sending them back to the rear CCP.

We were using our Humvee to drive into the dip to help evacuate the casualties as they exited the city and were coming under heavy ISIS fire each time. All who could shoot did so and we had to fight our way out of every evacuation. The Humvee was getting hammered—we later counted more than one hundred hits. Our engine began leaking transmission fluid, brake fluid, and coolant as the rounds took their toll. At one point, we were working on seven wounded soldiers when another one came running up the hill, yelling, "There's a family down there! They're shooting a family! They're attacking a family!"

Justin was gone, driving patients to the rear, so I grabbed Mohammed, who was standing nearby. "Mohammed, you drive, we gotta go help those people!" I climbed in the front of our Humvee, Kevin was still up on the gun and Sky and Slowly jumped in the back with Shaheen. Another Humvee loaded up with Iraqis and we drove down together. Once we got there, we could see the dad was down on the ground not going anywhere and it looked like he'd been shot in the leg. The mom was frantic, and there were two scared little girls, and a couple of boys. The Iraqis quickly loaded the mom, boys, and one of the girls into their Humvee and took off.

I jumped out at the same time, headed for the dad. Suddenly, the little girl started screaming. I looked and where her eye had been was now a bloody hole. A bullet had gone through her head and angled out her eye, but somehow, she was still alive. I grabbed her and handed her to Sky in the Humvee. He and Slowly immediately started to work on her while Kevin continued to fire away at ISIS from the turret. I scooped up the father, and as I did so, his whole body jerked, and he let out a moan. He'd been hit again.

I jammed him in the Humvee on top of Sky and jumped in the front. "Go! Go! Go!" I shouted at Mohammed, and he gunned it.

The Humvee lurched a little but didn't move. "Go!" I yelled. "We gotta get outta here!" Mohammed gave it more gas and the engine roared, but it wouldn't move. He jammed it into reverse and it still didn't go anywhere.

"I think broken," he said, looking at me, eyes wide. The intensifying ISIS fire had managed to complete the destruction of our transmission in just the two minutes we were there. ISIS bullets were peppering us, and I knew we wouldn't survive here long before they sent an RPG or something worse our way.

I got on the radio with Ephraim, who was up with the ambulances. "We need a Humvee down here now! We've got two badly wounded, and we're gonna have dead people in a minute if we don't get outta here! Get Mustafa to send a tank down to cover us and a Humvee to pull us out!" Ephraim was calm but urgent on the radio and said he would do his best.

In the back, the little girl was screaming as Sky held her down and Slowly bandaged her face; the bullet had entered near her temple and exited out her eye. A couple Iraqi BMPs flew by us, meeting ISIS's counterattack, but none of them knew we were in trouble. I yelled again into the radio. "Send a tank now, we have two badly wounded who will die!"

"We're working on it," came Ephraim's calm voice. "Should be just a minute."

Mohammed looked at me. "I go get help," he said.

"No, Mohammed, you'll get killed. I'm on the radio working on it." The door opened, and he was out as I lunged to grab him. The Humvee was too wide for me to reach him, and he was gone, running up the little hill we'd just come down. I slid over into the driver's seat and started trying to make it move. I worked through all the gears and got it to lurch a little up the hill, but then it lost power and slid back down as ISIS fire continued.

The girl was thrashing and moaning as Sky and Slowly worked on her. The father, right behind me, was spasmodically kicking me in the back of the head. Then, driving down the hill came Mohammed, back in another Humvee. He swung around to our right and parked next to us so that he'd be covered from the fire, which was coming mostly from our left. Shaheen and Slowly both jumped out to start transferring the patients from that side.

Instantly, Slowly was hit by three bullets that smashed into his webbing, one grazing his stomach, the other two ricocheting off the top of a grenade without detonating it. Quick as a cat, he was back in the Humvee. And then I heard Shaheen yell. Even in the middle of all the noise, the crying girl, Kevin's machine gun going nonstop, ISIS fire, I heard him yell, and it sounded like death. He went down, moaning. Mohammed saw it happen and jumped out of his Humvee to help him. What he didn't know was ISIS had circled around and was now shooting from a different angle.

As Mohammed ran to help Shaheen, six bullets went through his body, but he somehow did not go down. He hauled Shaheen off the ground, staggered over to the vehicle with him in his arms and loaded him in. His own blood streamed from his neck, and he put one hand up to stop the flow as he jumped into the driver's seat and took off back up the hill.

At the time, I didn't know Mohammed had been hit, but I knew we were still stuck. I got back on the radio, calling for a tank. Finally, an Abrams rolled down next to us and opened up on all possible ISIS positions. They fired away for a couple minutes and the ISIS fire decreased. Justin, just returned from the ambulance run, saw the situation and together with Hyder, grabbed another Humvee. They drove down to us, jumped out, hooked us up to their vehicle and pulled us out.

After sitting in that spot under fire for that whole time, expecting an RPG to blow us up any second, I felt pretty grateful for the courage of Justin and Hyder in coming to get us. This was not the same Hyder who had jumped out in front of the approaching suicide car near Al Rashidiya in January, but he was just as brave. And Justin was there with him—they became heroes to me that day.

Up at our CCP, we pulled the girl and her father out and finished bandaging their wounds as best we could before loading them into the back of one of our ambulances for evacuation. I found out Mohammed had been shot; he and Shaheen were already gone, evacuated by Bradley to the next CCP. We later heard they both survived initial evacuation and were flown to Baghdad.

It was still morning on the first day of the assault, and I'd already lost two men: Shaheen, who'd been with us since 2015, and Mohammed,

MUSHARRIFAH, WEST MOSUL
FAMILY RESCUE
4 MAY, 2017

36th Brigade
BMPs

CASUALTY
COLLECTION
POINT

H3

⑤

Iraqi
Command

④

HILL CREST

① ISIS SNIPERS
SHOOT CIVILIANS
FLEEING TOWARD
IRAQI ARMY

LOWGROUND
KILLZONE

ISIS
SNIPERS

③ H2
 H1

② DAVID & TEAM
DRIVE HUMVEE (H1)
DOWN INTO CITY TO
RESCUE WOUNDED FAMILY.
H1 IS DISABED BY ISIS GUNFIRE

②

①

ISIS
SNIPERS

③ MOHAMMED RUNS UPHILL UNDER FIRE & RETURNS
WITH A 2ND HUMVEE (H2). SHAHEEN EXITS H1 TO
TRANSPORT WOUNDED, BUT IS SHOT IN THE STOMACH.
MOHAMMED IS SHOT SIX TIMES HELPING SHAHEEN INTO H2

④ MOHAMMED EVACS HIMSELF AND SHAHEEN IN H2 TO CCP

N
▲

⑤ HYDER AND JUSTIN DRIVE A THIRD HUMVEE AND TOW H1
BACK UP THE HILL. THE TEAM RESCUES A GIRL & HER FATHER

50 METERS

Silver Horn, Slowly, Sky, and Ephraim work hard to save Aisha's life after we were pulled out of the kill zone where Shaheen and Mohammed were shot, May 4, 2017.

the new believer, who proclaimed, "We will die together." I prayed they would live, as well as all of us.

But we couldn't stop. Nothing was stopping, and the casualties kept coming. That day, we saw at least thirty casualties from the Iraqi Army and that many more civilians. Silver Horn, Slowly, Sky, Ephraim, Bradley, Justin, Kevin, Dlo, Zeb, and I were treating and evacuating people constantly.

That first day, the Iraqi Army managed to push about four hundred meters into the city. Then, right at nightfall, ISIS pushed them three hundred meters back to the first line of buildings. That's where we found ourselves as the night lull came, in one of those buildings right on the edge of the city. There were a lot of gaps all around us, but the Iraqis had some BMPs holding a line in front of our position. Still, it was a pretty vulnerable spot.

Some of the Iraqis were heading back to Mustafa's location, where they'd set up a headquarters and strongpoint. They suggested we go back with them and return to this position in the morning. It seemed to make sense, but then I realized that if we left there would be no medics here.

Our team after the rescue of Aisha and her father–Justin, Kevin, Sky, Ephraim, Slowly, Silver Horn, myself, Zau Seng, and Dlo, May 4, 2017.

I prayed and felt we needed to stay. I said to the Iraqi officer leaving, "There's no medic here. This is a dangerous place and we should stay with the soldiers. Sir, I'd like to stay. Is that okay?"

He shrugged and said it was fine. I made an announcement to the team: "Hey guys, we're staying here tonight," and went back behind the house to where our armored ambulance was parked to work on emails. The vehicles often were my best office because I could have quiet and charge my laptop. A lot had happened today and I wanted to make a report.

After about an hour, I went back to our house, where ISIS fire was intensifying. Some of our team weren't very happy about staying there.

"Dave, this isn't a tactically sound position. We're under pretty serious threat here. We can just come back tomorrow—what good is it if we're all killed here?"

"This isn't a wise decision. The Iraqis haven't picked a wise place to make a stand."

I looked around the group. "What do you all think? Does everyone agree?" Everyone agreed that this wasn't a great position. I agreed too; this was not a good situation.

I said, "Okay. Let's pray about it," and I prayed. I opened my eyes and looked at them. "I still feel the same. You can't run if the people can't run. These soldiers can't leave, and we're here to help them. They have no medics but us." Those were the main reasons, standing with the people and living by our motto, but there were some practical ones too, and I listed those: "Also, it's dark now. It's the wrong time to be moving around. You could be shot by the Iraqis or ISIS, or the Americans. And the Iraqis have BMPs right down there in front of us for security."

I added, "But tomorrow you can go if you want. You have freedom. But not as part of the Free Burma Rangers. We don't leave people if they can't leave, unless God tells us." These were brave men and professionals who would each save my life and others' lives and I did not doubt their courage. It was just a different situation and relationship than they had experienced before. We prayed again and I still felt we should stay. There were seven of us there—besides me, there was Kevin, Justin, Sky, Ephraim, Slowly, and Silver Horn.

Everyone nodded their heads and said, "Okay, let's do it," and they moved to the building we would strongpoint. When they saw the BMPs for themselves and realized the Iraqis had actually created a defensive position and they weren't as exposed as they thought, the feeling switched, and they were in. I was grateful to have these men on our team. They made us stronger and more capable and I appreciated their commitment all the way with us.

We fortified the building where it had been half blown up and set up the night watch schedule. I moved to the back room to sleep, thinking, *Well, I'll wake up when an RPG slams into here.* I hadn't slept much lately, so I actually had a great sleep that night.

The next morning, I went to where Colonel Haider, the battalion commander, had slept, to see what the day's plan was. He came up to me and hugged me. He said, "You stayed with us. That means a lot. You know, I haven't really slept in two weeks and last night you were with us, I could sleep. I feel like, sometimes, we Iraqi soldiers are trash. We're not worth anything. The world does not care about us. But because you stayed with us, it means we count. And I slept for the first time." Tears rolled down his face.

Now I teared up. "I slept too!" I said. Then I hugged him. "We'll never leave you. We love you. We're with you in this till the end."

I walked back to our house feeling closer than ever to the Iraqis. Even before I entered the blown-up room where the team had stayed, I could tell something was up. There was no banter, only quiet, urgent tones. As I walked into the half-lit dimness, I saw Dlo sitting hunched on the floor, sobbing. Justin sat next to him, also crying. Sky stood by, serious and silent. Dlo looked up. "Shaheen is dead," he said in a quivering voice. I took a deep breath. That was bad. I wanted to feel it, but I also felt I had to make sure the team held together.

"We need to confirm this," I said. "And we've got a job to do here. No one send anything out, no one post anything."

Rumors were rampant, but it was also very likely that Shaheen could be dead. I had Dlo call a doctor in the hospital where Shaheen was being treated. Dlo's whole face lit up as he found out he was still alive. The report had been false. I was even able to talk to him. He sounded good, and I felt good: our team was still whole—and those who were here were elated. It felt like Shaheen's life had been given back to us.

We could work undistracted, which was needed. There was more fighting, more people fleeing. The team continued treating the wounded. Those who escaped all had stories—lost family members, injured people left behind. One couple came out and we thought the guy might be ISIS. The wife was badly burned, her face nearly unrecognizable. Their building was hit by an air strike the day before. "Our daughter is still alive back there. She's trapped in the building. Please, please—can you find her?"

By then we were in the city, in the maze of streets and buildings and rubble. They were talking about us finding one destroyed building in blocks of them. Colonel Arkan said, "Okay, we'll try." He got some directions, then took his vehicle, with five other guys and me all jammed in, to see if we could find this building and the trapped girl. We went street by street, windows open, even as bullets sometimes pinged off the Humvee. *Wow,* I thought, as I had so many times before. *These guys are brave!* We were driving right into an ISIS-occupied part of town, without much recon, to find a little girl.

We drove through an abandoned area, trying to stay out of sight of known ISIS strongpoints. I looked up and saw an ISIS flag waving above us.

Finally, we went down a muddy little hill, past a vacant lot, and there was a collapsed building that looked like what the parents described.

In the back of the building, removed from the street and against the walls of the neighboring buildings—which had probably helped shelter her from ISIS fire—was the girl. She was alive, with one leg pinned under the rubble. When the air strike hit this building, the concrete came down in chunks, many too massive to move by hand. Getting her out would take careful planning and we'd need special tools to break up the concrete she was under.

Suddenly ISIS realized we were there and began expressing their displeasure; soon bullets were everywhere. Concrete chunks flew off the wall and hit me in the face, but no bullets. We pell-melled it over the chunks of debris back toward the Humvee. When I got to cover, I turned and shot back. Colonel Arkan was there, laughing at my running form. "Man, they couldn't hit you because your head wobbles so much. You look like a wounded animal running!" I was still healing from a torn hamstring and foot injury, so wounded animal was my style.

We jumped in the Humvee and barreled out of there, bullets bouncing off the back. I prayed the girl would survive one more night. Back at our position, General Kasem showed up and, with the general staff, made a rescue plan. They flew a team of firemen up from Baghdad with extraction equipment. Those guys weren't soldiers at all, big, fat guys—but they were dedicated to saving people regardless of the risk to themselves.

Our FBR team's plan was for Ephraim, Kevin, and Justin to set up in a position from which they could overwatch the rescue while Bradley, Sky, Dlo, Slowly, and Silver Horn prepared to reinforce us and take care of casualties.

The next day, May 6, we rolled back in, this time with three BMPs and three Humvees. Colonel Arkan was leading the mission. From FBR, I went and brought Zau Seng to film. We drove right into ISIS; our vehicles started getting shot up right away. ISIS had erected more blocks in the streets, which meant we had to find a new approach. Once there, the three BMPs anchored the corners of the block while the three Humvees screened the firemen while they worked.

Soon, all the vehicles were shooting back at ISIS as they fired on us from three sides. The soldiers fought them off while we lugged the extraction equipment over the rubble to where the girl was trapped in the back corner of the house. We formed a cordon around the corner where the firemen would be working, taking up positions behind debris from which we could defend the building. The firemen started cutting into the collapsed concrete roof under which the girl was pinned, breaking the big chunks into smaller, movable pieces.

I realized no one was defending the firemen, who were working on top of the rubble and a little higher than the surrounding debris field. If ISIS got a bead on them, they'd be totally exposed. I thought maybe I should get up there. But then I'd be pretty exposed. Then John 15:13 came to me, as it had before: "Greater love has no one than this: to lay down one's life for one's friends."

I ran out and laid low in the rubble next to them, looking out while they worked away with their backs to the danger. No, this wasn't a great position. One of the Iraqis yelled at me, "No, no, no, go back! American, get back, you're gonna die!" I compromised and moved off a little to one side, so I still had a good line of sight but was behind a bit of concrete.

I looked for targets but didn't want to shoot until I had to, so as not to draw attention to the men cutting the girl out. She was stuck in the back corner of the house, right up against the neighboring buildings and away from the street. This position must have saved her thus far from ISIS; it was also protecting the firemen. There was shooting all around us, but nothing came into this corner. After a few minutes of drilling, they freed her.

Firefighters from Baghdad and soldiers from the 36th Brigade free Rahab from where she was pinned for two days, Musharrifah, May 6, 2017

Colonel Arkan and the firemen lifted her out, her face twisted in pain, and carried her to their Humvee. I said a prayer of thanks—and we started taking more fire. We shot back as everyone safely arrived at the vehicles. Then the firemen started back toward me. *You've gotta be kidding me,* I thought. They weren't going to leave their tools for ISIS and were coming back for an air compressor, generator, and random cutting tools as ISIS fired down on us. I stepped out to help carry the generator, and we all ran back together, piling into the Humvees.

I was in the back Humvee as we pulled out, threading our way through the rubble. ISIS had moved in behind us and had taken the road we came in on. We turned down a different street with a berm across it we had to get over. The Humvee floundered on our first attempt, rolling back down to the street. Uh-oh. "Please, Lord, help us get out of here," I prayed. We were taking more rounds as we again started up then rolled back down the berm. If we got stuck here, we'd be in a tight spot, with ISIS right behind us.

For a third time, the driver gunned it and threw the heavy Humvee at the berm—and we were across. Suddenly, all the tension drained out of me, and I was filled with elation, surprise, and relief. Thank God, we were alive. And we had helped to save someone else's life—someone who would surely have died without help. I was so thankful. The previous two days—just the first two days of this battle!—had already been full of loss and pain, but here was a life snatched out of it. I was filled with joy and gratitude.

Once back at our position, Silver Horn and Slowly worked on the girl. Her leg had been crushed by the fallen concrete, but otherwise, she was okay. I thanked God again. After initial treatment and assessment, we loaded her into our ambulance and drove her to a field hospital in the rear. I wanted to spend more time with this survivor, so I rode with her to the CCP. I held her hand and talked to her while Faiz translated. "My name is Rahab," she said. "I am seventeen, and God sustained me throughout the time I was trapped. Thank you for helping me. I love you. If you have another daughter, please name her after me." She wasn't shy! She spoke with confidence and smiled up at me sweetly.

I laughed and said, "You are a tough lady! Yes, I will do that, if we have another daughter. I am your friend forever. I love you too and will help you in any way I can."

At the division CCP, the Iraqi medical staff, led by Major Muhammad, who was Major Naseem's counterpart, took excellent care of her, and I stayed until she was evacuated again an hour later.

That was a small spot of light in a lot of darkness. Every day we were taking care of casualties as the Iraqis pushed through Musharrifah toward the old city of Mosul. I missed Shaheen but was able to talk to him every few days. He said, "Don't worry about me, I'm getting better. And don't let the hospital cheat you with my bill!" He texted me some photos of himself, first on oxygen, then off, smiling and giving a thumbs up. Mohammed was there with him, in a neck brace, also doing well, which was hard to believe when I heard he was shot six times.

I talked to Shaheen on May 13, and he said, "You know, God, Jesus, and the angels saved me. I'm coming back to you guys soon." While I doubted he would be back soon, the knowledge that they were both alive gave me peace—our little team was still intact.

The next day, May 14th, someone called Dlo with another report that Shaheen had died. This time, we didn't believe it. He had been posting on Facebook just a few hours before. There had already been one false report, and we had our defenses up. We kept working while Dlo called around. Finally, it was confirmed, but it seemed surreal, and it was hard for us to take it in. He had been recovering and seemed stable, but suddenly got a blood infection that very quickly went septic and he died soon after. It was a deep loss, and I felt a sad resignation.

CHAPTER SEVENTEEN

A Walk on the Wild Side

"I wish no connection with any ship that does not sail fast for I intend to go into harm's way."

—JOHN PAUL JONES, AMERICAN NAVY
COMMANDER IN THE REVOLUTIONARY WAR

It wouldn't do any good to change our operational plan. We were going to stay in the city, stay in the fight, and keep doing what we were doing. I got some pushback from the team. Some wanted to go see Shaheen's family, or go to his funeral, but I was adamant. Lots of men were dying, and their friends and commanders couldn't—and weren't—leaving to mourn with every casualty. I saw us in the same position. As long as we could help people, we weren't leaving the city.

I had one variable: Syria. Last time we were there, I had promised Bashir we would come back in May. Now it was May, and we weren't there. No one had known how long this fight would drag on, but we were still in the thick of it. I was in touch with Bashir about this, and I didn't want to break a promise.

That's one thing I try never to do: break a promise. It's not just a prideful point-of-honor thing; it's how I feel we're called to be in this world—true. God is true and unchanging, and we're called to be like Him. If you only keep your word when it's easy or convenient, no one will count on you for anything, and ultimately, you're only living for yourself.

Anyway, I had promised Bashir we'd come to Syria in May, but I was hoping he'd let me out of it. I told him the battle was raging here, and we were useful, but if he needed us, I'd find a way to keep my promise. He said, no, don't worry about it, stay there and come to

Syria later. But I didn't want it to be a frivolous change, so I told him to pray about it again.

The next day, the day after Shaheen's death, I was up on the roof of a house under direct fire. Every time I poked above the wall on the roof, ISIS shot at me, but I couldn't get a signal down below. So I tucked myself in a corner against the wall with my phone lifted to hit the one spot where I could get a bar of service and not get shot at. I was checking email, and Bashir called me. I answered: "What did God tell you?"

"Well," he said. "God gave me a dream. In my dream, I was walking down this long wide street. And I saw many trees and flowers and it was very beautiful. There were birds in the trees, singing. And as I walked down the lane, the birds turned to me and said, 'Mosul. Go to Mosul.' So, Dave, you stay in Mosul. It's okay." I thanked God and thanked Bashir. We would stay.

The 36th finally established themselves in the city. We had co-located with the 3rd Battalion, Lieutenant Colonel Feras's men, where they set up right on the edge of Musharrifah. We got ourselves a house near his command post, abandoned by its owners, and cleaned it out. We hauled water over from other buildings, as there was no running water, and made a defensive position. It was really a nice house, with beautiful paintings inside and unusual murals on the wall in the yard. Lieutenant Colonel Feras was a great guy to be teamed up with. We had only been working together closely since we entered Mosul—only ten days, but it seemed longer!—and I loved him.

One night, we were hit pretty hard by an ISIS counterattack. We were all standing outside near the river as the sun set, and Lieutenant Colonel Feras, in his T-shirt, no armor, no helmet, had gotten behind a Humvee and started firing back with his M-4. ISIS was firing at him with machine guns, but he let them have it. He was a joker, a roly-poly, always-smiling guy who made us laugh all the time, but always stepped up when things got serious.

He spoke English and German, had visited the U.S. and was trained in Germany. He talked about his daughter, who lived in Baghdad, all the time. He told me about how, when he was not deployed, she always brought him the paper and snacks when he got home from work every day. Now that he was in the battle, they talked on the phone daily; they were very close.

Love begets love, and I saw and felt it living with the Iraqis day in and day out. As I saw Feras's love for his daughter, I loved him more—and I loved her, whom I had never met. The same happened with other soldiers—Mohan would call his family, get his kids on the phone, then put me on the phone with them. And I loved him more for it. I think this same love helped them, helped us all, risk everything for people we didn't know who were running away, and also sustained us through the seemingly relentless tragedy of what we saw.

I talked to Bashir on May15, the day after Shaheen died, and when I got off the phone, I was happy that I wouldn't have to say goodbye to these guys and head off to Syria. We were with Feras at a forward position and had been receiving fleeing families all day. They would finally reach us after sneaking through the streets to avoid ISIS, and we would help guide them to safety, treating the wounded, and evacuating them farther from the fighting.

This continued into the night. One family of five tried to escape, and all were shot; one girl died, and everyone else was wounded. A nine-year-old girl was hit in the stomach and her intestines were spilling out. The mom had a broken leg, and another man had a broken pelvis after being hit three times. We worked frantically to save them, with Slowly and Silver Horn doing the main medical care while Justin evacuated them through the perilous labyrinth of Mosul's half-destroyed neighborhoods.

Lieutenant Colonel Feras and his men defended this position and supported the evacuations. It was sad and dangerous work, but I felt, as I had many times, it was reservoirs of love sustaining us; this is God's love as we experience it in his gifts of relationship.

By now, the Iraqis had taken Musharrifah, and their next advance would be into a neighborhood known as Tammuz 17. ISIS was solidly entrenched here—this was one of the first places they had occupied three years earlier when they took Mosul, and it would be the last place they would leave. They were positioned to fire down the streets the Iraqis needed to across.

The day after helping the shot-up family was the day of the advance. The Iraqis attempted to cover their movement with cannons and machine-gun fire back at the ISIS positions. As the covering fire was laid down, the soldiers sprinted across the street one by one. Lieutenant

Colonel Feras's unit was the first to go. They got across a side street, and it was harrowing, but they managed without losing a man.

They started across the main road. ISIS fired them up right away, and they took immediate casualties. Feras called off the advance, yelling at them to retreat. At the same time, he ran out, firing up the street to cover his men as they ran back. I saw him up ahead of me, saw him run out and start shooting up the street, trying to protect his men. I was running toward him when he was hit. Right in front of me, his body gave a giant lurch, and he fell to the ground.

I ran up to him. The bullet went in his left shoulder and came out right behind his right shoulder—passed all the way through his chest. He was dead. ISIS was still firing, and some of his men started firing back to give cover as I grabbed him by his clothes and started dragging him back. He was heavy, over 250 pounds, and soon others ran out to help. Once we were out of the line of fire, I went to work; I had to try. I packed his wounds then tried CPR for a few minutes, but he was gone.

Tears rolled down my face. The loss of this laughing, jolly, brave, and selfless man, trying to save his men in the middle of this slaughter—and right in front me—it was terrible. We put him in the ambulance and it took off to the CCP. What would happen with his daughter when she found out, I wondered. With great sorrow welling up within me, I stood there in the street, watching the battered ambulance rattle off, and wiped away my tears. He was gone, but the battle raged on.

The 2nd Battalion was chosen to make the next attempt to cross the road to Tammuz 17, so we joined them to give medical support. The lead platoon was commanded by Lieutenant Hussein. I hadn't spent a lot of time with him yet but knew he was a good guy and spoke English well. I went up to talk to him that morning. He called me his uncle and asked me, "Why do you risk your life to help us?"

"God sent us, and we are with you as a family. We will take a walk on the wild side with you," I replied.

"What does that mean, 'walk on the wild side'?" he asked.

I smiled and replied, "It means we do not know what will happen! But we will walk on the wild side with Jesus. Can we pray?"

"Yes," Hussein said.

We prayed together, and I felt a peace come over me and Hussein smiled and said, "Let's go."

For three days, we were with Hussein and the 2nd Battalion, trying to cross that main road to Tammuz 17, and we were losing people all the time. The fighting was brutal, and with every street we took, we found more civilians. They poured out from hiding—big groups who had been huddled silently in a single room or hunkered down in secret underground holes. As the Iraqis liberated their street, the people somehow got the message and opened their hiding places. They came out cautiously, fearfully, at first, then hurrying, thanking us, old ladies and men, kissing us, passing babies to us to make sure they escaped safely, and then rushing on to get well and truly out. We all knew ISIS's ability to turn the tables quickly.

By the third day with the 2nd Battalion, we had cleared the side roads opposite Tammuz 17, and it was time to launch across the main road. Zau, Silver Horn, and I loaded into a BMP with Lieutenant Hussein. It felt like D-Day as our assaulting vehicles, with us buttoned up inside, lurched across the wide main street under heavy fire. Our BMP made it to the other side, the machine gun firing at ISIS the whole time.

At first, we couldn't get the back hatches open and, with RPGs screaming by, I thought for a minute we could all be stuck in a great,

Peter with General Walid and Lt. Col. Feras in West Mosul, 2017.

burning coffin as soon as one hit us. Then the hatch popped up and we all spilled out, sprinting for cover in the nearest buildings.

Bullets flew around us, and we shot back and forth for about thirty minutes before we were able to suppress ISIS enough to move at all. Then the civilians began coming out of the houses, fleeing. It seemed a little preemptive to me: we were still taking lots of fire from ISIS. But we ran out to help guide them out of the kill zone. One old guy wearing white and moving on crutches was going pretty slow; I picked him up and carried him to safety.

Later I found out someone had recognized him and told the Iraqis, "You better check that guy. He's an ISIS sniper." Sure enough, the Iraqis pulled out his cell phone and found pictures to prove it. I heard he was executed on the spot. I had risked my life to save him, but it didn't really bother me. We were just doing our best, and that's all we could do.

We had breached Tammuz 17, though at great cost. The neighborhood was full of "rat holes," and ISIS could go for miles through these holes without ever going into the street. We started barricading those and clearing the houses we could in our immediate area. It was getting dark, and we wanted to at least have a secure place to sleep. We didn't relish the idea of ISIS crawling back through one of their holes in the middle of the night.

The next day, the Iraqis began methodically clearing the buildings, starting at the toehold gained the previous day. We followed, ready to treat and evacuate the wounded. There were still many ISIS hiding, and sometimes the soldiers would start on a building and find two ISIS in one room and one in another, and then it'd be room-to-room fighting.

I was praying the whole time, *What should I do?* I wanted to lead these assaults; I was trained for it. Plus, I was an American, and Americans grow up throwing things—I could throw a grenade through a door without missing, I was pretty sure of that.

With the Iraqis, this sometimes became an issue. It would have been comical if it wasn't deadly. Following a clearing team, I'd hear, "Don't forget to pull the pin," as they prepped a grenade for the next room. Then they'd would pull the pin but toss the grenade into the doorframe by accident. It'd bounce around for a second or two before one of them kicked it into the next room, hopefully before it blew us all up.

As I prayed, I knew my job: stay in the back. Take care of the wounded, pray, be moral support any way I could, and if I had to, fight. But my job wasn't to take the lead in it.

Also, as the leader of FBR, like any organization, I am responsible for a lot of administration, and I answer many emails each day. Mosul did not change this, and I had to keep up with emails and the operations of then over seventy teams in Burma. Sometimes, I'd be crouched down in the corner of a room with my phone, reading and answering emails while the Iraqis cleared the next room. I'd be replying to something from a team in Kachin State and look up when I heard the big boom. Then I'd go back to the work of an admin ranger.

That went on until May 18, as we slowly pushed through Tammuz 17. That day, Silver Horn and Slowly left for Erbil to meet Karen, the kids, Eliya, and Hosie, who were all arriving from Thailand on the 20th. Silver Horn and Slowly were rotating out and going back to Thailand. Sky and Dlo were the drivers back to Erbil, so for the next two days or so, I was without a main medic. Our plan was the same: stay at the rear of the assault element and provide basic medical and evacuation support in case they took casualties or for any civilians we met. Silver Horn and Slowly left on the resupply BMP Justin rode in on. For the next couple of days, we would be just three: Justin, Zau Seng, and me.

After they left, it was a day like the others: constant noise, firing, short dashes over rubble between cover points, tense house clearings and firefights with ISIS as we progressed. One Iraqi soldier was shot in the face as he tried to enter the small driveway of a house that needed cleared. He lay in the open, his life ebbing away as his buddies tried to fight ISIS off and rescue him. The ensuing fight took an hour, and by then, he was dead. His friends carried him into the street, weeping.

In the late afternoon, our advance was halted by heavy ISIS fire up the next street, and there was a lull in the fighting where we were as we tried to get more air support. We strongpointed two houses, posting security on two three-way intersections that anchored both ends of our street. We thought our left flank was being secured by a sister unit we'd been in radio contact with. But in the labyrinth of Mosul, they confused one block with another and so, although we didn't know it, there was actually no one on that flank except ISIS.

Lieutenant Hussein and I were in the street near a wall and the remnants of a blown-up car. Most of the men were inside the house compounds behind us. It was a rare quiet moment, and Lieutenant Hussein sat down on the curb. Now it seemed too quiet. I had a bad feeling about us relaxing in the street. I sat down next to him, getting ready to suggest,

"Maybe we should get off the street." Before I got the words out, our world erupted in a blast of gunshots at close range.

From around the corner, three ISIS fighters came, AKs up, looking down the sight plane of their weapons and shooting rapidly. They advanced to seven meters, firing constantly. One of them shouted "Allahu akbar!" ("God is great"), grinning as he fired. It was like slow motion, except it was happening in milliseconds: I can remember the eruption of gunshots and as I looked up, I could see each of their faces as they came toward me, their weapons at their shoulders, professional and determined as they fired, intent on killing us.

Bullets hit Hussein and the ground around us. I had been sitting, with my weapon on safe resting between my feet. A very bad ranger. I said, "God help me," fully expecting to die. But I was still alive, and in one motion, I pulled my gun up, pushed off the safety, got on one knee, and started returning fire. I felt an impact in my left forearm, and it knocked my left hand from the AK. I put it back on the gun, thinking, *That was a wallop. I hope my arm is okay, but I can still use it so it must not be too bad.*

I first shot the man in the middle, who was smiling, knocking the gun out of his hands and hitting him multiple times. He staggered back and limped around the corner. I pivoted as the man on the right ducked behind the car between us. I saw him through the front and back windows and shot through the windows, hitting him in the chest. He went down. I spun back left, surprised I was still alive.

The last ISIS man standing had advanced to four and a half meters from us, shooting at Hussein and me the whole time. He hit Hussein again but missed me with every shot. I fired at him, and he fell back and ran back around the corner. I knew there might be more ISIS around the corner, so I pulled out a grenade and tossed it in that direction. As the grenade went off, the volume of ISIS fire reduced.

I pulled out another grenade and threw it. Hussein was lying on his back, a pool of blood spreading under him. He was saying over and over, "Don't leave me. Don't leave me. Uncle, please don't leave me."

Shooting continuously and under fire, I was shouting even though he was right next to me. "I'm not gonna leave you, but I can't help you until I push ISIS back." I threw another grenade and started yelling for help. "Somebody come out and help! I need help!"

Tammuz 17, where ISIS shot me and Lt. Hussein on May 18th. A bloodstain from Lt. Hussein is on the ground in front of me, May 21, 2017.

When the shooting started, the guys in the compound couldn't see what was happening. The most likely thing was a suicide vehicle, and there was no valor in running out to face one of those, so most of them hunkered down behind the wall. But when he heard me yell, Justin came running with Zau Seng following. That was no small act of bravery. They didn't know what was out there except death, but they came anyway.

Justin helped me drag Hussein back to cover as Zau fired down the street. Two Iraqi soldiers also leaned out from an opening in the wall and returned fire. Both were hit. In the driveway of the house where we dragged him, I started treating Hussein's wounds. That assault was just the beginning of an ISIS counterattack, and soon all of Hussein's men were back out in the street trying to hold off ISIS. Justin provided security at a rat hole connecting our house with the next one.

I prayed and tried to stop Hussein's bleeding. He'd taken three shots in his chest, two in his left arm, and one in his left leg. I was stuffing gauze into the holes and telling him, "Stay alive, keep stayin' alive, don't give up. In Jesus's name, live!" As I treated him, I asked the Iraqis to

ISIS ASSAULT: TAMMUZ 17
18 MAY, 2017

Abandoned houses

    ①

⑥   ③   ①

Sidewalk   Wall

DAVID

① THREE ISIS ASSAULT AROUND CORNER.
   LT. HUSSEIN IS SHOT SIX TIMES, DAVID ONCE

HUSSEIN   ②

② DAVID RETURNS FIRE THROUGH VEHICLE,
   KILLING ONE ISIS & MORTALLY WOUNDING TWO

③ TWO WOUNDED ISIS TURN & RETREAT

Rathole

④ DAVID, JUSTIN & ZAU SENG   ④
   DRAG HUSSEIN TO COVER, SECURE
   HOUSE & TREAT HUSSEIN

ZAU SENG   JUSTIN

⑤ HUSSEIN'S SQUAD PROVIDES
   COVER FIRE AS BMP FIGHTS
   ITS WAY TO SQUAD

⑤

⑥ BMP ARRIVES AFTER 30 MINUTES
   & EVACUATES HUSSEIN & TWO
   WOUNDED IRAQI ARMY SOLDIERS

Road

radio for a BMP and Sergeant Saad, a barrel-chested and very brave man, made the call. After about thirty minutes, an Iraqi BMP fought its way to us, and we loaded Hussein into it along with the two other wounded soldiers.

I knew I was bleeding; I'd been hit in my left arm, but as I looked at it, I realized it was not very bad and Justin bandaged me up for the time being. The fighting slowed but didn't stop. The unit had lost its leader, but Sergeant Saad took command as we realized our whole left flank was exposed.

To get to a position with more cover, we climbed precariously up and over a nearby building using rebar poking out the side to scale the three floors and traverse to another building. I'm sure we looked like heavily laden beetles crawling up that wall, but we did not want ISIS to know where we would end up that night as they clearly knew where we'd been.

We worked our way up through more rubble and made a strongpoint on the roof of another three-story building that had no easy approach. We barricaded the concrete stairwell with furniture and made a perimeter on the roof, careful not to be seen above the parapet. We took turns pulling security. I rebandaged my wound and started taking antibiotics right away.

I called Karen that night, let her know what happened, and sent out a quick email to my close friends and team to let everyone know I was okay. That was probably a mistake because people posted things right away, and I spent the next day, when we weren't fighting, trying to assure people my injury was minor. With Karen's help, and our media team, we worked out a low-key message that gave out the general story but not many details.

In the morning, we cautiously made our way off the building and back down onto the street. We ran a gauntlet of ISIS snipers as we pushed back to the location of the previous day's attack. Sergeant Saad and his soldiers in the lead killed two more ISIS in the street. At the end of a long block just past where we'd been yesterday, we stopped at a large house on the corner and strongpointed it.

We radioed our position and were told we had hit the limit of the advance. This time, the units on our left and right were on target, and we linked up, forming a cordon at the end of Tammuz 17. This brought us to the edge of Hawi Kanisa (which means "place of churches"), a formerly Christian neighborhood now empty of its Christian inhabitants, that formed a green belt running along the Tigris River.

ISIS was still around us, and bullets struck our building all day. To our right (south), ISIS controlled buildings, and the Iraqis called in air strikes to neutralize them. Iraqi helicopters joined in the fray, firing rockets with a deafening roar. Iraqi artillery fired missiles and we could see them clearly, very close to us as they rose to their apex then whistled in, exploding with tremendous blasts of shattered steel, concrete, and glass. Our building was showered with shrapnel and rocked by the explosions, but all the firepower prevented ISIS from taking our position.

The next day, a BMP came up to us with more food and ammo and out jumped Ephraim, a welcome sight and reinforcement. He had come back from Erbil with my family and our Burma team who had just flown in. We caught him up on what had happened, and he immediately slotted himself into the defense of our position.

The following day, I went back to meet the rest of our team, who were at the nice house at the edge of Musharrifah, and had a joyful reunion with Karen and the kids. Eliya, Monkey, Toh, Hosie, Zeb, and Noelle had just arrived too, and it was a big party as the Karen cooked and I took a proper dip bath. It was pure joy to see Karen and the kids. Pure joy, but also heaviness. In a way, much had changed since I'd last seen them, only a few weeks ago.

We had seen a lot of death in those short weeks. I had lost Iraqi Army friends. And we had lost one of our own, Shaheen. As I left the frenzy of battle, the absence of Shaheen opened up in me a big hollow place. I had time and space to feel it for the first time. So, we were happy to see each other, but sad, too. I had just come from the heat of a battle, and they were just getting ready to go into it. They wouldn't be in the front with me, of course—I didn't know exactly how it would work when we went back out there. But I prayed. I prayed that they would be ready for whatever this next phase looked like—and that I would too.

CHAPTER EIGHTEEN

ISIS Digs In

"Daddy, I don't want you to die."
—Suuzanne Eubank, in Mosul, May 2017

We spent a day back in the house of nice murals in the area of the 36th's 1st Battalion, at the edge of Tammuz 17. Eliya did a good job of cleaning the wound in my arm. Even though I had started antibiotics right after I was shot, I developed a fever because it was getting infected, so it was good to get a thorough cleaning and a new bandage on it. Tim Hayes came right about that time and brought his daughter, Maddie, who was in her junior year of nursing school. She stayed to help, but he went back.

Before he left, I decided to take a quick trip with everyone, back to the front between Tammuz 17 and Hawi Kanisa. We drove down the road where Shaheen was shot, and I showed them the spot where I'd almost died just a few days before. The body of the ISIS attacker I killed was still there in the street; the Iraqis told me they found the bodies of the other two further away.

Hussein's blood still stained the ground behind the shot-up car. Some of his men still occupied the buildings there, and it was good to see them again. They all came out, shook my hand, and invited us in. We sat around the courtyard and drank tea for a while. It was hard to imagine that just a few days earlier, I was nearly killed here.

The 36th was getting ready for the next push, but for the coming few days, they were in a holding phase as their sister unit, the 37th, pushed down through Hawi Kanisa, to our east. We did a few patrols with the 1st battalion through our sector. Then families started coming back to the neighborhood where we were staying. Many of them had been gone just a couple of weeks, having fled only when the fighting came close.

Most of them didn't have much, and their homes had been looted or damaged. We set up a distribution station out of our house, handing out food, water, diapers, baby formula, and providing medical care. We again had help from the Iraqi Army, who patrolled the streets around our house. This would save us in the next couple of days.

The house had a wall around it with a big metal gate; for distributions, we would back the armored ambulance up to the gate with the unarmored ambulance right next to it, so there was only room for one person to pass between them, to protect the opening and make the flow of people manageable. Once they were finished, we'd channel people back out the other side along the wall.

There was always a crowd trying to push through, and our house became a center of activity. One day, the soldiers helping outside our gate suddenly came to alert. They had received a radio transmission from a patrol in the neighborhood who had found a suicide bomber in his house assembling vests and preparing to use them. Upon interrogation, he spilled everything: he told them he was on his way to kill the Americans who were giving out food and water; also, there were more suicide bombers on the way to hit the same target, and ISIS would launch a counterattack on our location.

Immediately, we cleared all the civilians out and moved Karen and the kids into a back room of the house. We posted lookouts at all the avenues of approach to our house. I went out with the Iraqis looking for the other suicide bombers. One of the patrols found one and killed him right away, but we found nothing else and returned to the house, keeping security posted all night.

The next day, the same thing happened.

ISIS was infiltrating back and, for two days, tried to attack our house. As we were alerted to specific threats, the women and children would move to the safest room and we'd defend the approaches to the house. We had numerous small firefights, and one Iraqi soldier was shot in the foot.

One day, as we were unloading relief supplies ordered from east Mosul a few days before, we saw two ISIS fighters make a dash for it right next to our house. We shot at them and they fled, disappearing into a different house. We split up and Monkey, Sky, Eliya, and I started clearing the houses all around us. We searched each room, using grenades to clear them. We weren't taking any chances. The ISIS fighters fell back but came back the next night.

We prayed about where we should be and felt this was not a good position. Pretty soon, we would only be defending ourselves and not helping people. At the same time, General Mustafa asked us to move back to where he'd set up his headquarters and CCP. It was a little safer and further back out of the fight. We agreed and moved over to the nearby neighborhood.

The houses there were bigger and ours, just across the bumpy, unpaved street from Mustafa's, was a partially completed three-story home. It even had a fridge that could run on a generator. This was a luxurious touch that meant cold drinks were an option.

That became our headquarters until the end of the battle. It was the best battlefield setup we'd known. I'd get up at five in the morning, work out on the roof, take a dip bath, then assemble our team. We'd pray together and go to the front to take care of the wounded soldiers and the civilians who were escaping. We'd come back every night, clothes caked in dried blood, dust, and sweat, get a bath, change, and eat a great meal Karen and the Animals prepared. It was surreal. There was fighting going on all around us, but here we had a great little domestic setup—a place of love, light, and fellowship. In that little island of peace, I could center myself on prayer and our purpose there.

Karen and the kids did homeschool, and they helped the rest of the team with food and shoe distributions, which were done out of that house, as well as occasional medical care for patients who came by. Our team rotated in and out of the front and took turns making runs to Erbil to keep our food, medicine, and relief supplies stocked up.

At the end of May, the 36th started pushing into Hawi Kanisa. Hawi Kanisa is a sort of "green" area, irrigated by the Tigris and well cultivated with fruit and olive trees, fields and farms, and scattered houses and churches. That is, until ISIS took over and destroyed it. The churches were wrecked. All the Christians were chased out.

With the 36th, we worked our way through Hawi Kanisa, circling in from the north and working our way south toward the northernmost bridge in Mosul. One morning, after we prayed and as we were loading the Humvees, I noticed Suu with tears in her eyes. "Why are you crying, honey?" I asked, hugging her close to me.

"Daddy, I don't want you to die."

I put my hands on her shoulders, looked her in the eyes, and said, "I promise you before I do anything dangerous, I will pray, and I will think of you first, and I will be careful." She smiled and hugged me tightly. As it turned out, there were four different times where thinking of her helped me survive as I looked for different options in dangerous situations. After the battle of Mosul was over, I remembered this and as I hugged her, I told her, "Honey, thank you so much, you helped save my life."

We pushed south in an armored column, spread out from the river back to the first main road west of the river. As we got close to the first bridge, the terrain became more urban, with a higher concentration of buildings. We pivoted and did a broad armored assault toward that bridge, into the neighborhoods on the bluffs next to and above it. In front of us were scattered houses and farms, and just on the northwest side of the bridge, there was a huge hotel, formerly one of the most luxurious in the city. It had been bombed and was totally wrecked. It was just north of a major highway and was a strategic position because on the other side of the highway was Shifa Hospital.

By then, the hospital had been heavily damaged, but ISIS had strongpointed it and turned it into their northwest Mosul headquarters. They set up antiaircraft guns on the grounds and were reportedly using an elevator to move heavy weapons up and down. They had all kinds of defensive positions set up: Russian Kornet antitank systems, RPGs, and machine gun and sniper systems. They laid waste to anybody who tried to approach.

I heard the Iraqi government was reluctant to bomb the hospital because they said they wanted to preserve it, which seemed crazy to me because it was already badly damaged. Without help from the air, the only way to get the ISIS fighters out of there would be a bloody infantry assault, which would require fire support from tanks, artillery, and RPG antitank systems just to breach the hospital. Many Iraqi soldiers would die, and the hospital would still be further damaged. We all thought it should just be bombed. It was going to need rebuilding anyway, and there were certainly no patients left inside—though it was uncertain whether ISIS was holding civilians there.

This hospital was the eventual objective as we pushed south through Hawi Kanisa. As we reached the edge of the greenway and began to get into shops and houses, there was a pause in the battle as we waited for the next movement. Off to the side of the road, in a blown-up shop front, I saw an Iraqi officer taking a break as we waited. He looked familiar, and I looked closer and walked toward him – it was Lieutenant Colonel Ahmed from the 15th Division.

Theirs was the unit we had linked up with for a few days after Al Rashidiya on the east side—he was the one who told me ISIS snipers were bad shots, right before I almost got shot by one. He was a funny guy, and we had a lot of talks about Jesus and faith, Iraqi history, and Islam. I became close to him in that short time we were together. Suddenly, there he was, and we had a good reunion for a few minutes, together with Colonel Arkan of the 36th. Then our unit started moving and I had to go. I said a prayer with him, said, "God bless you," gave him a hug, and rejoined our guys.

One hour later, he was killed. His Humvee was hit by an RPG as his unit started an attack. I never saw him again, but I kept a picture of him with me. Once, after all this had happened, our team was trying to cross into a secured area on a bridge controlled by his unit, and they weren't letting anyone across. They saw my picture of Lieutenant Colonel Ahmed and they loved him too, so they said, "Of course you can cross." I posted his picture in our camp in Burma and also in Thailand, right next to Lieutenant Colonel Feras, Shaheen, and the other heroes who died in Mosul.

One day, I almost lost my own head in a less-than-heroic way. The tanks were lined up in an orchard at the edge of the Hawi Kanisa green area, firing south into the buildings between the highway and us. We were taking a lot of accurate sniper and machine-gun fire from those buildings and had already sustained a few casualties. I'd been moving behind the tanks most of the time, but now they stopped. A wall in front of us surrounded the farmhouse the orchard belonged to.

The tanks stopped behind the wall, and I was sure they wouldn't shoot through it. I wanted to cut across the orchard to my left, and the tanks' left, to get to my Humvee. It was a lot shorter to move around in front of them. I figured they'd see me, and I'd see them, and it would be easier than dancing around behind them. I crossed in front of the first tank, a T-72. My head was just at the height of the barrel, and I passed about three meters in front of it. The hatch flew up, and the gunner popped out, screaming. "What are you doing?" He was scared and angry, and I realized, oh—they're about to fire.

"Sorry! I'm sorry!" I yelled back, feeling like an idiot. I jogged off to the side. As soon as I was clear, they fired a round right through the wall in front of us. Wow. That was close. Only the tank crew's alertness saved me from getting my head blown off. That would have been not only deadly, but embarrassing. I knew if someone else on my team did that, I would have given them a pretty serious scolding and assigned a lot of push-ups. So, later, I told everyone what happened, did push-ups, emphasized what a terrible example it was, and did more push-ups.

Eliya, his eyes twinkling, grinned and said, "Thara, be good. God likes that."

The tanks continued to lead as we worked our way to the highway that crossed the first bridge. The next stage was the crux of our campaign: crossing the highway to reach Shifa Hospital. It was a bit of a conundrum: in order to assault the hospital, we had to cross the road. But in order to cross the road, we had to suppress the fire coming from the hospital.

By the end of May, we reached the hotel just north of the highway. The next attack would be the attempt to cross the highway. Success would mean the defeat of ISIS's northwest headquarters and their last major strongpoint in Mosul. The morning of the assault there was already a lot of fighting going on around us, gunfire everywhere. We started out all stacked up beneath the blown-up hotel, using it as a base for the assault; it later became our CCP. The assault would be carried out by a combination of a battalion of the 15th Division, led by a different Lieutenant Colonel Ahmed, and the 36th.

Lieutenant Colonel Ahmed's battalion was to start the proceedings. I had planned to go with this first assault element, but I prayed and thought again. I didn't really know where they were going. If I got pinned down with them, I wouldn't be able to help anybody. I talked to my team, and we prayed and decided to go with the second assault element.

The first element sprinted across the rubble- and rebar-strewn ground, bent over and racing for cover. They were headed left, down an embankment and through ruined buildings, toward the river. ISIS opened up with everything they had—rockets, mortars, RPGs, machine guns, and rifles—and they were lethal. Those guys began taking casualties right away.

It looked like the second element was going to go right, into a more open area, so I waited again. If I wanted to be best placed to help, I should wait for the third element, going right down the middle.

Neither of the first two groups made it anywhere close to across the highway before both were pinned down by the heavy fire coming from the hospital. The third element went straight up the middle, through the courtyard of the hotel, and made it as far as a big fountain surrounded by a wrecked and waterless pool.

Very quickly, the entire assault was halted, the men unable to move forward or backward and taking casualties. My team and I had tailed the third element by thirty meters and positioned ourselves behind a little wall just to the east of the main hotel. The wall was about two meters tall, three meters long, and a half meter thick. That became our spot for the day—which we spent dashing out to drag the dead and wounded back to the CCP, where Eliya, Sky, and Zau, along with the Iraqi medics, went to work on them.

With me behind the wall, working on casualty evacuations, were Monkey, Toh, and two Iraqis. We took turns shooting across the road to suppress ISIS in the hospital as we dashed out to drag back the wounded. At a certain point, ISIS figured it out and started shooting at our wall and sending RPG and mortar rounds over it. It was thick enough bullets weren't penetrating, but there was some metal scaffolding behind us, so they started trying to hit that and ricochet rounds off it and into us. It sort of worked, and I had a couple rounds hit me in the helmet on the bounce, but they didn't do any damage. However, the wall was slowly but steadily crumbling under the continuous fire, and it was only a matter of time before we lost it. After two hours, it was reduced to half its length and lost a foot of height.

Suddenly, off to the right in the fountain area, one of the men who had been pinned down took off running, back toward us. ISIS shot him in the back and he fell down about twelve meters away. Bullets were smacking all around him as he lay there, bleeding out. I knew if I ran to him I'd be hit for sure; but there he was, struggling to stay alive but totally exposed to ISIS. I saw, between me and him and a little bit to the right, a small depression behind a piece of concrete. I prayed with Monkey and Toh and told them, "Okay, you guys, fire as many rounds as you can and hit all the windows in front of us. I'm gonna run and try to get that guy out of the fire."

About three meters from him there were some partially collapsed arches. Under the arches were three or four Iraqi soldiers huddled away from the fire. I thought if I could get the guy over to those arches, we'd be masked from enemy fire.

Monkey and Toh started firing away—this was one of the first times they had ever shot at anyone in their lives—and I dashed out and made it to the little depression with bullets coming all around me. I prayed and then started to launch into the next four or five meters to reach the guy. Just then, one of the Iraqi soldiers under the arch crawled out and grabbed him by the arm, dragging him under the arch. He was shot again as they pulled him in. I scrambled over to them and started treating his wounds. He'd been seriously hit twice, once in the upper back and once in the lower. I started packing gauze and QuikClot in, trying to stop the bleeding, and prayed for him. He was still alive, but we needed to get him out.

At first, I thought we'd have to go back through all that open area but then saw there was a hole in the rubble we could crawl through and go back deeper into this wing of the hotel. Then we'd have to cover maybe twenty meters of open ground to get to the hastily set up CCP in the inner bowels of the hotel, in a sort of cave of concrete slabs.

There, Eliya, Sky, Zau, Faiz, and others were working to save lives. We dragged the wounded man through the rubble, me pushing him and two Iraqis pulling, scraping his face and chest across jagged points of rebar and broken concrete. It was really just a crawl space with no room to even kneel. By the time we got him to the other side, where we had to cross the open, he was dead from blood loss.

And this is what that day looked like. All day long, dashing out to help someone who'd been wounded, dragging them back and bringing them to the CCP. There was a three-hour period when the fire came in so heavily, we couldn't move. They had us. We fought back, but every time we stuck our heads up, they were firing away. Lieutenant Colonel Ahmed, commander of our partner battalion, was wounded, and Eliya took care of him. (A year later, while manning the border checkpoint we needed to get through, he helped us cross into Syria.)

After several hours, we had twenty-two casualties and managed to evacuate all of them. Six or eight died right there. We had a stack of blankets at the CCP in which we wrapped the dead.

The next day was similar, but this time, Monkey, Toh, Ephraim, and I were in the back with Colonel Arkan, looking for another way to cross the highway. Eliya, Zau, and Sky were at the hotel CCP that day and did the running back and forth, dragging casualties. That night, the Iraqis decided to try a night attack but that also failed. It was even worse, actually, as they ended up taking casualties from friendly fire by a sister unit to the west.

The situation was looking bad. The commander of all the Iraqi forces, Gen Yarala, called for a commanders' conference in Hulayla. It included the highest-ranking Iraqi generals and the Americans, including Colonel James Patrick Work of the 82nd Airborne advise-and-assist team. Colonel Work was previously in the Ranger Regiment and had a very good reputation. General Mustafa asked me to come to the meeting and I drove there in our Humvee with the Animals. They were dressed in a mix of uniforms with flip-flops and chewing betel nut as we walked into the meeting—not exactly standard high-command attire.

The meeting was led by General Yarala. He asked all the generals there, "Can you keep attacking and take the hospital?" No answer. He asked again, and again no answer. So he said, "I'll tell you the answer: you can't." He listed the casualties from every unit. He said again, "You can't, and I'm not going to let you. We have a new plan."

The new plan was to keep the Iraqi ERD as a blocking force at the hospital complex so ISIS wouldn't advance from there. Everybody else would swing around to the west and bypass the hospital, penetrating south all the way to the next bridge. Then they would advance back east and north, clear all ISIS out of the way, and seal off the hospital. Everyone felt this was a good plan.

We drove back to our little base with General Mustafa. I felt again what a haven it was and wondered if we'd have to move. I liked my routine that ended with peace and started with peace. Sometimes I'd eat dinner with Mustafa and his staff, pray with them, and talk about how we could help more. The families from this neighborhood were starting to return and lots of civilians were moving through. An American advise-and-assist team helping with air support moved in next door to us at one point as well, after their position got shelled closer to the front. It was a very civilized (yet still deadly) way to have a war.

After this meeting, the 36th was going to pivot south and pull out of the hotel/hospital area. Their guys gradually started leaving, setting up a headquarters further south and west. It would probably be a week before they started the next phase of the attack. We were still in our house but were packing to follow the 36th. Major Ali of the ERD contacted us and said, "Hey, we've got a lot of casualties coming in. Can the Rangers stay and help a few days?" I asked General Mustafa and he agreed we should help, because the 36th would need time before they were ready to attack again from the new position.

This was June 1st. We had Eliya, Toh, Monkey, Zau, Ephraim, Sky, Zeb, Sahale, Hosie, Maddie, and our Mennonite friends Darrell and Brent, who had brought along two nurses, Karen and Rhonda, working at the forward CCP. Bernard the journalist joined us right about then as well. Back at the house were Karen, Suu, Peter, and Noelle, going back and forth between the house and CCP. For translators, we had Dlo and Mahmood, a Christian Syrian refugee we met in Erbil.

We got the appeal for help and loaded in a Humvee and one of our armored ambulances, and I took Sahale down with me to help drive the armored ambulance if needed. We drove down to within about five hundred meters of the hospital, and ISIS was firing mortars, but they couldn't shoot us directly because there were buildings and terrain between us and them. As we turned into a side street, I saw about thirty walking wounded and about ten more being carried. Everyone was bleeding: shot in the leg, the arm, the stomach, holding themselves, crying, wailing. There were about a hundred more people, uninjured, walking along with them, helping them.

They were all terrified, relaying horrific stories. I remember one man, a little younger than me, who was screaming, "My daughters, my daughters, they killed my daughters! Oh God, oh God, what can I do? They were shooting everyone! Babies, babies, babies!" He couldn't go back to his daughters—they had been shot right next to him, he described it, two sniper shots, bang, bang, both girls hit in the head— because he had his other kids he was trying to rescue. My heart broke for him. I held him and prayed for him, for his two dead daughters, for the rest of his family, and for his heart, that somehow Jesus would restore him.

There were other stories: "They killed my whole family. Only I made it across, and I can't even go back to their bodies. This is not Islam! This is not Islam! Oh God, oh God."

We asked the people where this was happening because it was unusual. We knew ISIS was killing people, including civilians, but normally they focused on soldiers. They would kill civilians sometimes, but not en masse. They said, "People are trying to escape past the hospital and Pepsi factory"—maybe five hundred to seven hundred meters away. The "Pepsi factory" was a soft drink factory situated just west of the hospital. People were trying to sneak through its ruins, but clearly, ISIS controlled it.

We treated their wounds the best we could, stabilized them, and evacuated them. One nine-year-old girl I carried was bleeding profusely, and by the time I got her into the ambulance Sahale was driving, she died. Another older woman collapsed in the street, but I could not see where she was wounded. I picked her up and carried her over to Sahale and Hosie. We loaded her into the ambulance. Then I looked at my hands; they were full of blood. She had been shot in the upper thigh, and the blood had seeped through her thick black dress. Hosie, Sahale, and Zeb were driving back and forth to the new Division CCP that was bigger than what the 36th had been using.

Around 5 p.m the flow of people and casualties slowed for a bit, and Ephraim, Eliya, Zau, Bernard, and I drove the Humvee up to where the shooting was. We wanted to see where the slaughter was happening and if we could help more. There was shooting from two directions and an ERD soldier told us, "There are more people coming. Can you come back tonight and help?" We could see we needed to move here to help more.

CHAPTER NINETEEN

The Last Redoubt—Shifa Hospital

"Only one thing I shouted in my heart, was, 'This is God! He is in it.'"
—MONKEY

We drove back to our house and grabbed a few things to stay the night. Then Eliya, Zau Seng, Monkey, Toh, Ephraim, Sky, Bernard, and I returned to join the ERD, just a few hundred meters away from ISIS. As night came, people tried to take advantage of the dark to sneak across the road in front of the hospital and adjacent soft drink factory. There was shooting off and on all night as ISIS tried to pick off these civilians. Some had been lying in the road all day, faking dead, and as it got dark, made their attempt to cross. Others crouched under cover on the other side. ISIS had night vision and were still firing effectively.

All night long, the casualties came: men, women, and children, shot, bleeding, dazed, and moaning. We treated the wounded, evacuated them, lay back down in all our gear to sleep a few minutes, then were alerted again to help a new group. First morning light on June 2 came around 5 a.m. As the warm sun slowly appeared, burning through the war haze of the city, I went down to the road—the same one we'd been trying to cross for the last week—and poked my head out.

It was a four-lane highway. To the left, east, the road went down to the blown-up bridge, where I could just see the Tigris rolling by. To the right, the road went into the heart of Mosul. And to the south, in front of me, I could see the hospital complex and the destroyed soft drink factory with some other blown-up buildings in front, across the road. I looked carefully around the corner as ISIS bullets went by.

My gaze first came to a young lady lying on her back, shot. I remember thinking, *There's a really pretty young lady,* but she was dead, lying out on the road not far from me. This hit me; it made me deeply sad and determined to stand against the evil force that had killed her. My gaze moved a little, and I saw a bag of rags—no, that was a baby, wrapped in swaddling clothes, shot dead, right in the head. I saw an old lady, a grandmother, dead. There's a grandfather, dead. Slowly, I scanned the street, and it was like my eyes had to adjust; I realized all those little lumps were people and as the sun got brighter, I saw people, people, people. I saw an old man in a wheelchair, his head slumped over, and the young man who was trying to push the wheelchair was on his back, dead.

It was a horrifying scene. Every time I poked my head out too far in the street, trying to take it all in, ISIS shot at me. I called my team. We stood in silence as the horror of what we were seeing washed over us. We started trying to move along the wall and through the rubble of a nearby building to get a better vantage point, taking photos.

I looked across the street, which had been a double-lane highway and was now a rubble-strewn death trap; how far did this go? On the other side, I could see a low retaining wall, and there were about twenty more people dead there. What a massacre this was.

Then something moved. I looked more closely and could see a little girl sitting next to a dead woman. She was hiding under the woman's burka,and peeking out. It was probably the body of her mother. There was another movement, and I saw another kid, walking, a little boy. He was younger, maybe two or three years old, with only his shirt on. He was moving through the dead bodies.

I thought, *He's looking for water; he's probably been there a whole day or two in the hot sun. All those bodies are probably his family. He probably doesn't even really know or understand they're dead.* Anguish gripped me: "Oh God, what can we do? How can we save them?" This was the same street we'd been trying to cross for a week, the same street the Iraqi high command had called a special meeting about, in which he'd given up on crossing it.

There were Iraqi armored vehicles on the street, just down the way, all mangled. We couldn't cross on foot and we couldn't cross with armor. It was one hundred and fifty meters of open ground right in front of ISIS in the hospital. We'd heard reports there were up to two hundred Chechens, who came from Russia and joined ISIS, manning the hospital. They had .50-caliber sniper rifles, light machine guns, heavy machine guns, sniper systems, a ZSU-23 antiaircraft gun, antitank systems from RPGs to AT4s to a Russian Kornet that had already taken out many tanks. I prayed, "Lord, help us, how can we do this?"

I called the team back at the house and told them the situation, asked for prayer, and had Sahale and Hosie come up to our position to help treat patients and drive if needed. The Iraqi Army and ERD were planning an assault that day and there was still potential for more people to come. I kept going back to the edge of the street and looking at those people, the little boy moving around, the girl peeking out from under her mom's dress.

I prayed and made a plan; if I could get a tank to lead the way and blast at the ISIS positions, have an armored bulldozer follow it to clear a way, and then have two Humvees behind that, we could possibly drive up to the children and rescue them. In order for this plan to have a chance, we would need smoke too, and I would ask the Americans for that. I asked the Iraqi soldiers there, "What do you think? Do you want to go?"

They all agreed. "Yes, we want to help, but it seems impossible."

The exception was an Iraqi private named Zuhair. From the time we arrived, he persisted in asking us if we could help rescue any survivors. "Let's go rescue them, let's go rescue now. No one's going to help us, let's just do it."

I said, "Man, we'll be dead, but I do have a plan."

He said, "I'd rather cut my arms off than do nothing. I've got to help them—look at that baby across the street." He was the single encouraging voice all day, but he didn't have a plan; he just wanted to go. I prayed with Zuhair and told him my plan. Then I went up the street to talk to the ERD brigade commander at the house they were using as a headquarters. This house was next to the one we were using as the forward CCP. I told the general my plan and asked him for the armor. Two tanks and a bulldozer were parked on the street across from us, and I pointed to them while we talked. He said he wanted to help but the tanks and bulldozer were needed right then for an attack.

"And even if we could spare the armor, they're all going to get blown up. ISIS has antitank systems. It's a trap. They'll just blow you up. Plus, we're fighting ISIS right over there. Our attack starts in about fifteen minutes." He was sorry and said maybe we could use them later. I prayed with him and told him I would check back all day. I called U.S. Army General Efflandt, who had returned and replaced General

Richardson, and described the situation to him, asking for smoke so we could attempt a rescue.

I told them, "This is where we are; here are our coordinates; these are the ISIS coordinates; there are some living civilians trapped in this spot." I said, "We need smoke. If you can drop smoke to screen us, we have a chance to use the Iraqi Army to get in close enough to rescue whoever's left alive."

General Efflandt said, "Yes, we are on this and will coordinate with the Iraqis and get you smoke. Let us know when." That was a comfort, and I thanked God for him and the U.S. Military.

All morning, I was going back and forth between the spot where I could see the children and the base up the street. I sent out a quick message with a couple photos to our wider team—back in Chiang Mai and all over—and asked everyone to pray we could save these people somehow.

Noon came, and we still could not get any armor. Sahale came up to me and said, "Daddy, the Iraqis brought up food. You should eat."

I looked into her sweet, trusting, and firm eyes and felt gratitude and love well up in me. I hugged her. "I love you, Sahale, and am so proud of you." We sat and ate together, and just as we finished, my chaplain, Paul Bradley, called from Thailand. He said, "I'm praying for you. God will show a way. He'll give you what you need for this mission."

We prayed together. This time, I said to God, "Lord, thank you. You'll show us a way." I felt a surge of power and of hope; I felt God do something through Paul's prayer. I called General Efflandt and his team again, and they told me to ask the Iraqis to call them to coordinate. I got the Iraqis to call and coordination began. The Iraqis asked me to keep communicating with the Americans, and I did.

By now, it was about 1 p.m. Those surviving children had been out there in the heat for going on three days. I wasn't sure this would work. The Iraqis were getting ready to launch their own attack to the west of us. I kept praying and thinking about alternate plans in case this didn't work out. I thought, *Well, if we can't do it now then we'll go at night.* The problem at night was, ISIS had night vision. Second, if we moved at night, other Iraqi units in different positions could shoot us. They'd think we were ISIS.

It had already happened on this road, when they tried a night attack earlier in the week. Also, by then, there might not be any survivors.

Night was actually a pretty bad option. But we seemed to be out of good options, and I thought, in the worst case, we could try that.

A couple hours later, the Americans were standing by to drop smoke, but I still could not get the needed tank and bulldozer from the ERD. I decided I would ask the U.S. to drop smoke anyway, and we would have to go for it with whatever we had. Around 3 p.m. the first smoke drop came, a practice round to make sure the location was correct. I gave the feedback that it was on target and ran to the Iraqis. There, Colonel Mohammed had taken the general's place. I told him, "Look, we've got smoke! Please come with me." He followed me down the street, ducking behind the wall on the corner. We dodged ISIS bullets and ran to the building we were using as overwatch.

He looked and said, "That's not enough smoke. I'm not going to give a tank or a bulldozer or any Humvees."

The U.S. dropped more smoke, and I said, "If Allah tells you to help, will you?"

He looked at me in surprise and answered, "Yes."

I bowed my head and prayed, "Dear Allah (God), please tell the colonel what to do, in Issa's (Jesus's) name. Amen."

He looked at me, paused, and, holding up one finger, said, "One tank, one tank only." That was it, no bulldozer, no armored Humvees. It also meant we couldn't bring our Humvee because without the bulldozer, the road was too full of debris to be able to follow the tank. We were going to have to go out there on foot. Take it or leave it, the moment was now.

It was about 3:30 p.m. Zuhair had just been called away to another duty. I was standing inside this little blown-up house, right on the edge of the street, just out of ISIS's line of fire, looking at the little girl. I turned to my team: "We got one tank. We will have to run behind it. I'm going now. Who wants to come? Volunteers only."

Monkey immediately said, "Zau Seng, he can be camera."

Zau answered, "Monkey, that is not the meaning of volunteer!"

Monkey looked sheepish and said, "Okay, I will go. Zau, you film from here."

Sky and Ephraim said they were coming, and Mahmood said he would also come in case we needed a translator. Bernard, the journalist, was with us at that moment as well, and he'd been getting good photos and video of the whole situation. Dlo, Eliya, Toh, Sahale, and Hosie would be the support team and stay back.

Our rescue team went outside, running low along the wall as ISIS fired at us until we got back around the corner. There, we gathered and said the Lord's Prayer. Just then, the Iraqi tank rolled around the corner and got into position. It was now or never. I looked at the tank and our team, got the thumbs up from Colonel Mohammed, and shouted above the roar of the tank, "Whoever wants to go, let's go!" and took off running to get behind the tank. Sky, Ephraim, Mahmood, and Monkey followed.

We ran across the road, and ISIS started shooting. We caught up to the tank, keeping it between us and the ISIS fire. The tank pivoted around to face the ISIS positions in the hospital and soft drink factory complex. It fired its guns at ISIS and took off straight toward the hospital, its jet turbine engine screaming. We ran behind as bullets hammered into its steel hull and deflected off in all directions.

The tank wove around the dead bodies, and I recognized the two girls shot in the head the father had told me about the day before. As we got closer to the corner where the little girl was, an ISIS RPG or mortar impacted nearby but missed us. ISIS rifle and machine-gun fire intensified, and bullets were flying over us and hitting the ground all around us. We were trying to stay behind the tank and stay covered from the ISIS positions on three sides of us.

As the tank stopped across from the wall, the first smoke drop began to dissipate, so I called the Americans again, shouting into the phone: "Thanks for the help! Sorry I'm shouting but I'm right behind the tank. The smoke's gone. It was awesome! You got us here alive, but if we don't have more now there are kids that are gonna die, the tank's gonna get blown up, we're gonna die, and—how much longer before you can send more smoke?"

General Efflandt's battle captain said, "Ten minutes."

I said, "Okay, we can make it." Waiting for the smoke, I noticed the little boy was nowhere to be seen. The little girl was looking at us from under her mom's dress and two men were feebly waving at us, but the little boy was gone. Eight minutes later, a barrage of smoke came, and it was beautiful, a thick screen in front of us.

I came to the edge of the tank, Sky and Ephraim were getting ready to shoot, and I said, "Okay, this is what I'm gonna do. You guys give me cover, I'm gonna run." What I thought was, *There's no way I'm going to live through this.*

Sometimes, you do something and think, *I might get hurt, but I have a chance.* This wasn't one of those times. This was, *you're not just going to get hurt, you're going to get killed.* But I looked at the girl and thought, *What would I want for my kid?* And I prayed to God, and I felt: it's now or never. And I also felt, if I get killed, my wife and children will understand, it's for this little girl. I prayed again: "Jesus help me," and took off at a run. Ephraim and Sky opened up at ISIS behind me, giving me covering fire and exposing themselves to ISIS bullets as they did.

I ran up to the girl and grabbed her by the arm. She was holding on to her dead mother and didn't want to let go. I had to wrench her off. I got her in my arms and actually tucked her under my right arm and took off running back to the tank. ISIS was shooting at us, and either they hit the rock under my foot, or I just tripped but, either way, I went down hard. The girl was tucked tight under my arm and I didn't want to let go, so she slammed down hard too, face-first into the ground. I got up, never loosening my grip on her, and ran back behind the tank. I handed her to Mahmood, who started talking to her in Arabic. And I prayed right there, "Thank you, Jesus, and bless this girl."

We still had to get the men, and this time, I took Sky with me while Ephraim continued to shoot. But soon we needed him too, and it took the three of us to drag the two men back behind the tank. They'd both been shot multiple times. Now we had to move all these people back. In our original plan, we'd have Humvees, but that hadn't worked out. We couldn't put the people on the tank for two reasons: the back of an Abrams tank is cooking hot from its jet engine (I lost the hair on my arm from being too close to the Abrams when they were shooting). And the second reason we couldn't put people on the tank is because ISIS would just shoot them from above.

We had to carry everyone back and stay behind the tank as it began to back up and out of ISIS fire. I took the girl. Sky carried the smaller of the men. Ephraim and Mahmood dragged the third man. Monkey continued filming. ISIS was shooting the tank, and bullets were pinging everywhere. The tank was driving backward now, firing its main gun as well as the coaxial machine gun to cover our retreat.

We were trying to stay just ahead of the tank and not get run over, but not get too far out in front either and expose ourselves. As we ran, the man Mahmood and Ephraim were dragging somehow rolled out-side the tank coverage area and was killed by ISIS. Now we had two survivors. Then I saw Ephraim stumble—one knee dropped to the ground and he almost fell over. The tank kept rolling, and he was almost crushed. But he popped up quickly and kept moving, with a limp and blood soaking his pant leg. He'd been hit.

Up ahead, I saw our Humvees and yelled, "Humvees, c'mon!" The Humvees didn't move. I kept yelling, and we kept moving. Finally, Bernard jumped in one of the Humvees and drove it up to us. Bullets bounced off it as he raced over. The tank was still shooting its main gun, hammering away at ISIS. I had the little girl against me, and I told her, "If no one adopts you"—and I prayed before I made this promise—"I will. I will never leave you. You'll always have a parent. So if we can't find your family, or if there's not an Iraqi family to adopt you, my wife and I will adopt you." She just stared, glassy-eyed.

We got everybody in the Humvee—the wounded man, the girl, and the rest of us—and drove into the safe area before stopping to reassess. Eliya and Toh treated Ephraim's wound. Darrell was there with our armored ambulance, and we put Ephraim in there to evacuate him to the CCP. He had a through-and-through in his calf but was okay.

I looked more closely at the little girl in my arms; she seemed unwounded. It was a miracle to me we both were alive. I didn't want to let her go, so I walked with her in my arms up the little hill to where our base was. The Iraqis were jubilant and taking photos and video; this was a spot of life in the middle of a massacre, and we were all joyful.

The wounded man stayed in the Humvee. Dlo switched out with Bernard behind the wheel so he could film and drove up after us. I got back in and took Sahale with me. I told her, "Come and film this. I want you to film this girl." The wounded man, Sahale, Bernard, Dlo, and I headed out to the CCP. The girl was in my lap, and I started giving her water. She went through six bottles on the drive; she hadn't had water in three days, sitting there in the sun.

As we drove, I called Karen, who was at our house with Peter and Suu. I said, "Go to the CCP, I'm going there right now. I've got a girl. She's not shot. She's the only one not shot. She's lost her whole family, and she's gonna need a mother."

We got to the CCP, where the medics had begun to work on Ephraim. We started the little girl on an IV. She was in shock, scared

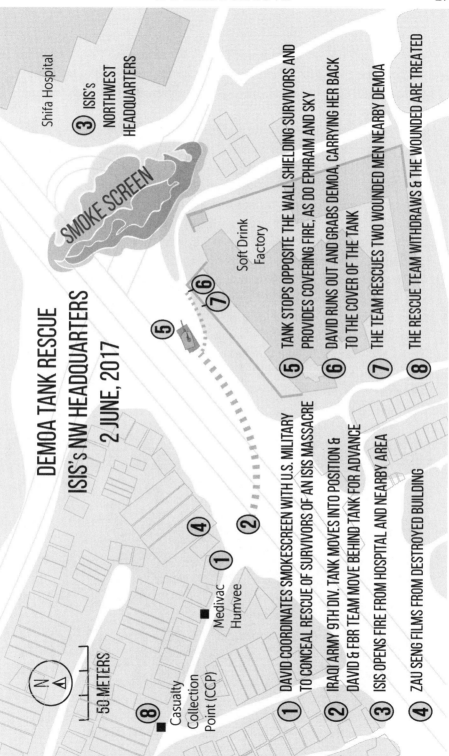

DEMOA TANK RESCUE
ISIS's NW HEADQUARTERS
2 JUNE, 2017

N
50 METERS

Casualty Collection Point (CCP)

Medivac Humvee

Shifa Hospital

③ ISIS's NORTHWEST HEADQUARTERS

SMOKE SCREEN

Soft Drink Factory

① DAVID COORDINATES SMOKESCREEN WITH U.S. MILITARY TO CONCEAL RESCUE OF SURVIVORS OF AN ISIS MASSACRE

② IRAQI ARMY 9TH DIV. TANK MOVES INTO POSITION & DAVID & FBR TEAM MOVE BEHIND TANK FOR ADVANCE

③ ISIS OPENS FIRE FROM HOSPITAL AND NEARBY AREA

④ ZAU SENG FILMS FROM DESTROYED BUILDING

⑤ TANK STOPS OPPOSITE THE WALL SHIELDING SURVIVORS AND PROVIDES COVERING FIRE, AS DO EPHRAIM AND SKY

⑥ DAVID RUNS OUT AND GRABS DEMOA, CARRYING HER BACK TO THE COVER OF THE TANK

⑦ THE TEAM RESCUES TWO WOUNDED MEN NEARBY DEMOA

⑧ THE RESCUE TEAM WITHDRAWS & THE WOUNDED ARE TREATED

and whimpering. Karen picked her up gently, and within about five minutes, she was asleep in Karen's arms. It was probably the first time in three days she'd slept, because she'd been in the middle of the battle, in the middle of a massacre, among dead bodies, and with bullets flying around her all that time.

We checked on the man we had brought out and were getting ready to send Ephraim out to a hospital in Erbil with Darrell and the Mennonite team. At that moment, there was a commotion, and I saw Iraqi Federal Police dragging the man we had just checked on out of the CCP. His IV was ripped from his arm, and he was bleeding from his wounds. He was terrified. I pushed my way through the mass of police and grabbed the man. The police looked at me in surprise, then anger, and tried to pull him away from me.

I said, "Please, please—I'm not questioning your authority. We're on the same side. I will release him, but, please, he's been shot. We just risked our lives to save this man. He was shot by ISIS. One of my men was also shot by ISIS when we rescued him."

"He is Daesh. He will die. Let him go, and get out of the way," one of the policemen replied, pulling out his pistol and gesticulating angrily at me.

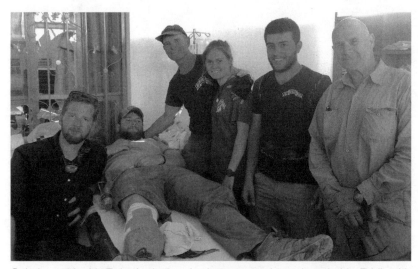

Sahale and I with Ephraim before he is evacuated to a hospital in Erbil, with Zeb, his brother; Mahmood, our Syrian translator who was also on the rescue; and Bernard, who helped drive us to safety in a Humvee, June 2, 2017.

The injured man slid to the ground, and I sat down next to him, putting my arms around him. He was trembling. I repeated, "I'm not challenging you. I know ISIS has done so much evil, and you all have lost so much to them—you have lost more than any. But I have lost many friends too and have been wounded four times and have seen ISIS kill women and children. You are the authority and have the right to arrest this man. I am on the same side as you, and I am under Iraqi authority. I am with you, but please don't kill him. Let him be treated and then question him after that."

Then I started to choke up and finished with, "I will not let him be killed like this."

At that moment, the doctor in charge there came up and started pleading with the police too. "This American is a hero; he has been with us during all the fight in Mosul. He just saved a little girl and this man, who were both shot by ISIS. We are treating them. We must take this man back into the hospital. Once he is stable, you can question him."

I decided I would not let this man be taken, even if it meant dying with him. I would stand my ground. Or, rather, sit my ground. This thought made me laugh. It made me think of tree huggers, and I felt like a tree hugger; this guy was my tree. I hugged him and smiled.

The police were nonplussed: here was an American, hugging a suspected ISIS member and being defended by one of their own. This was a new situation for them. They relented and said, "Okay, we will ask him a few questions with you here, and then he can go back inside."

I sat with the man as they questioned him and then helped him back into the hospital. We decided to take the little girl back to our house as no one really knew what to do with her. It was just about a mile or two back to our little headquarters with General Mustafa, who hadn't quite moved to his new place yet. Once back at our base, Karen put the girl on our bed, then held her as she cried softly. General Mustafa and Major Naseem came in saying, "We heard you rescued a girl. You really love our people. We love you and thank you. We will help find the girl's relatives."

She was sitting with Karen in the back room of our house, where there was a bed. Now she was kind of catatonic, but awake. We thought about her mom, her brothers, her sisters, her family who were probably dead. We tried to talk to her, but she wouldn't answer. General Mustafa, trying to speak to her in Arabic, started crying. So did Major Naseem, and so did I. We cried for this girl and for all she'd lost. General Mustafa held her, and she allowed herself to be held by him, and he rocked her and cried for her. He said, "If we don't find your family, I'll adopt you."

Throughout the rest of the day, different soldiers came in and out to visit the little girl. Almost all left crying. Several others offered to adopt her. Through it all, she stared listlessly, slept, or cried silently. The only words she would say were, "Take me to my mama."

Her life was saved, and, in turn, she cracked open the hearts of Iraqi soldiers, generals, our team, and people all over. God used us to pull her from the abyss and in so doing we were touched, imbued with new life and love. This was powerful. Monkey later wrote our whole FBR team about this rescue. Below is his letter in its entirety:

> Dear Brothers and Sisters,
>
> I want to write and share what happened with God and me during our last mission in Iraq.
>
> With every mission, after I get the call from FBR headquarters, especially for an international mission, I pray to God to make sure it is His time for me or not. It's a very simple prayer: "God, is it your call or not? If so, I will go. If not, please give me some action to stop me." I have had confidence every time I went—except during this last time in Iraq.
>
> This time, I met very difficult situations, so that deciding to help the people in need was also difficult. I remember the time when we rescued the little girl: we saw many, many dead bodies in the main road and by the road. We also saw that some were still alive among the dead bodies. Some wounded men waved their hand for help and some children were walking, and some were playing among the dead bodies. It made me very sad, but it also made me afraid to help them. I tried to drive away the fear, thinking, 'what if it is my kids or family.' I thought of John 15:13 from the Bible, which says, "No one has greater love than this, that someone would lay down his life for his friends." But I said in my heart, "Lord, I am not ready for this word."
>
> I also remembered one of the mottos that all the Free Burma Rangers must follow: "Do not be led by fear or comfort." This rule also did not encourage me to do the rescue, as I am a person with fear, and lazy. When our leader, Dave, asked me, "Who will go with me?" I said, "Zau Seng," (another FBR cameraman) instead of myself. I knew many people all around the world were praying

for us but still I was weak to make the decision to go on the rescue.

When we talked about possible ways to do this rescue, we needed two things: One is the Americans to drop a smoke bomb; the other is a tank to go in front of us for our cover and to shell ISIS as well. I thought, if we got smoke and a tank, I might dare take part in the rescue. But I did not want to pray for the smoke and tank because I was not 100% sure I would go even then, and I had ignored answers from God many other times in my life. I could not imagine how we could get the smoke from the US Army, and the local authorities had already refused our request for a tank. But Dave did not give up. He prayed and talked to friends, and our team talked and prayed together.

Then, while we were talking about how we could do the rescue, standing in a building by the main road, a smoke bomb from the air was dropped. We stopped talking and ran down to the corner of the road. A big tank came and turned toward the main road. Dave started running and shouting, "Whoever wants to go, let's go!" and led in front.

I did not have time to think and make a decision. Only one thing I shouted in my heart, "This is God! He is in it."

I ran and followed the group. I could not believe that we got the smoke and a tank. The tank was even bigger than I thought. After the rescue, Toh, our medic, and Zau Seng, our other cameraman, and I stood among the Iraqi soldiers. One of them looked into my eye for a while, saying nothing, but his eyes were kind. Then he turned into the building and came back with a hat: it had 'S.W.A.T.' on it, and he placed it on my head. "Wow, that is an honor," said Toh and Zau. I could not think too much. I was re-concentrating my mind.

That night, I reviewed what had happened and what I had done:

1) We did the rescue.

2) I refused God's word: John 15:13.

3) I refused the Ranger motto.

4) I refused my leader's call.

5) We got what we wanted and needed, even though I personally did not even want to pray for it.

Just think. I was a part of it because of God's mercy and faithfulness. I realized the honor is His, not mine. I do not deserve it because I refused everything to do the rescue. Only because of His mercy and faithfulness to all His creation, did I dare go. This is why I want to write and share with you, and give all the glory to Him.

He is very merciful and faithful to you, me and all.

I want to thank God for His mercy and faithfulness to all of us. I want to thank people all around the world for being in prayer for us. I want to thank our team for working together as a family. I want to thank our leader for leading us boldly and in love.

God bless you,
Monkey.

That night, we went back out to the front. Clearly, God wasn't finished saving—and changing—lives in Mosul, and we still wanted to be part of it.

CHAPTER TWENTY

In the Valley of the Shadow of Death— And Out Again

"God is either the God who parted the Red Sea or He isn't."

—DAVE, DURING RESCUE

Winston Churchill is credited with saying, "When you're going through hell, keep going."[7] In Mosul, we kept moving. The next day, June 3, we were back on the little rubble-strewn street just a couple hundred meters from the body-strewn street we ran down the day before. ISIS was still pouring death out from the gaping wreckage of the hospital and the buildings around it. It was a bit like the situation David in the Bible found when he showed up to bring his brothers food: a sort of stalemate with Goliath coming out to threaten and abuse the Israelites every day. Every day, ISIS sat up there in that hospital, maximizing the destruction they could wreak from their one strongpoint.

People were still trying to escape, and the Iraqis were still trying to figure out how to take the hospital. That morning, the morning of June 3, a small, disheveled man with intense eyes came up the street. He had somehow made it through ISIS's lines, and the Iraqis jumped out and pointed their guns at him. They wanted to make sure he wasn't going to blow himself up; he had a beard and a wild look that made us think of ISIS, but he convinced them he wasn't. His name was Omar. He told us his mother was old, sick, in a wheelchair, and stuck back behind the ISIS lines. He asked for help to get her out of ISIS territory. He also told us there were a few more people, wounded but alive, stuck back across the road. He'd seen them on his way over.

Zuhair, the Iraqi private who encouraged us in the rescue a day before, was back too. He was waving a phone. "There's more people!

We've got to go get them. Yesterday, you did a heroic thing. Thank you for risking your life to help my people. Please help us again." He'd actually talked on the phone to a woman who was stranded in the soft drink factory, wounded.

While escaping with her family, she was shot twice in the leg, crippling her. Her family stayed with her a little while but then kept moving. Her brother had promised to go back and get her, but once he had made it across the Iraqi lines, they wouldn't let him go back. She was lying over there somewhere, waiting for help. She saw our rescue the previous day from her hiding place and managed to make a phone call out to her brother, who made contact with Zuhair and had talked to the woman.

It wasn't an easy conversation. "Where are you?"

"I'm not sure—it's a little room, in the Pepsi factory."

"Where in the factory?"

"I don't know."

"Can you see anything from there?"

"Before, I was outside the room, and I saw Daesh shooting a lot of people—I also saw the tank and rescue yesterday. I was afraid Daesh would come, so I crawled in here and now I can't see anything."

Zuhair started to get agitated. "I can't help you if you can't tell me where you are!" He yelled into the phone.

The woman got angry too, then. "Fine! Don't come!"

Omar intervened. "I know where she is. There, you see the dead man in the wheelchair to the left?" He pointed to a man slumped over in a wheelchair with a woman shot dead at his feet. Her dress was flipped up over her head and one of her hands was stretched toward the chair. "Behind that wheelchair, see a small building attached to the factory? She is in there, I think."

Zuhair turned to me and said, "We've got to help that girl and those people. Come on!"

Omar confirmed he'd seen the other people too. He'd help us find them after he got his mom. I called the Americans again to see if they could drop more smoke. They did, and Omar took off, crawling through the rubble back across the street. On the other side was a wall with rubble piled up against it. He climbed up the rubble and over the wall and disappeared into a hole in the soft drink factory.

Thirty minutes later, he was back. We saw him appear with his wheelchair-bound mother at the hole in the building above the wall.

He muscled the wheelchair through the hole and then lifted his mother out of the chair. He carried her over to the edge of the wall and started lowering her. She was limp and looked heavy.

The wall was about eight feet high, and Omar could only lower her so far. There she dangled and leaning forward as far as he could so as to lessen her fall, Omar let her go. She dropped the remaining four feet, hit the rubble and rolled down. Omar jumped down after her but couldn't stop her from breaking her leg and striking her head. But she was alive!

At this point, Iraqi ERD troops had pushed forward on the other side of the street and were close to Omar and his mother. They helped pick her up, loaded her in the Humvee, and hauled her back to us. She was eventually evacuated back to the CCP.

Zuhair took charge. He grabbed Omar and started getting all the information he could about the location of the survivors. Again, he told me urgently: "There are living people in there. We have go help them. I'll go alone if I have to, but you are Special Forces. You can lead us."

"Yes, but this is not a movie. We will all die. ISIS controls all the soft drink factory, hospital and surrounding area," I answered.

Zuhair looked at me intently and asked, "Are you a soldier or a doctor?"—meaning if I was a soldier this was my job, but if I was a doctor I could stay back.

I stopped, prayed, and listened to God. Then I thought, "I am an ambassador of Jesus, he sent me here to love and help these people. That means I go. Also, I was a soldier." I looked Zuhair in the eye and answered, "For this, I am a soldier. I go."

He grabbed my hand and smiled, "Yes, yes, let's go!"

I told him, "You lead, and I will follow you with my team. We will do this together." I would not be the leader of this mission; Zuhair would. The day before, I led. I prayed a lot, we prayed together, I called people, and I conceived the plan. I coordinated with the Americans, I coordinated with the Iraqis, got smoke, led the rescue, went to get the girl, led everything. This time, it was Zuhair.

I had told him I'd follow him, but he was still a private. We went and talked to his immediate superior, a major, and tried to get some resources to help. The major said the same thing the general did the day before: "No. This is a suicide mission. We can't do it."

Zuhair begged to be allowed to go. "Sir, please, sir, there are living people in there, women and children wounded, trapped by ISIS. They will soon die. We are their only hope. Please let me try. There are four of us who want to go help. We are all volunteers." I asked the major if we could pray about this and told him that, in addition to the four Iraqis, I would go and bring my team to help.

We prayed together, and the major looked up and said, "Okay. I cannot send anyone on this mission, but whoever really wants to go can go. No one has to go, but I will give all who want to eight hours off, so this is on your own time."

"Thank you, sir!" Zuhair and I replied in unison.

We now had to get our team across the street. We found out that after the smoke drop for Omar, there was no more available at the moment. Since we would be moving through buildings, we were not getting a tank either. But ISIS was still blasting anything that moved, so we made another plan. We would drive our Humvees and follow an armored bulldozer that was going to cross the street a few hundred meters down the road, away from ISIS, and link up with the ERD troops who were already across the road—the same troops who helped evacuate Omar's mother.

Our team was Zuhair and three other Iraqi soldiers in a Humvee in front of us, and in our Humvee was Zau Seng, stationed up in the turret to film and wearing his trademark big grin, Toh, Sky, and me driving. Due to the number of hits we had taken from ISIS in this, our second Humvee, I could not properly keep the armored windows up and also had to hold the door closed.

I followed Zuhair's Humvee behind the armored bulldozer, and we wound through a labyrinth of alleyways, working our way further away from ISIS. Finally, we got to the crossing point. The bulldozer revved its big engine and started across as fast as it could. Immediately, ISIS opened up with cannon, machine gun, and sniper fire. The bulldozer made it halfway as bullets bounced off its thick armor before an armor-piercing 23mm cannon round hit the engine, stopping the dozer in its tracks.

Right away, more rounds hit, there was an explosion, and the bulldozer started burning. The driver leapt out of the cab, using the dozer as a shield, and ran back across the road. I watched him until I saw he was clear, said, "Lord help us, in Jesus's name," and shot out across the road as fast as I could.

As we bounced past the burning dozer, bullets hit the armored side of our Humvee, cracking and gouging the plexiglass windshield. At the same time, my battered side window came down, exposing me and everyone inside the Humvee to the ISIS fire. I could do nothing about the window, but I held the door closed with my left hand and steered with my right. It was scary, but I couldn't help laughing at the absurd picture we must have made, bouncing along in front of ISIS, with doors swinging and windows dropping open. As we cleared the street and reached the cover of the ruins on the other side, we said a collective "Thank God." Zau popped down from the turret grinning and said, "Very good, sir."

We linked up with Zuhair and his team. There were two other ERD Humvees here strongpointing the narrow lane running up to the wall of the soft drink factory. There was an embankment of rubble leading up the wall, and then we had to scramble up about eight feet to get over it. Before we started, I asked our combined team to stop. "Dear God, help us be an instrument of peace in Jesus's name."

I felt very afraid, but praying helped, and I felt my priorities were aligned with God's: to bring peace, to bring help to people in need. We were not going in to pick a fight but to try to save lives. Mortal danger and accompanying well-founded fear have a way of exposing our motives. Fear helps strip away any pride or aggression. My motives were clear: duty to help those in need and love for people who were in danger and in great need. Good motives didn't take away fear, and I wasn't feeling like a superhero; I was terrified.

Unlike yesterday, when we went in behind a giant screen of smoke with tank guns blazing, this time, we had no help. Silence was our best defense here, and we carefully helped each other up over the wall. To the right was the hole in the wall through which Omar had carried his mother. Zuhair and his men led the way through the hole, and we were inside the ISIS-occupied compound.

In front of us was the wreckage of the factory. Giant concrete roof slabs were half fallen in, concrete pillars were broken off halfway, and twisted pieces of rebar poked out everywhere. Small and large blocks of busted concrete covered the floor as we crept through the damaged machinery.

We left one of the Iraqi soldiers at our entry point as rear security in case ISIS came around the corner. We carefully and quietly picked our way over, under, and through the rubble. Zuhair was leading and kept turning around and encouraging us, in a whisper, "Come on, come on—ssshhh." I was right behind him, and my eyes must have been huge. We knew our lives depended on silence. If ISIS found out we were here, they would smoke us.

I told my team not to shoot, even if ISIS fired in here. If we shot back, all the ISIS fighters around would know we were here and it would be over. We would only shoot if we were trapped and had no other way.

We carefully ran across a large open space and reached one end of the first room. The fear in me intensified. *This is crazy*, I thought. *If ISIS comes through any of the doors or sees us, we're all dead.* Then I remembered the end of an email I received from a church earlier that morning: "Be bold," it said. This gave me courage. When you are afraid, no one needs to tell you to be careful. You already are. But when you are afraid and trying to do good, you need help to be bold. I thanked God for all our praying friends who helped us be bold.

Now we came to a smaller open area; at least, the roof was destroyed so there was sunlight filtering in, and it felt open. As we climbed over big chunks of concrete with metal sticking out everywhere, ISIS started shooting at something in front of us, and a coalition bomb hit the hospital area with a boom.

We kept silently moving and entered a second part of the building. It was a high-ceilinged room, and here the roof was mostly intact, although the walls were blown out. Rebar spidered out from the ceiling. Suddenly, Zuhair stopped in front of me, and I stepped up to his side to see what he was seeing. I drew a quick breath.

The entire next room was full of empty soda cans; they covered the floor from wall to wall. It was a giant, room-sized pile of cans, rising from the entrance where we stood to a depth of about three feet at the opposite doorway. We had to go through that to get to the outer courtyard. The absurdity of it hit me, and I laughed to myself. "Wow, we are really in it now. No way." But the laughter quickly drained away.

There was no way we could do this without ISIS hearing us. We were lost. It felt like that moment on a climb when you're just shy of the summit but realize getting there is probably going to cost you your life. Except this wasn't just my life. It was also the lives of all these brave guys, my team. And it wasn't just a mountain summit. It was the life of a woman I'd never seen, who had been gunned down but hadn't given

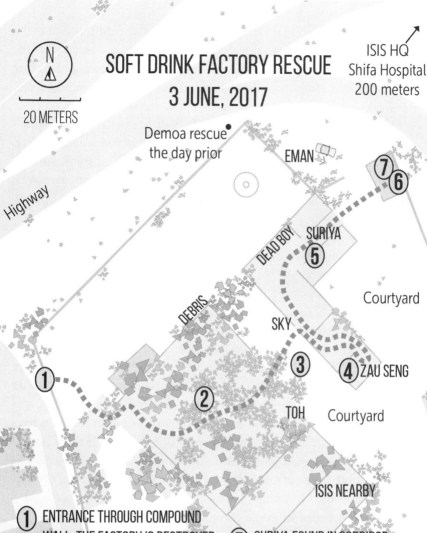

SOFT DRINK FACTORY RESCUE
3 JUNE, 2017

N

20 METERS

ISIS HQ
Shifa Hospital
200 meters

Demoa rescue
the day prior

EMAN

⑦
⑥

Highway

DEAD BOY

SURIYA
⑤

Courtyard

DEBRIS

SKY

③

④ ZAU SENG

①

②

TOH   Courtyard

ISIS NEARBY

① ENTRANCE THROUGH COMPOUND WALL. THE FACTORY IS DESTROYED, & THE TEAM MUST CLIMB THROUGH THE WRECKAGE

② HALL OF CANS

③ OPEN COURTYARD. TOH POSTED TO SECURE EXIT & SKY & ZAU SENG POSTED TO SECURE COURTYARDS

④ MAN SHOT THROUGH KNEE FOUND

⑤ SURIYA FOUND IN CORRIDOR

⑥ DAVID & TWO SOLDIERS FIND KHOFRAN & ABDUL RAQMAN

⑦ DAVID SEES EMAN WOUNDED & TRAPPED. ZUHAIR, SURIYA & DAVID RESCUE EMAN BY PULLING HER INTO COVER WITH WIRE

THE TEAM EXITS WITH WOUNDED THROUGH THE WAY THEY ENTERED

up. Though I was yet to see her, I'd seen the ones who didn't make it: the old man in the wheelchair, the two little girls whose dad I'd hugged, the husband who'd collapsed in my arms over the lifeless body of his young wife. I couldn't bring those lives back, but maybe I could save this one.

I said a prayer and thought again of the message I had read before deciding to join this rescue: "Dave, be bold, in Jesus's name." And I thought, *Well, God is either the God who parted the Red Sea, or He isn't. He can do this if He wants to.* And I told God, *Lord, I believe you are the same God, and you brought us here. Help us make it through.* Then, with a smile and a shake of my head, I motioned to our team to keep moving through the cans.

One by one, we ran through. The noise was tremendous; it was loud crunching, cracking, and popping. Again, I laughed to myself at the ludicrous nature of this expedition. We all got to the far side of the hall of empty soda cans and stopped. There, in front of us, was an open courtyard and, beyond that, the hospital loomed high.

I could see their positions in the hospital—if they looked, they could see us. We did not know if ISIS was in the next building on the other side of courtyard, but we did know they were in the buildings behind that one, and in the buildings to our immediate right. I placed Toh behind a chunk of concrete to guard our right flank and cover the courtyard in front of us. "Stay here and cover us, but don't shoot unless you have to," I whispered to him. He nodded seriously and fixed himself behind the pylon, eyes scanning intently. I felt a wave of love for him. He was our gentle but tough medical director from Burma, standing in the gap. I knew he would let nothing pass as long as he was alive. I also didn't know if he or any of us would come out of this alive.

I looked across the open courtyard and thought, *If ISIS is in the buildings directly across from us, we'll be dead if we cross here. We'll probably be dead anyway.* It seemed like a big gamble. I asked God what to do and felt I should use his name with faith and with nothing in the way. I turned to Sky and said something I've never said in combat, on a climb, or in any dangerous situation. I said, "Sky, I'm afraid."

I've been afraid before, in combat and on climbs, but I never admitted it. It's not wise, it's irresponsible as a leader, it's not useful, and it only causes doubt and confusion for the people following. When you're on an airplane and it has trouble, you don't want the pilot to volunteer that he's afraid; you need him to focus on flying, not his fear. Later, you can always say how you felt. Or, if someone asks, tell the truth and admit it. But in times of danger, when you're a leader, it is usually not useful to confess fear. John Paul Jones said, "If fear is cultivated it will become stronger, if faith is cultivated it will achieve mastery." We need to overcome fear, not dwell on it.

For me, this situation was different. We could feel the power of darkness so thick, the power of fear so thick, the danger so great, and we were so small. I felt I needed to be transparent and clean before God and my team, who were both with me in this—and so I whispered, "Sky, I'm afraid."

Sky said, "Me too!" I smiled and reached out and took his hand.

"Let's pray." I whispered. I prayed against ISIS. I said, "ISIS, you can't hear us, see us, or stop us, in Jesus's name. And Satan and demons, you cannot stop us either, in Jesus's name. And if you do not like our prayer, then talk to Jesus because we are moving forward behind him."

We stood in that opening with death in front of us: two men, afraid, hands clasped, praying—both committed but without the power to do more. And then I nodded to Sky, and we launched off across the open courtyard; it was also full of cans and rubble. *Don't lose your footing*, I told myself as I sprinted over the jagged chunks of rubble and thousands of cans.

We got to the other side and into the building with no hail of gunfire erupting from the walls. ISIS was shooting but not at us. We entered the building, rifles at the ready, and saw a man lying on the floor. He had a fist-sized hole in his left leg where his kneecap used to be. Flies were buzzing in and out of the wound and terror twisted his countenance. Behind him and outside a partially opened doorway, I saw a man and woman dead in the next street.

Sky knelt and bandaged the man's leg. I tried to reassure him we were here to help him, not kill him. He looked at us wide-eyed. As Sky tended to his wound, he began to moan, and we gave him a shirt to bite on to help stay quiet.

Then we heard noises coming from beyond the open door. Was ISIS out there? I motioned for Zau to stay with the wounded man, to pull security on the open back door, and to stop ISIS if they came through. I put Sky in the opposite position, one room over, to guard our left flank as we went forward searching for the woman who had called us. Zuhair,

Omar, and his two remaining soldiers led the way as I followed, with confidence growing that this was God's mission.

We came out into the left side of the courtyard and moved along the walls, and this time, we had the building to block ISIS's view. We ducked into what had been a corridor between buildings, and there was a little girl, maybe six years old, with her back pressed against one of the walls of the narrow hallway, looking at us with the blank stare of shock and fear. She was dirty, her clothes stained with blood, but she was not wounded.

Directly across from her in a small room lay a little boy, dead. Blood seeped out of his head where he had been shot. There was a trail of blood from outside the building into the hallway and this small room. He had been shot, and then crawled into this room and died. He looked about five years old. I took his picture and bent down and prayed for him.

Where are his mother and father? I thought, filled with sadness. I motioned to the girl, smiled and put a finger over my lips, "Don't be afraid, we are here to help you, shhh," I whispered.

We went through the hallway, which emptied into another small courtyard. We dashed across it, about ten meters, to the last building of the soft drink factory. The buildings with ISIS fighters were right behind this small building and in the buildings to our right. Immediately to our right was an entrance to the courtyard, and to the left was a gate that opened out into the street and served as an entrance to the factory. The little girl followed us, eyes wide, as went into the last room.

This room, like the others, was demolished. There were bullet holes in the concrete walls, overturned chairs and tables, blankets and mattresses strewn all over the floor. There was a couch against the wall and, huddled on it back in the corner, was a wounded and crippled boy, maybe sixteen years old. Somehow, he'd escaped this far and then been left. In the middle of the floor, lying twisted on her stomach and left shoulder, was a woman. As we came in, she turned to look, eyes wide in terror, shielding her face with her hands at the same time. She thought we were ISIS.

It was the woman who had called us. She'd been shot twice in her upper leg, with one of the bullets breaking her femur. Once she realized we weren't ISIS, she smiled up at us. The crippled boy moved out from

the corner and sat on the couch against the wall. One of the Iraqi soldiers gave him a cigarette and he sucked the smoke down frenetically.

We had moved through the entire factory from back to front. These
were the only living people we'd seen, and I was sure there were no
more. We had four people we'd have to move out the way we came: the
first man with the hole in his leg, the little girl, the crippled boy, and the
woman with the broken femur. They would all need to be carried.

I went back outside to look around and start planning how we
were going to evacuate them. I looked out the front gate of the factory.
Beyond the gate was an entrance parking lot and, beyond that, the street
we'd come up yesterday, running behind the tank. The hospital was to
our right as I faced the street but the ISIS in the hospital couldn't see us
because we had this small building between them and us.

Then I heard them, the voices of ISIS behind this building. They
were very close but did not know we were there. We had to get out fast.
I looked back out to that entrance area and there were dead bodies all
over. Beyond it was the street we had been looking at from the other
side; lots of dead people there too. Flies buzzed everywhere but nothing
else moved. I could see the man in the wheelchair with the woman at
his feet. There was a blown-up car about thirty meters away, with three
or four bodies beside it.

Then one of them moved.

I looked again. "No way," I thought. A woman I had thought dead,
lying flat on her back, lifted her hand just a little and waved. A hoarse
and whispered call for help came floating over to us. Zuhair was next to
me. *Oh God*, I thought. *There is no way to save her*. If we went out there,
not only would ISIS from the hospital shoot us but the ISIS fighters on
the other side of our building would know we were there and attack. All
of us, including the three wounded and the little girl, would die. "This
is not about courage," I told myself. "This is about foolishness. There is
no way we can save the woman out in the street and the others too. We
would all die here."

I didn't know what to do and what to pray. I said silently to God,
*God, please just take her to heaven now. Let her die and go to you. It
would be better for us all.* It was a horrible thought and I'm ashamed to
tell it, but my heart sank in that moment and I saw no other way.

I looked at Zuhair. "We can't go out there," I whispered.

"I'll go alone, even if we all die, I will go. I will not leave her," he said softly.

Suddenly, with alarm, I realized, *He will! We're going to have to do this—I'd better pray again. Lord, we don't have a solution, please help us!* I grabbed Zuhair's hand and prayed with him, out loud but quietly: "God help us."

I opened my eyes and Zuhair looked at me, hesitated, cocked his head, then pointed up to the electrical wiring running along the outside of the building about seven feet up. He mimed using the wire to pull the lady in. We ripped it off the building as quietly as we could, and I cut off a length with my knife and tied it together. We had about a thirty-meter length of wiring.

He motioned for the little girl to come and whispered in her ear. He handed her the ball of wiring while he hung onto one end. The little girl took the roll of wire and ran out about twenty meters as it unraveled and threw it toward the woman in the street. It landed on the woman's chest and she grabbed it. The little girl dashed back as, from the hospital, ISIS shot and missed, kapow, kapow! She arrived back, breathless and untouched. I guessed she was so small ISIS didn't see her until it was too late, and the building behind us blocked her from view of the nearest fighters. The woman was on her back behind the destroyed car and was too low for ISIS to see from where they were shooting.

I started praying for her then, that she could get the wire around her hand. In the best conditions it's hard to tie something around your arm with just one hand. And she'd been shot, lying in the sun, we found out later, for five days. What strength did she have left, what kind of concentration? If she didn't tie it right and it came off halfway, we probably wouldn't get a second chance. I prayed it would stay on. When she seemed ready, we started to pull. I was helping Zuhair pull while the two other Iraqis were providing security. And I thought, *this is an important moment.*

With one hand, I used my phone and filmed for about fifteen seconds because I thought, this is something that needs to be recorded. Zuhair pulled with two hands and I helped him with one. She was on her back, being dragged across rubble, bumping through rocks and concrete, and I could hear her voice, low.

At first, she was saying, "For my children, Allah akhbar, Allah akhbar (God is great, God is great), thank you, God, you saved me, you saved me. Thank you." As we got her into the compound, she looked at me: "Shukran, shukran," which means thank you. She reached us alive and without a hail of gunfire descending, and I looked at her in awe and was humbled. I did not save her. God helped Zuhair find a solution and I was just there. I had reached the limit of my courage and was out of ideas. Zuhair had not run out of courage; his persistence scared me into asking God again for help. And God helped.

Now we had five people to get out. We shuttled them, section by section. Omar carried the woman who had phoned us, Sky carried the woman we dragged off the street, I carried the little girl. Zuhair had the crippled boy. As we worked our way back to Zau, he told us he could hear ISIS out on the street behind us, just past the open back door. We tensed and all raised our weapons.

The sounds faded and we crept out to the big courtyard, crossing the noisy cans and rubble again. Shots rang out over our heads, but it seemed ISIS still had not seen or heard us and were shooting at the Iraqis across the street again. We got the four back to the middle of the factory and went back for the first wounded man. We put him on a broken door and used it like a stretcher.

Khofran reacts to our arrival, at first thinking we're ISIS, June 3, 2017.

Eman, right after we dragged her to us in the soft drink factory, June 3, 2017.

With Zuhair, Eman, and
Suriya, June 3, 2017.

We'd get a couple people through one section, crawling over and under giant slabs of building, rubble, and rebar, put them down and then go back for the others. Little by little, we got all five out. It took us almost two hours to move them all, but ISIS never found us.

Once they were all out of the factory, we still had to go over the wall where Omar dropped his mother earlier. Some of us went over the side to help catch the people as we lowered them. As we were moving these wounded through the hole, other people started to appear, who'd been hiding. They wanted out too. We told them we'd come back. We got out of the ISIS area to the Humvees and loaded the people.

We drove to the same crossing we'd used earlier; the bulldozer was still in flames in the middle of the highway. We stopped at the edge of the street and prayed earnestly, then I revved the engine and we shot across the road, zigzagging as we went to avoid the burning dozer and ISIS bullets. ISIS shot at us, hitting the Humvee but not stopping us. We were across! Smiling and laughing, we jumped out of the Humvees, thanked God and congratulated each other. It was good to be alive. It was good to have helped others live.

And it was a huge relief. Tension had built at each stage: the cans, the open courtyard, dragging the lady—and we survived it all. But I didn't have time to feel it. We pulled all the casualties out of the Humvees, put them in ambulances, and sent them to the CCP. Then we turned back around and drove back to that hole in the wall, back through ISIS fire. We'd promised those other people we'd be back.

Our vehicle was hit each time we crossed, and each time, my door came open, facing ISIS where all this fire was coming from. It was a total Mr. Bean extraction, us bouncing over the rubble, doors swinging open and shut, armored windows dropping open of their own accord. Bullets were hitting the side of our vehicle, but nothing hit us, and we returned safely each time. We picked up as many people as we could, brought them back, dropped them off, and went back. It took two more trips to get everyone out.

I got out of the Humvee, back in the safe zone, and took a deep breath. Relief washed over me. We did it. We'd got those people out and survived. It was a miracle. Suddenly, I wanted to see them all again, to make sure they were really okay, to rejoice with them in life—theirs and ours. We all came so close to death but were saved. I wanted to celebrate, to laugh, to hug them and rejoice at life!

I found Sahale, who was there, ready to help, with Noelle. "Honey, thank God, we're all okay! Drive me to the CCP, I want to check on those people." Sahale drove the ambulance, and I jumped in next to her. Noelle (Sky's wife) was in the back, cheerful as always, and rode with us. Back at the CCP, I found each one of those people who'd been trapped and found out they were all living, and fine.

The lady we dragged with the wire—she had been wounded for five days—was fine, and it turned out the little girl was her daughter. The lady who called us and initiated the rescue after being shot twice in the leg was fine. The man with the hole in his leg was going to live. Omar was there, with his mother, grinning from ear to ear.

I thought, *Wow, God, wow. Thank you that we could be part of that, thank you we lived through it.* I didn't think we were going to live through it. And we got all those people out, including the people from the day before. I was so thankful: for the Americans, who dropped smoke; for the Iraqis, who had the courage to send a tank; for Zuhair and the other soldiers, and Omar, who went on foot; for my teammates, all of them, they all had an important part to play; and for my wife and kids, who were behind me in spirit every step of the way.

In the midst of being overwhelmed with gratitude, in that moment I thought of those all over the world who sent me messages, Scripture, and prayer. A lot of people sent me Scripture. I would start to get scared, and I'd remember a verse, or a message: "Dave, be bold. In Jesus's name." Or Psalm 23—many people sent me that psalm during this time: "The Lord is my shepherd.... Even though I walk through the darkest valley, I will fear no evil for you are with me; your rod and your staff, they comfort me. You prepare a table before me in the presence of my enemies." That psalm took on new meaning for me, through the battle: it means God has us. He gives us trust when we need it, gives us strength when we need to be brave, protects us in the valley, and takes us through and gives us good things. But not without enemies: "in the presence of my enemies."

The enemies are free in one sense; people are allowed to be wicked. They'll be all around you. Don't look at them; look at the feast, and the good things God gives you. If we look at our enemies, we'll have no taste and we'll lose that good meal. It says, "You anoint my head with oil; my cup overflows. Surely your goodness and love will follow me all the days of my life, and I will dwell in the house of the Lord forever."

We have to die one day. Whether it's tomorrow, or when we're in our teens or twenties, or a baby, or when we're a hundred—one day, we'll go. But we're not going to go to nothingness. We're going to go to Jesus, who died for our sins, who shows us how much God loves us, and we'll be with him.

These verses and messages came to me while I was in the middle of those rescues, when I was making decisions that could cost my life. I needed them.

CHAPTER TWENTY-ONE

The End: Victory, but No Parade

"Go. Tell Americans we love them; tell them, please, love us."
—GENERAL MUSTAFA TO DAVE, JUNE 2017.

The next day, we moved our front-line operation and rejoined the 36th where they were repositioning after the initial failed attempts to take the hospital. The new attack was going to be from the west and south of the hospital, working toward the second bridge. We drove south to the new CCP, which was at a major highway intersection, with overpasses and underpasses and an old shop with a big, wide-open front entrance. General Mustafa and the 36th were staying in some houses behind it.

The team and my family stayed in the same house we had been in on the edge of Hawi Kanisa, even though most of the 36th was gone. Some of the neighborhood families had moved back and an American fire support team moved in next door to us.

A friendly, generous, multigenerational Arabic family had moved back into their house across the street from us and had swooped up the little girl whom Karen was still caring for. They gave her new clothes, spoke to her in Arabic, and had other kids and kids' toys for her to play with. She still hadn't told us her name, or really said anything besides, "Take me to my mama."

By then, Justin was gone, Ephraim was back in Erbil recovering from his leg wound, and Sky and Noelle also left. Our frontline Humvee element was the Animals and me, with Dlo or Mahmood for translation. Dlo and Zeb were driving the ambulance with patients back and forth between the CCP and us. At the new CCP, my family, Maddie, and Hosie were helping with patients—sometimes we'd go back there to meet them and get supplies. We also met up with journalists there and sometimes took a few with us to the front.

It was June and starting to be smoking hot. The fighting was fierce again and we got shelled heavily. Once, just after exiting our Humvee, a mortar landed right on it, a direct hit on top. It wrecked the machine gun mount and showered fragments inside the vehicle. Zau Seng had set his helmet up there and it got a huge dent, but we were all okay.

Right after that, we were in a little compound, eating between casualty evacuations. Zau was sitting with his legs stretched out in front of him, body armor off when a mortar hit the building next to us and a fist-sized piece of metal flew over, missing his head and landing right between his legs in the grass. We all laughed and then ran, following Zau to the relative safety of a building. Better to laugh than cry.

The 36th was pushing further in and as they took more of the city, we were seeing bodies everywhere. Many of them were so desiccated by the heat they were flattened like cardboard. We often had no choice but to drive over the flattened bodies as we moved under fire to help survivors. We had daily casualties and Toh and Eliya were keeping busy treating people.

One day, around the sixth or seventh of June, some Iraqi soldiers from 1st Battalion of the 36th came up to me and said, "You know, we know about your rescues. Can you do another rescue?" The leader of this group was an Iraqi soldier who, after an earlier battle, had pointed his RPG at me in anger after I caught him stealing food we gave to his buddies.

I had prayed quickly and controlled my temper. I looked him in the eye and walked up to him. "My brother," I said and hugged him. I then gave him more food in front of everyone. His buddies immediately began to make fun of him.

Since that incident, I had been with him in battle and saw he was one of the bravest and most effective soldiers in the brigade. We were meeting again, and I hugged him and said, "My brother!" We both laughed and I asked him, "What is it?"

"There's an eighty-four-year-old man trapped in a house over there and he can't get out." They told me he didn't really want to leave, actually, but just needed food.

I thought it was kind of strange but prayed and said okay. We had nothing to carry food in, so we dumped some canned food into pillowcases from the houses we were pushing through. I grabbed a black-and-red polka-dot pillowcase, filled it with cans, and put it on my back.

They pointed to the spot and we headed out—Eliya, Toh, Zau, Monkey, Mahmood, and me—running through the streets. When we crossed the street with our pillowcases of food, ISIS shot at us, probably wondering what kind of an assault force we were.

We got to the old man in a shell-damaged building and through Mahmood, I said, "Hey, we brought you this food. I heard you might want to stay. I think you'll make it because we're gonna push through this whole area and the Iraqis will secure it and ISIS won't be able to get you."

He looked at me: "Stay? I don't want to stay! Get me outta here! ISIS will kill me like they have my family." Tears came to his eyes.

I teared up too and told him, "You will be like my father, I will not leave you. We'll get you out of here." I hugged him. Taking him with us did change our return trip a bit because he was a big guy, six feet tall or so, just like my real father. With Mahmood's help, I got him on my back, and we moved out. Because we weren't going to be sprinting across the street, we went back a different way, through a series of rat holes knocked in the walls of the houses, so we could move without being in the open.

We got to the point where we had to cross streets and I looked out the window to check it out. Whoa. There, running down the narrow street, were about three hundred people. They heard the Iraqi Army had come, there was liberation, and they started running, literally for their lives, screaming as they fled. And ISIS opened up on them. It wasn't as dangerous a position as the street in front of the hospital because it was narrower and there was more cover, but ISIS was still trying to inflict as much damage as possible.

We joined all these people in the street, running. I had this old, heavy man on my back and bullets were whipping around us. I saw a man right in front of me, my age probably, carrying his old mother. He got hit in the back and went down. His mother was thrown to the ground alongside him. He lay there on the ground, bleeding out, and she was there, watching her son slowly dying—and there was nothing she could do.

There was nothing I could do with this man on my back, so I stepped over them both, turned a corner, set the man down, and ran back. Toh picked up the old woman and carried her around the corner and the rest of us lifted the man and moved him. Eliya tried to save him but he died quickly. In about fifteen minutes, right where I was, ISIS shot eight people and killed five.

On June 6, ISIS started launching sulfur mustard and chlorine chemical attacks. These weren't directly on us but on the unit operating next to the 36th. The first one affected a few men and the next day there were more than twenty casualties. I heard that maybe six of those died, choking and unable to breathe. We loaded some into our ambulance and I prayed with them. We had six gas masks but left all but two at the office in Erbil. We hadn't seen ISIS use gas since Bashiqa in 2016. It was our mistake to not be better prepared. I thought, *Well, we'll do our best.*

We'd evacuate these guys and their eyes would be bugging out; they'd be gasping for breath, holding their throats, spitting, gagging. Before, ISIS used sulfur mustard but this time, it was also chlorine. Zeb, Dlo, and sometimes Sahale, drove people back to the CCP, washed themselves, and hosed out the back of the ambulance. This went on for three days. Meanwhile, we were moving with the 1st Battalion of the 36th, pushing farther in.

One day, I went into a just-cleared building and found a dead ISIS fighter. He'd probably been dead for three or four days and was starting to smell pretty bad. He had an ISIS flag draped over his body and I thought, *People have been asking for ISIS flags—I'll grab it.* I took it and shoved it in my pocket. Then I smelled my hand and it stunk. I realized what I'd just done and whipped the flag out of my pocket and threw it on the ground. But I smelled like death now; this wouldn't help any meetings I might have, or my reunion with Karen, or the kids. I had to dig around in that blown-up house for soap and water, take off my pants and wash them and my hands and my whole body to get out that stench.

Right then, a Vice News journalist came up and a few other news people. More journalists were coming, and more of them wanted to talk to me. For one, I spoke English and was easier to communicate with than an Iraqi. But also, I had a different story for them. The video of the rescue of the little girl behind the tank had been released; CNN broke it first as part of a bigger story about civilians being targeted by ISIS. It was picked up and shared and was starting to get big, and news outlets wanted a piece of the story—it was good news and something interesting for an audience tired of bad news.

While I talked to the journalists, some more civilians started moving through our position. They looked worried but at this spot, we were actually out of range of ISIS. At one point, I saw a man trying to carry a woman, struggling and panicked. She was big, maybe two hundred pounds. Bullets were hitting the walls above us but from the angle ISIS was at, I knew they could not hit us. I walked over to him and said, "You don't need to run. There's no way ISIS could shoot you right here." They were trying to get around the corner thirty meters away, where they'd be completely safe.

I should have just picked her up and carried her at a walk around the corner. With a crowd of journalists watching, I picked her up and started running—running with a two-hundred-pound woman. As I ran, she shifted her weight and started to roll out of my arms and I leaned forward to not lose my grip, but then started falling forward so my legs couldn't keep up and I knew I was going down. It flashed in my head, *Oh no, I'm going to hurt her.* I rotated as I went down and landed on my shoulder and head with her full weight on me. I cut my face and hurt my shoulder a bit but she was fine. Wow. That was embarrassing.

I apologized to her. She was scared and I picked her up again and, this time walking, carried her around the corner. There was a wheelchair her husband and some of her family had, but they hadn't been able to maneuver it in the rubble. We put her in it and got her out and I apologized again. Pride is a dangerous thing, especially when combined with journalists, and I was very sorry.

We were with the 1st battalion still, and some of their men came over and told us there was a family beneath one of the buildings. "They've been hiding there for three months, the woman and kids. The husband's dead out there in the yard." We had to drive through fire but found them, all huddled under a building, all looking scared except for this thirteen-year-old boy, who was angry. You could tell by looking at him: he wanted to kill us. The soldiers told me, "His dad was ISIS and he really hates us."

His mother and another lady with a newborn baby were there. They were sick and needed help. We went down and prayed with them and Toh and Eliya examined them. They were anemic and had some skin problems, and one of them had a respiratory infection. We had medicine for all of this, plus food for the kids. We started treating them, then had to leave for more supplies.

There was one dangerous place we had to cross between this frontline position and the CCP, about fifty meters of open area at an intersection. By now, we were back in the vicinity of the hospital and, with its height, the ISIS men in positions on the upper stories could see down into some of the surrounding streets. They started shooting at us with a .50-caliber sniper rifle as we crossed this intersection. One of the rounds went through the turret and on through the magazine of Zau's AK that was slung across his chest—hitting the gun and going out the other side without hurting anyone.

A flurry of bullets impacted our windows, cracking them and making it hard to see through them. One round hit the door and destroyed whatever was left of its latch: it just swung open on its hinges, two hundred pounds of steel banging open and closed. But we made it around the corner and then to the CCP to stock up on supplies.

We returned to the house with food for the family and as we headed down to the cellar, where they were hiding, the boy met us on the stairs. "You can't go there. It's not your job. They're women, they're my women."

I stopped for a minute. "Hey," I said. "That's your mom and your sister and they need medicine and food, they need help. The baby is sick."

He just looked at me. "No."

"Hey, man." And I prayed quickly for the right words. "It's over. It is over. We're not your enemy. I'm really sorry your father died, but that whole ISIS idea was wrong. I know you face many injustices and that's partly why ISIS came up—and those injustices need to be settled. But the way it happened is wrong, and it's over. They lost."

I stopped for a minute. Then I looked him in the eye. "I pray for your dad. I hope you'll see him in heaven. But right now, we're going to go down there and help your family and you're not stopping us." I took his hand and held it and prayed for God to give him peace in his heart, and for a new Iraq, and that he could forgive his enemies. Then I gently moved him out of the way. We went down and treated the women and gave the family food.

They were happy we were back. The Iraqi sergeant who was with us told me, "You know that when we turn our backs that boy could kill us, easy. But we won't kill him unless we have to." That struck me as a lot of mercy. He continued, "We want to build up a new Iraq." On the way out, I prayed with the kid again and gave him an FBR T-shirt. He smiled and relaxed a little bit.

As we came back into the street, some of the Iraqi soldiers came up. "Hey, we heard about that rescue of the little girl you did. We want to see it. Can we watch it, please?" Monkey's video was all over the internet, and news of the rescue was circulating around the front line. I didn't have the video on me, though. It felt a little bit weird actually—I wasn't sure what to do. Go out of my way to show them a video of myself? But I loved these guys and it was something they asked for. So, I prayed and asked our team. "This is for love, we should do it," they agreed. I told the soldier I'd go back and get my computer and show them.

We drove back through that intersection, under fire again, got hit again, but made it back to the CCP. When I got back, Victor was there. He'd come for a quick visit and was staying with the family at our little headquarters. I said, "Sorry, I've got to go back again, these guys asked for this video." He said it was no problem, but he had a friend, a Canadian security guy who was there as his bodyguard, who wanted to come with us.

He came along and we got shot up again crossing the intersection; this time one of our tires got blown out. The Canadian helped us change the tire and we showed the video to the guys there on the front line. I also presented FBR's Star of Valor medal to some of the soldiers who I knew did heroic things but hadn't received one yet. I took down the names of others who we would give them to later. The 1st battalion started out the battle with around four hundred men back in October. I estimated now there were about sixty left who could fight.

I prayed with these men, hugged them, and got back in the Humvee to head out again. I was avoiding talking about it, but we were at a decision point in our mission. We planned to return to Thailand, then the U.S. on June 12. But we had thought the battle would be over by then and it wasn't. As I left those men, I wasn't sure I'd be back. But the drive to the CCP soon distracted me from those thoughts.

This time a .50-caliber round came through the vehicle, punching through the cupola. Another hit our window but did not come through. The tire we just changed was shot out and we limped back to the CCP. Our Humvee was practically in pieces now.

Back at the CCP, I met with Victor again. Our armored ambulance was there, and he got in that and our whole team drove back to the house, the same little haven we'd been staying in. I was going to turn the Humvee in to General Mustafa. I showed it to him and said, "Sorry, man. This vehicle is pretty much shot to pieces—it's basically ruined now."

He just laughed. He said, "Dave, you're like me with hospitals." He was beaten at the Salam Hospital and the Shifa Hospital had taken its toll. "We should stay away from Humvees and hospitals, you and I. We're both zero and two." He laughed again and hugged me.

I'd been praying about whether we should stay to the end of the battle because it looked like it could go on longer. I asked Mustafa and he said it was pretty much done, they were mostly mopping up. They were very close to the river and were just going to stop and be a blocking force while the Golden Division finished up the old city. And he said, "You should go to America and tell the story of what's happened."

We went over to our house to talk about it and had a little prayer meeting. I really wasn't sure. The team thought we should go, and I felt like we should stay—but I wasn't sure if that was from God or just me. So we prayed about it and just then General Mustafa walked in. He said, "Hey, I know you're praying about America. This battle is almost over. Please go. Go. Tell Americans we love them; tell them, please, love us." Later he told me, "Thank you for showing us what it means to follow Jesus."

There was our answer. We went across the street to the Iraqi family who was helping with the little girl. She still wasn't talking. General Mustafa promised to help look for any family members and Dlo was on it also. He took down everyone's names and numbers and we gave the family some money to help with the girl's expenses. We were going to stay part of her life; I was going to keep my promise.

Then we packed up our gear and drove back out through east Mosul. It was amazing to see that place coming back to life. It was bustling with shops where you could get shawarmas and cold Cokes. In Erbil we cleaned ourselves and our gear and were able to meet up with Ephraim and Mohammed, who were both recovering from their wounds. Ephraim was hobbling around the office, laminating things for us, and Mohammed showed up looking almost like nothing had happened to him. It had been just over a month since he'd been shot six times trying to rescue Shaheen. He still had a piece of bullet in his neck which had lodged there just shy of his spinal cord. The doctors hadn't wanted to risk the surgery to take it out.

He told us of going to see his family after he got out of the hospital. They were all crying and happy to see him, happy he survived. His sister told him of a dream she had around the same time he was shot. She saw him lying on a bed in a white room. He was completely still—dead, in fact. Then into the room came a beautiful shining man, and he walked up to Mohammed in the bed, took his hand, and told him to get up—and he did! This man she knew was Jesus.

I hugged him and felt so grateful. It was a real miracle. We still had one more duty to perform before we flew out and that was to visit Shaheen's family. So on a sunny day, we all got in the Land Cruisers and drove to where they were staying near Dohuk. They had a sort of farming house in the countryside outside Dohuk, where they went at certain times of year. It was a small adobe place with a few rooms.

We drove up a little hill where the house was perched overlooking some fields and a hillside, and we all went into a small room, sat on cushions around the wall like we did in innumerable other houses. We could tell they were grieving. His sisters were there, and his brother, and there were no smiles. Everyone was sad.

I gave them the FBR Medal of Honor for Shaheen and told them how much he meant to us, told them how brave he was and the love I'd seen grow in his heart that gave him courage and made him selfless. His dad was really sad and didn't say much, but his mom was mad. "I told him not to go," she said. "Why did you take him to those dangerous places?" And she cried. We all cried.

Shaheen died a hero—which is only a small comfort to the family he left behind. We talked and then they served us a big meal, a meal of mutton from his dad's sheep, which was something Shaheen had promised us for a long time. We had a good visit with the whole family over the food, and the mood lightened as it usually does over a meal. Then we left.

We spent a couple more days in Kurdistan, visiting and thanking people who helped us. We drove to Soran and thanked General Bahram and visited different KRG leaders and offices in Erbil. We stopped in at the U.S. Army base there and said thanks to General Efflandt and the team who helped us so much at different points in the battle. Then, on June 13, 2017, we all got on a plane and flew back to Thailand to prepare for the U.S. trip.

I thought of the people we had a part in saving: Rahab, the girl in the collapsed building; the little girl and the man we carried out from behind the tank; the shot woman who had not given up but called us in to help her and the other four people who were saved because of that; the old man; and a few others.

I thanked God we could do something good in the midst of evil and in spite of our own weaknesses. I prayed for those people who did survive, for comfort. I prayed that Jesus would do something with them in their hearts, to heal them, to give them comfort and purpose, that they could follow Him, and they could see their lost relatives in heaven.

The battle of Mosul was a devastating loss of life and livelihood— one composed of thousands of small private and public tragedies. The sadness of these weighs on me. It feels like I have a core of sadness inside me, stretching from my belly up to my chest. It does not fill me, but is there and I cry easily when I think of all who died. The loss of life, the people we could not save, even the men I killed, whose hearts had somehow become so twisted with hate and lies that they were not only willing to kill but willing to die for it.

They did not win, their hate did not win, and so the sadness will also always be shot through with joy and love and awe at the courage, love, and sacrifice of the men I fought beside, the men who gave everything, even their lives, to defeat this evil in the hope of a different and a better future.

I learned at Fuller Seminary from Chuck Kraft, my old Gandalf-like professor, "You can live well with sorrow, but you can't live well with shame." Through confession and the light of mercy and truth, Jesus comes in love to take our shame away. Sadness stays with us and may fade over time, but, intense or fading, it is a feeling based on love and so we can bear it. I learned too that sadness shared is divided, while joy shared is multiplied. We shared and divided many sorrows, yet we also shared and multiplied many joys. This is real life and it is a good life.

There is a verse in the Bible: "Therefore we do not lose heart. Even though our outward man is perishing, yet the inward man is being renewed day by day. For our light affliction, which is but for a moment, is working for us a far more exceeding and eternal weight of glory, while we do not look at the things which are seen, but at the things which are not seen. For the things which are seen are temporary, but the things which are not seen are eternal" (2 Corinthians 4:16–18).

We are always looking at the things that are seen; God gave us eyes, and we can't help it. After all I have seen, I cannot say the affliction is light; I will always carry the weight of those lives lost. But I believe their love and sacrifice carry a surpassing weight of glory and are reverberating throughout eternity.

Our Karen friend Dr. Simon once wrote a poem about his people's situation called "Our Living Testimony." I thought of it as we prepared to leave Iraq.

> They call us a displaced people,
> But praise God we are not misplaced.
> They say they see no hope for our future,
> But praise God our future is as bright as the promises of God.
> They say they see the life of our people is a misery,
> But praise God our life is a mystery.
> For what they say is what they see
> And what they see is temporal,
> But ours is the eternal.
> All because we put ourselves
> In the hands of God we trust.

Epilogue

The battle of Mosul lasted nine months, from October 2016 to July 2017. It was the largest deployment of Iraqi troops since 2003 and the world's single largest military operation in nearly fifteen years, since the 2003 invasion of Iraq. It was the largest urban engagement involving U.S. troops since the Battle of Huế in Vietnam.[8] It was also some of the most prolonged and destructive urban combat since the battle of Stalingrad in World War II.

The combined forces of the Iraqi Army, PMU, and Peshmerga numbered over one hundred thousand.[9] They faced up to twelve thousand dug-in ISIS fighters embedded with civilians.[10] The Iraqis and Peshmerga lost around fifteen hundred men combined, with more than seven thousand wounded (this does not count PMU casualties).[11] Over one million civilians were displaced,[12] and fifty-four thousand homes were destroyed in Mosul and its outlying areas.[13] Estimates indicated that a staggering eight million tons of rubble filled the city where homes, shops, and schools used to be.[14] Estimates of civilian deaths were around 10,000,[15] and the weight of sorrow and loss hung heavy across the land.[16]

My family and I spent the following three months in the U.S., thanking supporters and sharing the story. The video of our team rescuing the little girl from behind the tank went viral. CNN broke the story, and it was covered by outlets all over the world. We were on NPR, *Fox and Friends*, Channel 4 News, NRA TV, the Christian Broadcasting Network, EWTN Global Catholic Network, CNN, ABC, and CBS. The *Washington Post*, *Los Angeles Times*, and other papers around the world told the story.

We learned what a "green room" is and spent hours there; a lot of makeup was put on me for TV that summer, but it did not improve my looks. I was impressed by the professionalism and skills of the media, who really cared about what was happening and told the story well.

But the story I was telling hadn't ended. Mosul, a giant living city, was coming to life again—even as it was enveloped with death and destruction. Even as we traveled around America, embraced and overwhelmed by its natural and manmade beauty, the love of the people and the wonderful churches we visited, the opportunities to do the things we love as a family—climb, surf, hunt, skydive, rodeo—part of me was still back in Mosul.

Those lives we helped save, their stories were just beginning. They needed help, I knew. And I had made promises to them. The soldiers we were with in battle were still there, trying to bring order from destruction, to fashion some sort of peace; having lost so much, they were still there in the wreckage, working for something better.

No one was walking off into the sunset; instead, they were walking into the ruins of their former lives, suffused with sorrow and looking at what seemed an endless horizon of anger and vengeance. I didn't want to disappear into a sunset either.

I was in touch with Dlo, General Mustafa, and many other friends who were there. Dlo and Mustafa were working to find the family of the little girl. The story of the rescue was broadcast all over Iraq as well and many people saw her face. Dlo put inquiries on Facebook. She continued to live with the Iraqi family who had happened to move back to their home, which had been used by General Mustafa, right when we were living across the street. Victor Marx, whose specialty is trauma recovery and therapy, visited her with his family, and it was wonderful to see his videos of her in a fancy hotel, laughing.

Finally, Dlo and General Mustafa got a lead: someone saw her picture on TV and contacted them. General Mustafa was able to check their story, and it turned out her aunt and grandmother were still alive and wanted to take her back. They were from Diyala, which is an area east of Baghdad. Dlo talked to them and found out the girl's name. It was Demoa—which translates as "tears" in English. They came and got her and brought her home.

Within a couple months, Dlo was also able to track down the injured woman who called us from the soft drink factory with two bullet holes in her leg. Her name was Khofran, and she was from a small village about twenty kilometers south of Mosul. Her family was among those ISIS had swept up with them on their retreat from the Iraqi Army. Sky and Noelle were in Erbil, and they sent pictures of their visit with her;

she looked peaceful—calm, beautiful, and poised. And Omar—the brave man who army-crawled back and forth across the street of death to rescue his mother and then helped us rescue five more people—had shaved off his beard and smiled brightly at the camera.

I felt a longing to see those people again—to shake hands, smile, and laugh and remember those days of horror—but in the past. I wanted their physical presence as assurance that life had indeed prevailed.

In the meantime, there was upheaval in Iraq/Kurd politics: after the defeat of ISIS in their territory and nearing their total defeat in Iraq, the Kurds decided to conduct a referendum on independence. In the still-fragile post-ISIS milieu, they were warned against it—the Iraqi government was adamant, and the U.S., in general a staunch Kurdish ally, warned that they wouldn't be able to support them. But the Kurds had just helped rescue the world from ISIS: they stopped them in their tracks in their rush across Iraq, held them for years while the Iraqi Army got itself together to launch a counteroffensive, and were continuing to shelter and care for more than a million refugees. They weren't declaring independence; they were taking a step to see if their people were ready for it.

Resoundingly, they were—and just as resoundingly, the rest of Iraq and the world were not. Iraq, with help from Turkey and Iran, instantly shut down Kurdish airspace and its international airports at Erbil and Sulaimaniya. Two weeks after the referendum, Iraq Army and Hashid Shabi forces took Kirkuk from the Peshmerga. There were accusations that American weapons were used against the Peshmerga in the Kirkuk fighting—and the Kurds were deeply hurt. The U.S. had been a friend and ally, and the U.S. stood by silently as Iraq put the Kurdish dream down.

That would affect our trip back: We could no longer fly into Erbil. Previously we never traveled to Iraq with an Iraqi visa—we'd been able to get KRG visas, which was a much simpler process. Americans could get a visa on arrival for thirty days, and after the first few difficult visa situations with our Burma guys, the system was streamlined for them as well. The border between Kurdistan and Iraq had been very fluid—when there was fighting, and you were helping, no one cared. We were unable to get visas until November 2, and then only for my family because of our Iraqi friend Dr. Haitham Al Mayahi, who helped us. The rest of the team came through Turkey, and we were all back in Iraq by November 8, five months after we left.

First, we drove from Erbil to the new/old front line looking over Bashiqa and other towns that the Kurds had won in blood, then lost when the U.S. did not support their call for independence nor stop the Iraqi advance. On the Iraqi side, it was felt that the Kurds asked for and took too much. On the Kurd side, it was felt they were abandoned and lost what was rightfully theirs. Saddam Hussein had earlier driven the Kurds out of Kirkuk and other historical lands and now the Kurds had reclaimed these—only to lose them again.

On the new front, we met with Kurd Peshmerga soldiers with whom we had worked for three years; these were bitter and sad but sweet meetings. It was bitter for the Kurds, who had just lost so much, and sad for both of us because of our friends lost in battle. In the end, however, it was sweet because we were back together, and our bonds of love had only grown deeper.

Up at the front positions, we met with Kurd generals Afandi, Nooradin, Mutaa, and Bahram—all great leaders with whom we had worked and lived and served closely. They were all glad to see us but were disappointed in America. Everywhere we went along the front, we heard, "America betrayed us. You did treason to us. We used to be friends but no more." "Our friendship is broken forever. We cannot trust America." Farhang, the cosmopolitan son of General Afandi, said, "I could not eat or sleep for a week after you betrayed us and did not help us in the face of the Iraqi attack."

We heard these and other words again and again and could only apologize and pray with them. We told them we felt the U.S. was wrong to abandon them, but we also had friends among the Iraqi Army and the PMUs. I was wounded in battle four times: once alongside the Kurds, twice with the Iraqi Army, and once with the PMU. I lost many friends with each. So, with each group, we were bonded in love and hoped the U.S. would work with all sides to help find solutions.

After spending the night in a Peshmerga tent next to their trenches at the front, we drove to Mosul to track some of the injured civilians we rescued in May and June. We drove through a Kurdish dirt berm they closed each night and then through the PMU lines and Iraqi Army/ Police checkpoints into east Mosul. Here we passed through the ruins of Mosul neighborhoods just beginning to rebuild. Every few blocks were Iraqi police checkpoints, and the feeling was still tense. Most of the people here were under ISIS for three years, and many supported them.

Our first stop was the rescue site. It wasn't so easy to get to, with checkpoints and traffic and new routes. Mohammed, who was shot six times while rescuing Shaheen, was now working with us full time. He and Dlo helped us get through the many checkpoints and the mazes of rubble that were Mosul streets now.

Returning to Mosul and the site of the rescues was unsettling, and I felt a weight in the pit of my stomach. As I walked down the street where we had run behind the tank, I felt a wave of awe too—how close we came each day to being killed, how overwhelming the odds were on the side of ISIS. I couldn't shake the feeling of sadness and horror, and the memory of everything that had happened came back, as strong as the stench of death. As I walked through the rubble, picking my way over debris and scattered bones, I felt a palpable evil. It was still here. I could feel it and the fear that accompanied it. It was sharp and powerful, and I felt dread. I stopped and prayed against the evil. I felt it was still there, but it receded, coiling back down into the ruins.

I felt I could hear the bullets crack by me again, see the sprawled dead children and their shot parents, feel the heat and roar of the tank as it fired at ISIS. Again, I seemed to feel the bullets whiz by and mortars crash, looking into the blank face of a little girl as we stepped over her body. Our survival was a near thing and seeing it all again made me realize why we should not have made it.

All around had been ISIS-controlled buildings, and in one area, they were just twenty meters away. It was a gift from God that we had made it; but it was still a near thing. Looking at the scene, with bits of bone and scattered clothes, a little girl's shoes and bullet-pocked walls, I felt sad for all those who did not make it, all those who died slow, agonizing deaths as their family members died around them. As I walked the ground with my family and our team, I prayed for all who survived and those who did not. I got down on my knees, and as I prayed, a sob rose in my throat—I felt the sorrow of the loss of so many precious lives and the sadness of those left behind.

It was good for me to see that place, and hard too. But we didn't come just to remember the dead, but to see the living.

Omar was first: To get to his house, we drove through the ruins of a Mosul neighborhood just starting the rebuilding process. Every few blocks were Iraqi police checkpoints. We went into Omar's small, bullet and mortar-scarred house and had a joyful reunion. "I love you," he said.

"I love you too," I said.

"I love you four," Omar replied with a big laugh. His smiling wife and four boys greeted us, and we had a good evening together. We gave him and his family funds to help them, prayed with them, and went to visit another family.

We met them in the green riverside belt of Hawi Kanisa, the place of the tank battle near the hotel. It was in their field I walked into the tank's line of fire and got roundly berated by the tank driver. They had a grandmother who had lost her legs and a little girl who had lost her foot in an air strike. The grandmother and Sahale became especially close.

When Sahale sat on the floor beside the grandmother's bed, the old woman stroked her hair and told her how much she loved her and all of us. With a smile of deep contentment and joy she said, "You came when we were in need. God sent you. I thank God for a new granddaughter and for your family. We love you." We spent the night with them, listened to their stories, gave as much help as we could, and exchanged contact information so we could be in touch with them in the future.

The next morning, our destination took us across Mosul—very slow going with more and more people and vehicles returning, multiple checkpoints, and rubble everywhere. A tunnel was discovered near the place we spent the night. Three ISIS fighters had escaped from it and were at large. Every checkpoint was on the lookout, not only for the three ISIS fighters, but the many others known to still be hiding in Mosul.

Khofran's house was where we were headed, about twenty kilometers south of Mosul. When we got there, she was beaming, and it made our day to be with her. She told us her story and, at the end, said, "Even my family abandoned me and ran for their lives, but you, an American, came and risked your life for me. You have great mercy."

I said, "This is love, and it is from God. Jesus helped us do this and helped us help you." I told her how we prayed that God would shut the eyes and ears of ISIS and stop Satan and his demons, and it was God's power that saved her. She smiled at all of us and thanked us. We gave her money to help with her surgery, prayed with her and her family, and said goodbye.

Our next stop was the western edge of Mosul to meet Private Zuhair. We met on the side of the road and embraced each other a long time. He is a hero to me; I told him how I had retold the story of his bravery all across America. I told him how his courage and his words—"Even if I am the only to go and help and even if I fail and die I will go. I cannot leave those wounded people to die without trying"—had helped me on both rescues. We awarded him the FBR Star of Valor and Medal of Honor, which has only been won by three other living people—one of whom is Mohammed.

We returned to Erbil the next day. Dlo and Mohammed had been on the phone with the family of Demoa and were trying to convince them to come to Erbil to visit. They were nervous about traveling, so we sent Mohammed on a six-hour taxi ride to get them.

As they pulled up to our office in the taxi, we were all out in the street to greet them. They stepped out of the car, Demoa dressed in a pretty winter jacket, with her hair pulled back, and I dropped to my knees to thank God. She was nervous and held herself back, clinging to her aunt. Her grandmother began to cry and thank me: "I have seen your picture and have been hoping to see you to thank you. You not only saved Demoa's life, you saved mine. If she had died, I think I would have died also. I have no other grandchildren and only one daughter left. But God had mercy. Thank you for risking your life to save her." She cried and dropped down to kiss my feet.

I was embarrassed and lifted her up and hugged her. I told her, "This was God who did this—God loves Demoa and helped us save her. And it was not just our FBR team, it was American smoke, an Iraqi tank, the FBR support team, and people praying for all of us all over the world."

It took a while for Demoa to feel comfortable, but when Noelle, Sahale, Suu, and Hosie began to play with her and brought out toys they brought for her, she brightened up. Soon we were playing hide and seek, and she laughed and giggled as she ran around our office.

My heart felt full, and I was grateful for this new chance at life. It felt like there was a completeness. Demoa was rescued, then cared for by Karen and our team, then by an Iraqi family, Victor Marx, and finally reunited with her own family. Her aunt had seen her picture on social media and contacted Dlo, who put her in touch with General Mustafa. Demoa is happy and thriving. I do not know the depth of the emotional, psychological, and spiritual wounds she bears, but we prayed for her and trust God to keep healing her.

Her grandmother choked up at one point and said, "After the rescue, I had a dream. Demoa was hiding among the dead and beside her was a foul- and evil-looking stream. A man, shining and beautiful, appeared. He lifted Demoa up and carried her across the filthy stream, bringing her safely to the other side." The grandmother began to cry again and said, "I am so thankful."

I told her, "I believe that was Jesus who helped Demoa, and you can call on His name when you need help. He loves you and Demoa."

We took Demoa to a local mall, and she played on everything in sight: jungle gym, slides, go-carts, toy horses, and then the girls took her to buy toys. We finished with a big dinner and gave the family help to support her; the next morning, she went with her grandmother and aunt back home. As they drove away, I felt relief and joy that we were reunited, she was doing so well, and we could be part of this.

After that, we went to Baghdad. We loaded up all our vehicles and all our team—even though only my family had visas—and took off like a gypsy caravan over the contested roads between Erbil and Baghdad.

The way to Baghdad was longer than it should have been, as we had to go via the Sulaimaniya route—first through Kurd checkpoints and then into Iraqi territory and through the checkpoints manned by the Iraqi Army, police, and various PMU forces. Most just waved us through, but some stopped us and asked for our names and what we were doing. We were allowed through all the checkpoints and treated with courtesy. Due to heavy traffic, bad road conditions, two flat tires, and the many checkpoint stops, it took us ten hours from Erbil to the Green Zone in Baghdad.

We had no escort, but phone calls to Dr. Haitham cleared up any problem for us. Dr. Haitham is a dual Iraqi and American citizen who is a political and foreign affairs advisor to many Iraqi leaders, including Mr. Hadi Al Amiri, one of the heads of the PMUs in Iraq. He is a helpful coordinator between worldwide media, NGOs, and the government of Iraq. He was enthusiastic about bringing us to Baghdad, with a desire to foster better and more personal relationships between the Iraqi government and the U.S.

It was around 9 p.m. before we reached the Green Zone, where we were met by Dr. Haitham, who took us to meet Hadi Al Amiri, a serious-looking and controversial former minister of transportation of Iraq who left his post to fight ISIS. He organized the Badr PMU and is known as a brave fighter, brutal to those he felt were his enemies.

As we sat at a long conference table in his office building, he told me, "Where you are sitting, U.S. Ambassador Ryan Crocker and General Petraeus have sat, as well as leaders from Iran—and I tell them all the same thing: 'We want to be your friends but you will not control us. We need your help but not your domination.' We are grateful for all the U.S. help and consider you all to be friends."

He went on to say the Iraqi Army and the PMUs would not attack the Kurds, that this was the time to talk and that no further territorial disputes should be resolved by fighting. "The Kurds are part of our Iraqi family and they need their own way, but we can work this out together."

I asked him about Iran, and he replied with four main points:

1) We feel a spiritual connection with Iranian people since the Islamic revolution that removed the Shah and his oppression.

2) Iran helped us when we were in great danger from ISIS. We do not push away people who have helped us.

3) We share a fourteen-hundred-kilometer border with Iran; what do you want us to do, move our country?

4) We will not be dominated by Iran or the United States, but we want to be friends with both.

We had dinner together and came away from that meeting feeling we had some understanding. We respected each other and could talk.

The next day, Dr. Haitham arranged a meeting with Dr. Khalid Al Mulla, one of the top Sunni leaders. He was kind and serious and welcomed us warmly. He told us he was thankful for our help in Iraq and he considered America to be a friend. He said both Sunni and Shia were united to defeat the evil of ISIS but went on to say ISIS was indeed following the Koran literally, though brutally. Thus, they were wrong. He said, "Now that ISIS has been defeated, we need to reeducate our people, especially our young people. They need to learn how to think and believe on their own and rebuild our country. We need help to do this and now is the time for action not words."

From this meeting, Dr. Haitham led us back to the Green Zone to meet with Dr. Walid Al Hilli, senior adviser to the Iraqi Prime Minister, Mr. Abadi. Dr. Walid was imprisoned by Saddam Hussein before

Hussein was defeated by the U.S. Dr. Walid is an open-minded man with an excellent command of English. He educated us on Iraqi history and also reassured us the Iraqis and Kurds would work for a peaceful solution to their problems. "The U.S. is our friend and so is Iran and we want to be able to work with both. We are thankful for your humanitarian help for our people and your part in the liberation of Iraq from ISIS." We closed our meeting with prayer.

That night, we stayed with General Mustafa at his house in Mosul. That was a great and joyful reunion and it was wonderful to see him relaxed and with his family. His brigade suffered great losses, having started the campaign with 105 BMPs and more than forty Humvees but finishing with only twelve BMPs and five Humvees. He lost over 50 percent of his men and machines fighting ISIS.

Thirty of his troops who were killed were close friends of ours and we felt the loss together. General Mustafa did not only fight and defeat ISIS in his area of operations throughout the campaign, he also helped to provide lifesaving food, water, and medical care to over seventy-five thousand civilians. We love him, and reuniting with him was like being with family.

His neighborhood was one of the most dangerous in Baghdad and still is not completely stable with Iraqi Army and police covering numerous checkpoints. Staying in his house, we could see the bullet holes and damage done by an Al Qaeda attack years ago. At that time, an Al Qaeda cell attacked his house, trying to come through the front door. His family ran upstairs and Mustafa grabbed a machine gun, fired from the hip point-blank, and killed one of the assailants while wounding two. He kept the rest at bay until his soldiers arrived. Here, ISIS was just the latest threat.

The next day, we linked up with the 36th Brigade of the 9th Division—Mohammed arranged for us to meet them on the side of a highway on the outskirts of Baghdad and we sat for an hour or so in our cars while traffic flew by. Then a couple of army vehicles pulled up, Major Naseem got out of one of them, and we had another happy reunion. We followed them through Fallujah and Ramadi, both heavily damaged but slowly being rebuilt.

We continued to the Syrian border in the vicinity of Al Qaim and Rawa and spent the next three days with the 36th as they moved first along the Syrian border area and then east across to Haditha Dam and north to the destroyed, mostly empty town of Baiji. We distributed medical supplies and funds for food for civilians the soldiers expected to find in their next push west.

We had a good meeting with General Kasem, the 9th Division commander and a local PMU commander. Most of all we were reunited with old friends and handed out photos and awarded medals for valor and wounds. The next day, the 9th Division launched a sweep west back toward the Syrian border to clear possible remaining ISIS remnants.

From Baiji, we drove at night to Mosul, again passing through numerous checkpoints with PMUs controlling the outside of Mosul and Iraqi police inside. The west side of Mosul at night was an eerie, dark, and destroyed place. There, no one walked at night on the main roads, nor did we see shops. At night, there were only cars passing through the Iraqi police checkpoints.

Once we crossed the pontoon bridge to the east side, suddenly there were lights, shops open, and people walking and shopping. We spent the night with friends in east Mosul and the next day drove through the open berm into Kurdistan. We left grateful for the opportunity to reconnect with old friends and planning together how to help when we returned.

It was December, and we had missions to do in Burma. Our planned return to the Middle East was for the end of January. This time, we had no visas to Iraq, so our whole group went through Turkey. While we spent much of this trip in Syria, we also went back through Mosul. We still had business there.

We were back from Syria in February 2018 and came to Mosul to remember Shaheen's life and death and to celebrate the eventual victory over ISIS that allowed us to do so in peace. We received funds from Reload Love to build a playground in his honor. Dlo and Mohammed coordinated this while we were in Burma and then worked hard to get us through the checkpoints that were getting stricter as time went on.

After stopping at the site where Shaheen was shot, we went to a nearby park to see the new playground. It was full of kids, recently returned to their homes and enjoying the newest construction in their neighborhood. The next day, we did a GLC program there and dedicated the playground to Shaheen.

At the same time, Dlo and Mohammed continued to work on finding the people we helped rescue. As the GLC program ended, we got word they were able to track down Rahab. She was the girl trapped under a collapsed building; two of her brothers were killed while the rest of her family escaped and told the Iraqi Army about their trapped daughter. We had rescued her just a couple of days after Shaheen was shot, with the help of the firefighters from Baghdad. Rahab and her family were coming by taxi to meet us.

We pulled up behind their taxi on the side of the street; she got out, limping and on crutches, but smiling. After her rescue, the Red Cross helped get her an initial operation, which partially repaired her knee while determining the extent of the damage. Part of her kneecap is gone, and she needs further operations and physical therapy to be able to walk well again. But she has a future now, and when I asked her what she wanted to do in it, she beamed as she said, "I want to study to be a doctor." We hugged her and gave her parents what assistance we could for the next step—another operation.

As we stood in joy on the side of the road, visiting with Rahab's family, a thin, trim man walked up and joined us. Beside him was a young girl with a lively and beautiful face, with one eye covered by a patch. We soon realized they were the father and daughter who were rescued the day Shaheen was shot. Incredibly, they both survived. There they were, standing on the muddy side of the road on the edge of a still-destroyed Mosul, just minutes from where they came so close to dying. ISIS was not there, we were, and we rejoiced at life snatched from the brink of death.

We learned the girl's name was Aisha. Her eye was gone but she was otherwise healthy. I embraced them both and they smiled and thanked us again and again. The father invited us to their house to meet the rest of the family.

We said goodbye to Rahab and her family before stopping to visit the site from which she was rescued. Two of Rahab's brothers were still buried there.

As we walked around the rubble of the collapsed house, we could see where ISIS had been and how much the Iraqi Army and our team risked to get Rahab out. It seemed like a miracle.

We prayed over the site and then went on to Aisha's house. It was a joyful visit, steeped as it was in the joy of resurrection. The father told us, "You saved our lives; thank you so much and we thank God. You did not leave us. We honor the man on your team who gave his life that we may live."

On the way back to Erbil, Mohammed, who had decided to follow Jesus a year earlier, asked to be baptized. We baptized him and Jason, a medic newly working with us, in the Tigris.

A few months later, we were reunited with Lieutenant Hussein, who was recovering from his wounds. "I have become a follower of Jesus now," he said with a smile. "I used to call you Uncle but now I call you Father; you saved my life."

I was grateful for all those reunions, for the opportunity to continue to be part of those people's lives, whom God had performed miracles to save. Yet there was one more person I really wanted to see, and I prayed we could find her: the woman we dragged to us at the soft drink factory. The woman who taught me never to give up, who survived five days after being shot and lying in the June sun of Iraq, right under the guns of ISIS, and came out praising God. Her name was Eman and the little girl was Suriya, but that was all we knew.

We returned to Thailand and Burma in March, after meeting Aisha and Rahab. We returned again to the Middle East in May. Most of this mission was also focused on Syria, but we revisited our friends in Mosul and did a more concentrated search for Eman and Suriya.

We drove through all the neighborhoods of that part of Mosul, asking the local leaders if they knew her or anyone like her. We heard rumors: she was dead, her husband was an ISIS fighter, so she was hiding, or people just didn't know.

Mosul is a big city. It was hard to account for one civilian casualty after a war that had lasted for nine months, following an occupation that had lasted three years, in which thousands of people were killed, kidnapped, or fled.

We returned in late September, again to do a mission in Syria. This time, we brought Chris Sinclair, a close friend and videographer working on an FBR documentary, with us. He had been on many missions in Burma with us but hadn't yet been to Mosul and wanted to get some of his own footage, on location, of the rescue sites. On October 1, after checking up on Aisha, who had a new prosthetic eye, we prayed again: "Lord, help us find Eman today, in Jesus's name."

We went again to the rescue site at the destroyed soft drink factory so Chris could film it. As we pulled up and climbed out of our vehicles, a man, a normal passerby, walked by carrying a small engine. But he stopped and, with a light in his eye, asked: "Who are you and what are you doing?"

We told him, "We're visiting the place where we did a rescue last year."

His eyes widened and he said, "That was my wife and daughter you rescued. We have been looking for you for over a year. Thank God!"

Neither of us knew the other would be there that day at that time. In awe at what we knew God was doing, we hugged and prayed, and tears of gratitude came.

Mohammed was his name. He grinned happily as he spoke with Mohammed and Dlo in Arabic. We took photos in front of the car Eman had lain next to for those days. Then he led us to his house. We walked inside and there was Eman, sitting on the floor on a thin mattress, still too injured to stand but smiling and with peace in her eyes. They called in Suriya, who was outside playing. I knelt and hugged them both. It was a beautiful reunion.

Eman told us how much of a miracle it was to her to be alive. She thought she was dreaming when we came and rescued her off the street by the factory. Now she was pregnant but could not walk; she kept telling us how wonderful her husband is and how he is caring for her and their five children.

Together, they told us about that day: Mohammed had been ahead of her, helping four of their children flee, when a mortar barrage and ISIS gunfire erupted. After realizing they were separated in the chaos, he knew he could not stop and go back, but he had to save the children still with him.

In the week following his escape, he searched every hospital and displaced persons camp without success. He started to think his wife and daughter were dead. He told us of the joy they all felt when he finally found them alive. We gave Eman, Suriya, and Mohammed medals for bravery and being wounded, and also funds to help them.

Just a few months later, Eman gave birth to twin girls. She can now walk, though she is still working on returning to full activity. With the help of Tim Hayes, we were able to facilitate buying a used taxi for Mohammed, to give their family a livelihood in post-war Mosul.

Khofran is mostly healed from her injuries, and we are hoping she can come to work for us in Erbil, or perhaps come on a mission with us at some point. Her family is conservative Muslim, so this is not an easy negotiation.

Rahab is in a similar situation; while she expressed a desire to become a doctor, she does not get much support from home. We hope we can help her follow her dreams for her future, but it will be a slow process.

We see Aisha and her family regularly as well; most recently, we stayed the night at their house, where she and her sister kept Sahale and Suuzanne up all night, giggling and whispering and doing normal girl things.

Demoa is still with her aunt and grandmother; right now, that is the best place for her.

These reunions and the follow-up medical care are unexpected gifts from God and people. Tim Hayes and Victor Marx have come to help, while others have paid for the multiple surgeries needed and brought teams of physicians to help with the care and healing of each person. Without them and other supporters, we could do none of this.

I am constantly in awe of how people come from all over to help and together we can do what none of us could do alone. It seems I can do many bad things all by myself, but I cannot do much good alone. I thank God that in this world we are not alone. We have each other and we have Jesus to help us.

Our friends in the 36th continue to do the duty of soldiers—trying to keep the peace and fighting if they have to. After ISIS was mostly pushed out of Iraq, the 36th Brigade and 9th Division were redeployed to Basra in southern Iraq, a volatile region near the Iranian border. We visited them and helped buy food and medicine for civilians there as they risked their lives daily against a new enemy—this one the face-less enemy arising from corruption, mismanagement, and propaganda, fomenting rage from afar by creating conditions of injustice and oppression while blaming others.

While we have expanded missions into Syria, we continue our missions in Iraq and Burma and we recently brought Dlo, our Kurdish team coordinator, Mohammed, the Iraqi soldier who was shot saving Shaheen and is now on our team, and Edo, our Yezidi friend from Sinjar, to Burma on missions. This is a blessing. It seems like a miracle, and we are grateful.

Peter with local kids near where Shaheen was shot, where we erected a playground in his honor, 2017.

Meeting Rahab again, seven months after her rescue, 2017.

With Aisha and her father seven months after the rescue, 2017.

Khofran with my family at her home outside of Mosul, 2018.

My family with Lt. Hussein after his recovery, at our office in Erbil, 2018.

With Eman and her family more than a year after her rescue, 2018.

+

"...live in such a way that one's life would not make sense if God did not exist."

—**CARDINAL EMMANUEL CÉLESTIN SUHARD**[17]

The time for miracles is not over. The time for gratitude is just beginning. That I, a soldier at heart, and one who thrives in battle—could give up a place in the strongest fighting force on Earth to be a missionary among peace-loving Thai and Burmese villagers—and to do it in love, is not my natural self; it is a miracle.

That I would find myself called again into battle, this time on behalf of those villagers, helping each other to survive and thrive in the midst of their war, standing with them in the fight, no longer from the position of power but from the position of weakness—and learning much from them and much of the ways of God in battle in the process—that is a miracle.

That I would be sent and be accompanied by these humble villagers, back into the vortex of massive military might and violence, against one of the most ruthless foes in modern history—that is a miracle.

And that I would, once again surrounded by the might and power of the U.S. military and the Iraqi Army, take my stand from a position of weakness and, having the most powerful machines of war on my side, but not at my disposal, have God guide us like Gideon to lives He wanted to save—that is a miracle.

To do all this in love and freedom with my family, our team, and all our new friends is the greatest miracle.

We are part of a long line of happy warriors, from David, boldly fighting Goliath in the ancient past, to John Paul Jones in the war for American independence, who said, "I wish to have no connection with any ship that does not sail fast, for I intend to go into harm's way," to us who now have new challenges before us.[18] With God's and each other's help, we will go into harm's way to help others. We will meet these challenges with courage, forgiveness, love, and the fruit these bear, reconciliation. We will meet them with joy.

We don't know our next steps. We don't know what God has for us in the future. We are all caught up in His present: working in Syria, in Iraq, in Burma still, and in Bangladesh, and our eyes and our hearts are still with our friends in Sudan. All these are places of suffering; all of these places are home to people we love. In all of these places, we live in gratitude and we pray we can act in love. And we do it all while having faith that the time for miracles is not over.

Afterword

NOTHING DONE IN LOVE IS CRAZY

Do this for love. Love sets us free and helps us overcome fear, pride, and hate. Love may compel us to take great risks, but anything done in love is not crazy. When we run out of love, God has an unlimited supply. When love helps us overcome fear and self-interest, some may call us brave or even heroes. A journalist once asked me, "Aren't you just trying to be a hero?"

I answered, "Yes, we should all want to be brave and help others. To be brave is hard. It means you may lose everything. When you're risking everything, then pride, or wrong motives fade away; they are trumped by natural self-preservation. Love overcomes this and helps us do what is needed in spite of our weaknesses, selfishness and limitations."

Love is a powerful force. It is not neutral, and it is radical in its power.

> Love is patient and kind; love does not envy or boast; it is not arrogant or rude. It does not insist on its own way; it is not irritable or resentful; it does not rejoice at wrongdoing, but rejoices with the truth. Love bears all things, believes all things, hopes all things, endures all things. Love never ends. As for prophecies, they will pass away; as for tongues, they will cease; as for knowledge, it will pass away. For we know in part and we prophesy in part, but when the perfect comes, the partial will pass away.
>
> When I was a child, I spoke like a child, I thought like a child, I reasoned like a child. When I became a man, I gave up childish ways. For now we see in a mirror dimly, but then face to face. Now I know in part; then I shall know fully, even as I have been fully known. So now faith, hope, and love abide, these three; but the greatest of these is love.
>
> 1 CORINTHIANS 13

Love is radical in how it infuses us with joy as it forgives, transforms, frees, and empowers us to love and help others. Hate too has power, and it also transforms. But the result of hate is enslavement, misery, and destruction. To be fully human is to be free and to give ourselves to something higher than us. We have to make a choice to be transformed by love or by hate.

We have a desire inside us to reach for something higher, for something to love and give our whole selves to. Most who join ISIS or groups like them are searching for a higher spiritual meaning for their lives. They are willing to sacrifice everything for it. The problem is not their zealousness—it is that what they worship and follow is full of hate. Deradicalizing ISIS and others who hate and do evil is not the answer. Trying to neuter or tame people is crushing to the human spirit and against who we are created to be.

God is love and is on the side of love. We all need to choose a side. There is no middle ground. If we don't choose love, we will either be like ISIS or others, radicals for evil, or we will be indifferent and run over by evil.

The apostle Paul was gifted, disciplined, and zealously committed for the wrong purpose until he met Jesus and was transformed into a force for love. Compelled by love, he committed all he had to help others. The founding fathers of the United States, who wrote at the end of the Declaration of Independence, "We mutually pledge to each other our lives, our fortunes, our sacred honor"—these men and their families were willing to give all they had for the cause of love and liberty.

Amy Carmichael, who worked to stop child prostitution in Indian temples, wrote, "While we are counting the costs, Satan is busy buying up the territory." She was a force for human dignity, love, and freedom. Martin Luther King was called a radical but his willingness to sacrifice everything changed America and the world for good. Mother Teresa and Nelson Mandela willingly gave all to help others. These were all called radicals. It is not a question of being radical or not; it is a question of what we are radical for: love or hate.

You can and you might have to stop the human heart with a bullet, but you can only change a human heart with love. God gives love freely to all who ask. I have experienced how when I ask Jesus to help me: He changes my heart, forgives me, helps me forgive others, and gives me love to share. Thank you for allowing me to share this story with you and to share of what Jesus has done for me in spite of my weaknesses, limitations, and failures. Jesus's love keeps setting me free.

May God bless you,

Dave, family, and all the Free Burma Rangers

Endnotes

1   Elie Wiesel, "Nobel Prize Acceptance Speech," Nobel Prize, accessed March 2020, https://www.nobelprize.org/prizes/peace/1986/wiesel/26054-elie-wiesel-acceptance-speech-1986/.

2   Paul B. Spiegel et al., "The Mosul Treatment Response: A Case Study," Johns Hopkins Center for Humanitarian Health, February 2018, http://hopkinshumanitarianhealth.org/assets/documents/Mosul_Report_FINAL_Feb_14_2018.pdf.

3   *Oxford English Dictionary* (2019), s.v. "miracle."

4   Howard Thurman, "Don't ask what the world needs…" accessed January 20, 2020, https://www.azquotes.com/quote/518260.

5   Winston Churchill, *The Story of the Malakand Field Force* (London: Dover Publications, 1898).

6   The Mosul Study Group, "What the Battle for Mosul Teaches the Force," U.S. Army, September 2017, https://www.armyupress.army.mil/Portals/7/Primer-on-Urban-Operation/Documents/Mosul-Public-Release1.pdf.

7   Churchill, "If you're going through hell…" https://www.brainyquote.com/quotes/winston_churchill_103788.

8   The Mosul Study Group, "What the Battle for Mosul Teaches the Force," U.S. Army, September 2017, https://www.armyupress.army.mil/Portals/7/Primer-on-Urban-Operation/Documents/Mosul-Public-Release1.pdf.

9   Tim Hume, "How ISIS Is Fighting to Keep Its Iraqi Stronghold," CNN, October 25, 2016, https://edition.cnn.com/2016/10/24/middleeast/iraq-mosul-isis-tactics/.

10 ARA News, "Over 12,000 ISIS Militants Fighting for Mosul," June 27, 2016, https://web.archive.org/web/20170516043248/http://aranews.net/2016/06/12000-isis-militants-fighting-mosul/.

11 Helene Cooper, "Revived After Mosul, Iraqi Forces Prepare to Battle ISIS in Tal Afar," *New York Times*, August 18, 2017, https://www.nytimes.com/2017/08/18/world/middleeast/iraq-tal-afar-isis-battle.html.

12 "One Year on from the Start of the Battle for Mosul, Hundreds of Thousands of Civilians Need Assistance," October 12, 2017, https://

reliefweb.int/report/iraq/one-year-start-battle-mosul-hundreds-thou-sands-civilians-need-assistance-enarku.

13   Linah Alsaafin, "One Year After Battle for Mosul, a City Lies in Ruins," *Al Jazeera*, July 10, 2018, https://www.aljazeera.com/news/2018/07/year-battle-mosul-city-lies-ruins-180710105827500.html.

14   "Hidden Bombs and Eight Million Tonnes of Rubble Keep the People of Mosul from Returning Home," ReliefWeb, February 20, 2019, https://reliefweb.int/report/iraq/hidden-bombs-and-eight-million-tonnes-rubble-keep-people-mosul-returning-home

15   George, Susannah. AP. "Mosul is a graveyard: Final IS battle kills 9,000 civilians," December 21, 2017. https://apnews.com/bbea7094f-b954838a2fdc11278d65460.

16   These statistics are from the UN; Iraqi, Kurdish and U.S. military sources; and other unclassified sources, as well as our own observations.

17   Michael Garvey, "Believing: Lives That Make Sense," *Notre Dame Magazine*, August 5, 2010, https://magazine.nd.edu/stories/believing-lives-that-make-sense/.

18   Willis John Abbot, *The Naval History of the United States* (New York: Peter Fenelon Collier, 1890), 82.

Learn More About FBR

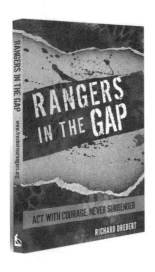
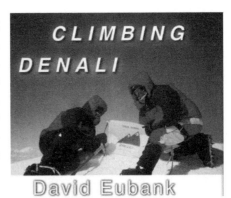

Watch the movie, Free Burma Rangers, available for purchase from Vimeo On Demand or www.christiancinema.com.

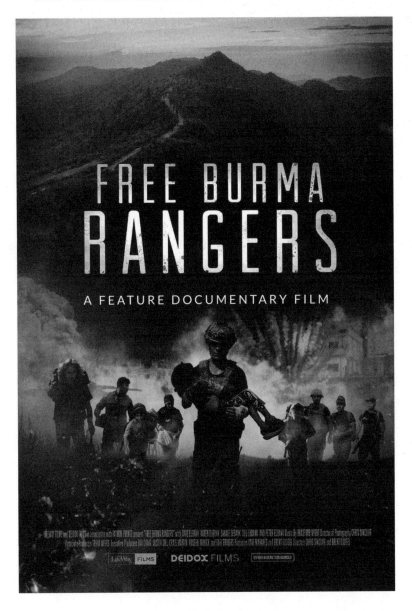

AVAILABLE NOW ON DIGITAL AND DVD

FOR MORE INFORMATION,
AND TO PURCHASE, VISIT:

FBRMOVIE.COM